The World of the Roosevelts

Published in cooperation with the Franklin and Eleanor Roosevelt Institute
Hyde Park, New York

General Editors:
William E. Leuchtenburg William vanden Heuvel, and Douglas Brinkley

THE DIPLOMATIC EDUCATION OF FRANKLIN D. ROOSEVELT, 1882–1933

GRAHAM CROSS

palgrave
macmillan

THE DIPLOMATIC EDUCATION OF FRANKLIN D. ROOSEVELT, 1882–1933
Copyright © Graham Cross, 2012.

First published in 2012 by
PALGRAVE MACMILLAN®
in the United States—a division of St. Martin's Press LLC,
175 Fifth Avenue, New York, NY 10010.

Where this book is distributed in the UK, Europe and the rest of the world,
this is by Palgrave Macmillan, a division of Macmillan Publishers Limited,
registered in England, company number 785998, of Houndmills,
Basingstoke, Hampshire RG21 6XS.

Palgrave Macmillan is the global academic imprint of the above companies
and has companies and representatives throughout the world.

Palgrave® and Macmillan® are registered trademarks in the United States,
the United Kingdom, Europe and other countries.

ISBN: 978–1–137–01453–5

Library of Congress Cataloging-in-Publication Data is available from the
Library of Congress.

A catalogue record of the book is available from the British Library.

Design by Newgen Imaging Systems (P) Ltd., Chennai, India.

First edition: June 2012

10 9 8 7 6 5 4 3 2 1

Printed in the United States of America.

For Susan

Contents

ILLUSTRATIONS

Cover photo "Assistant Secretary of the Navy Franklin D. Roosevelt in his office at the Navy Department February 26, 1918" (National Archives 19-N-1207).

ACKNOWLEDGMENTS

FDR's views on international relations are a complex interest to pursue, and luckily I have been able to access a great deal of expertise and assistance to guide this book to publication. David Reynolds has been an understanding and inspiring teacher. His interest and help on countless occasions has aided this project immeasurably. John Thompson did much to increase my understanding of US international relations. Andrew Preston was an enormous help by giving me the opportunity to try out early ideas at the Cambridge Graduate Seminar on US history and through his enthusiasm for my topic. Brendan Simms kindly let me try out early versions of chapters 3 and 5 as papers at the Cambridge International History Seminar at Peterhouse College. I am also immensely grateful to Richard Rex for the support and interest he has shown on so many occasions during my time at Queens' College. David Woolner, executive director and senior fellow at the Franklin and Eleanor Roosevelt Institute at Hyde Park, and Chris Chappell, Sarah Whalen and Joel Breuklander of Palgrave Macmillan have been instrumental in bringing this project to print. I also wish to acknowledge my anonymous reviewer for the many insightful comments provided. To all, I extend my sincere thanks. Any errors, of course, remain my own responsibility and in no way belong to those who have given of their time to help this project.

A grant from the Franklin and Eleanor Roosevelt Institute enabled me to complete my primary research at the FDR Presidential Library and Museum in 2007. The archival team were extremely helpful in accessing material and photographs on FDR's early life. Bob Clark and Mark Renovitch were of particular help in this respect. At Cambridge, the trustees of the Sara Norton Fund were kind enough to arrange two grants that enabled me to continue my work. In 2010, a grant from the Board of Graduate Studies literally made completion of my PhD thesis, on which this book is based, possible. To all, I wish to express my heartfelt gratitude.

Finally, thanks must go to my family—as a mature student with a young family trying to negotiate the challenges of a return to academic life while still maintaining a level of financial and familial stability I have incurred many debts. My mother and father, James and Jeanne Cross, gave encouragement and a quiet refuge where much of the writing took place. My parents-in-law Sheila and Vic Grayson have made heroic efforts with childcare and the countless other things that a father not writing a book would do to keep family life going. My wife Susan and children Edward and Sarah have endured my many hours of study—their love, patience, understanding, and support has made it all worthwhile.

ABBREVIATIONS IN THE TEXT

CPI	Committee on Public Information
DNC	Democratic National Committee
LEP	League to Enforce Peace
LFNA	League of Free Nations Association
LNNPA	League of Nations Non-Partisan Association
UMT	Universal Military Training
WWD	Woodrow Wilson Democracy

ABBREVIATIONS IN THE NOTES

ASNP	Assistant Secretary of the Navy Papers, FDR Library, Hyde Park, New York
EP	Election Papers 1924, FDR Library, Hyde Park, New York
FDRL	Franklin D. Roosevelt Library, Hyde Park, New York
Fl	Folder
FP	Family Papers, 1920–1928, FDR Library, Hyde Park, New York
GPC	General Political Correspondence 1921–1928, FDR Library, Hyde Park, New York
MSF	Master Speech File, FDR Library, Hyde Park, New York
PF	Publications File, FDR Library, Hyde Park, New York
PL	Elliott Roosevelt, ed. *The Roosevelt Letters: Being the Personal Correspondence of Franklin Delano Roosevelt* (3 vols. London, 1949–1952)
PPA	Samuel I. Rosenman, ed. *The Public Papers and the Addresses of Franklin D. Roosevelt* (13 vols. New York, 1938–1950)
PVPC	Papers as Vice Presidential Candidate, FDR Library, Hyde Park, New York
PWW	Arthur S. Link, ed. *The Papers of Woodrow Wilson* (69 vols. Princeton, NJ, 1966–1994)

INTRODUCTION

FRANKLIN D. ROOSEVELT (FDR) IS ONE OF THE most popular US presidents of all time. The American public consistently recognizes him along with other "greats" such as Washington and Lincoln, whereas historians regularly place him in the top three in scholarly polls.[1] Evidently FDR's famous charm has a long reach, but he was also president during extraordinary times that command the attention of historians. The Great Depression and World War II provide a dramatic context to his greatness. Scratch the surface of FDR's reputation, however, and one quickly encounters controversy and disagreement. His policies seem sketchy, incoherent, and hard to tie down. Personally he appears just as enigmatic—the "chameleon on plaid" of Herbert Hoover's famous 1932 portrait. This is particularly true in foreign affairs, attempting to understand FDR's views on international relations as president can appear almost impossible. His intentions on the world stage often seem confused, contradictory, and impossible to fathom.

The historiography concerning FDR's internationalism and foreign policy is a highly contentious field. The first area of disagreement concerns FDR's world outlook and whether he was an internationalist or nationalist. Both are complex and contested terms. For the purposes of this study the terms internationalism and internationalist are taken to indicate the broad array of positive attitudes Americans held toward governmentally organized structures and methods for interacting with the rest of the world. It does not include such broader definitions as nongovernmental organizations or more cosmopolitan, cultural connections unless they are directly relevant to particular discussions. Attention centers on the processes that interested FDR and investigating his changing attitudes toward his county's formal relations with the world across the military, economic, legal, diplomatic, and political spectrum.

The terms nationalism and nationalist in this study refer to an outlook that eschews formal connections to the rest of the world. They indicate a preference for a unilateralist approach to world affairs and an overriding concern for the welfare and interests of the United States. They are also closely associated to American notions of geographic isolation and security in the Western Hemisphere. Nationalism is preferred to isolationism that is a loaded pejorative term that FDR himself used to describe opponents of his foreign policy and that some historians have applied to his actions during his first term. The United States was never truly isolationist in advocating severance of all economic and cultural ties with the rest of the world and if the term is used it refers to a very specific context that will be detailed in the text and footnotes. Nationalism is a much harder term to restrict and define because it resists more strongly the connection to formal structures. It crosses the many social, cultural, political, and geographic definitions of nation that are all ultimately *imagined* because people's national identity is not founded on face-to-face knowledge and experience. Nationalism can therefore also refer to a sense of cohesive national identity, values, and ideals that influence the thoughts, beliefs, and actions of all Americans to varying degrees and in many different ways. In the American sense this was often at the expense of support for international political and diplomatic ties. If this sense is meant the term Americanism is used as a pragmatic approach to avoiding confusion.

Historical interpretations of FDR's presidential internationalism were initially negative. Early accounts charged him with pursuing an internationalist course only to resolve the domestic problems of the Great Depression.[2] More positive studies soon replied to these charges arguing for a consistent internationalism that contained varying degrees of forethought and planning. Criticism of FDR for his primary motivation by domestic concerns, however, has been a persistent theme and there seems little prospect for agreement on this score.[3] Sympathetic historians see him as forced by public opinion and lack of support in Congress to rein in his internationalism prior to 1937 while others see a firm nationalist who eschewed foreign entanglements throughout his presidency.[4]

When historians do agree on FDR's internationalism they are just as often likely to disagree on its form. This debate has centered on whether he adopted an idealistic or realistic ideological approach to international relations. The situation was never that simple or clear-cut. Both terms are a product of the post–World War II historiography and would likely not have been recognized by the protagonists of this work. Idealism is taken in this study to describe an approach to relations with the world that can place cultural values and connections above calculations of national interests or at least view them as a function of that interest. Realism, however, is taken to mean the reversal of this approach to prioritize those calculations of interest above any other concerns. In its most extreme interpretations it can indicate a belief in a strict determinism of world forces that preclude individual human agency. This is not to say that FDR did not adopt positions that could be described using either term as president. A central focus of this study is therefore the origins of this tension in FDR between notions of ideological separateness from and connectedness to the rest of the world.

Ideology, of course, is another notoriously slippery term that warrants definition. Michael Hunt has described it as "an interrelated set of convictions or assumptions that reduces the complexities of a particular slice of reality to easily comprehensible terms and suggests appropriate ways of dealing with that reality." Inspired by the work of cultural anthropologist Clifford Geertz, Hunt rejected narrow definitions of ideology to trace a vision of national greatness, a hierarchy of race, and an animus toward other people's revolutions as the core ideas of US foreign policy.[5] Such a broad-brush approach is helpful to understanding the wider cultural influences FDR encountered and does feature at times in this study, but a more narrow definition of ideology is also used. FDR was an individual with his own thoughts and experiences that contributed to his unique ideological worldview. He also encountered other individuals, such as Theodore Roosevelt and Woodrow Wilson, who pushed powerful personal ideological approaches to international relations. Understanding the nuances of these individual ideologies fully and FDR's interaction with them forms a central focus of this study.

By far the strongest interpretations of FDR as an idealist have come from his realist critics. George Kennan famously castigated FDR for fighting World War II under the banner of a Wilsonian defense of democracy and individual rights that gave unrealistic hopes of an amicable postwar settlement with the Soviets. Idealism has undoubtedly acquired a pejorative connotation in the hands of realist theorists that suggest it is an impractical, unworldly doctrine in comparison to their hardheaded schemes of deploying power to defend national interest. This view of FDR was not supported by the first generation of intellectual studies of his presidency that were unable to identify a coherent Wilsonian imprint on FDR and instead could offer only a bewildering array of generalities and inconsistencies.[6] This has not, however, deterred later scholars from seeking to link Wilson's promotion of democratic government, self-determination, collective security, disarmament, liberal economic globalization, and involvement of the US in world affairs directly to FDR.[7]

The Wilsonian interpretation of FDR's presidency has prompted revisionists, attracted by the many apparent similarities of background, style, and rhetoric with FDR's fifth cousin TR, to assess his internationalism along more realist lines. They note in FDR a keen appreciation of power on the international stage and an expanded geography of US security originating in TR and others such as naval theorist Alfred Thayer Mahan.[8] More specifically they have seen a series of ad hoc calculations and tactics by FDR

as president designed to protect America's interests. In the face of such contradictory claims, and a president notoriously difficult to pin down, many
historians have opted to sit on the fence. They suggest a combination of
Wilson and TR acting as joint tutors to the young FDR—TR providing a
realistic appreciation of geopolitics and power; Wilson providing the idealism that prevented FDR from having too narrow a conception of US interests.[9] The claim that he was heavily influenced by TR and Wilson is rarely
substantiated in any great detail by historians and is, in Warren Kimball's
words, "an unverified assumption."[10]

Both the idealist and realist interpretations of FDR's foreign policy, and
indeed much of the wider historiography, focus predominantly on FDR's
presidential years. If there is a unifying factor among historical studies of
FDR's foreign policy, it is perhaps the scant attention paid to his early life
and career before he became president. Even Robert Dallek's detailed study
devotes only 18 pages of 550 to the period. Instead, the period has been
largely left to biography that does not necessarily have foreign policy as its
primary concern and also often prefers to focus on the presidency. There are
exceptions that prove the rule—Frank Freidel's three-volume study of FDR's
prepresidential life published in the 1950s is still one of the best accounts
available and does cover FDR's early views of US foreign policy. Freidel's
main aim though was to trace a progressive heritage to the New Deal and,
that done, did not feel the need to extend his study into FDR's presidency.
On the whole biography, primarily due to space or focus, has failed to look
sufficiently for longer-term trends and connections between FDR's early
internationalist views and those he held as president.

The historiography's failure to focus on FDR's prepresidential life and
biography's failure to relate FDR's early attitudes on internationalism to
those he held during his presidency highlight an important question—what
exactly was FDR's early international outlook? Answers to this question
have the potential to shed new light on the existing debates detailed above
and generate new questions to ask regarding the form and development of
FDR's presidential foreign policy. The abundant and neglected source material provides a second motivation for considering the period. FDR is often
accused of rarely giving clear statements of his thinking, but there is danger
in making this an a priori assumption about him. During the prepresidential period, for instance, he produced some 22 articles relating in some way
to foreign affairs—including two major opinion pieces on foreign affairs
during his supposed "lost-decade" of the 1920s. This relatively prodigious
journalistic output in this period has gone largely unexamined by scholars
for many years. In addition to his writings, there are in the Roosevelt Library
detailed transcripts of hundreds of speeches given by FDR between the start
of his political career in 1910 and his winning of the presidential election in

1932. Some of these speeches are well known, particularly several concerning the League of Nations in 1919, but others have gone unnoticed in that year particularly because they fail to mention the League, even though they have important, even pivotal, things to tell us about FDR's internationalism. Together these provide an extensive and previously unmined body of source material. Thus, it is possible to trace the influences and development of FDR's internationalism during this period and state with confidence what he thought.

There is one further point to make about the existing historiography and body of biography—almost unanimously historians approach FDR as an intellectual subject adopting positions after rational and logical mental reflection. They do this, perhaps, because of the attractions of causative explanation contained in the intellectual currents of the day, but ultimately it leads to the big disagreements detailed above. From the experience of his presidency it seems enormously difficult to convincingly tie down FDR's thoughts when there are so many competing interpretations. This study aims to address this problem in three ways. The first is the simple idea that fresh analysis on previously neglected material will illuminate further the contentious areas of debate.

Second, analyzing what he was trying to accomplish with his speeches and writings as well as their immediate meaning can provide a good indication of his longer-term thinking at important junctures. In this methodology gaps and omissions become as important as what FDR actually said or wrote to persuade the public, party, and Congress to support his political agenda. By way of illustrative example FDR chose not to comment directly in public on the League of Nations for virtually a whole year from the summer of 1919 despite this period being the height of the League Fight. Instead, he advanced a consistently internationalist position that was still close to Wilson in many respects while avoiding the increasingly negative connotations of association with the president and the League. His rhetoric on the League, or lack of it, indicates a much more complex position than simple categories of support or rejection and enables deeper understanding of the formation of his internationalist outlook as a whole.[11]

Finally, this study rejects the a priori assumption that all FDR's positions were intellectually conceived. Secretary of Labor Frances Perkins wrote of FDR that he was "the most complicated human being I ever knew." Despite this common assessment, FDR was not an intellectually complex man or deep thinker and it is a mistake to view him as such.[12] Thus, the existing historiography has largely restricted itself unnecessarily by focusing on the impact of key individuals such as Theodore Roosevelt, Alfred Thayer Mahan, and Woodrow Wilson. They are still important influences to be analyzed, but we also need to focus on the practical experiences of FDR's life that may have contributed to his internationalism. The realities of international relations he was exposed to during his service in the Wilson administration, for instance, may well have been just as important to him as any intellectual communion with the president.

This focus on experience does not, in itself, require any complex methodology, though it can be aided by an awareness of the recent developments of cultural interpretations in the history of international relations. FDR's understanding of race, class, and gender can in certain instances illuminate further what he drew from particular experiences or ideas. Using them as categories of analysis to evaluate FDR's relations with other people and wider society, rather than as reified concepts can at times be instructive—for example in teasing out the different basis of FDR's racial assumptions from those of Wilson as a motivating and co-opting force for the US Caribbean interventions of 1916 onward. Ultimate causation with such approaches, however, is a notoriously difficult point to prove and this is particularly true with FDR's actions. Thus they in no way provide the central theoretical approach of this book. Instead, where appropriate, the newer historiography is brought in if it can help us understand something specific about FDR's internationalism or its context.

This work then aims to trace the development of FDR's international thinking in the years before he became president—the diplomatic education of the title. This detailed exegesis would appear vital not only as a point of departure from which to study his developing presidential foreign policy, but also to bring clarity and precision to the many existing shorthand descriptions of his earlier life. It also demonstrates the benefits in broadening interpretations of FDR to include not just his presidency and his intellectual influences, but his whole life experience. Understanding the complexities of FDR's prepresidential life and career promises a deeper and richer appreciation of his core international views.

CHAPTER 1

A PATRICIAN INTERNATIONALIST, 1882–1910

FRANKLIN D. ROOSEVELT'S (FDR) PARENTS WERE LONG ESTABLISHED members of the Hudson Valley gentry. Their wealth and lineage guaranteed their son's position in society and a privileged upbringing as a member of the patrician elite. Yet by the time of FDR's birth in 1882, cracks were appearing in this exclusive world. The country was changing and his childhood coincided with huge upheavals to domestic society and the international position of the United States. Both tradition and change would combine to shape FDR's early views of his country's relations with the wider world.

Generations of Americans considered the United States geographically isolated from the rest of the world. This common view was beginning to break down in the face of modernizing forces, but traditional hemispheric nationalism continued to hold an almost hegemonic status among the American people during FDR's early life. There was a strong parochial and pacifist strain to traditional American nationalism clearly evident in Jefferson's belief that the best way to protect democracy and liberty was to stay at home and rely on a civilian militia to rush to the defense of the country if an enemy ever approached its shores. FDR was certainly aware of this hemispheric outlook during his childhood—at Groton, in 1898, he argued against the annexation of Hawaii claiming: "We should look to the defense of our own coasts." Expanding this geographic point he argued, "All our territory is on this continent and all of it except Alaska is continuous...At present we have no vulnerable point...Why weaken our strategical [*sic*] position?"[1] These visible traces of FDR's Jeffersonian heritage at Groton provide a stark contrast to his views as a war president. During World War II, he clearly saw international political boundaries as secondary, the oceans as an integral part of the connected global system, and the earth as an integrated strategic whole.[2]

Such tightly conceived geographic conceptions of security were already being challenged during FDR's early years. Even in his youth he was not entirely comfortable with Jefferson's pacific and nonmilitaristic vision and the evidence indicates he already believed in an expansive geographic conception of US security with an assertive military protection of US property and interests, wherever they lay. FDR's privileged upbringing actually worked against him accepting a restricted view of the Western Hemisphere. His mother's family, the Delanos, had a long and fondly recounted seafaring tradition that included New England whaling and trade with China. FDR was himself an accomplished sailor who made full use of a succession of family yachts in his leisure time and held a lifelong fascination for maritime charts and prints. A succession of tutors, some foreign, and the elite private school at Groton also augmented FDR's wider appreciation and knowledge of the world outside the United States.[3] Groton, like many other elite private schools at the time, aimed through regular talks and debates covering international topics to develop a keen awareness of the wider world among the future leaders of the United States. One only has to note the numbers of influential Groton alumni such as Joseph Grew, Sumner Welles, Dean Acheson, Francis Biddle, and Averell Harriman who became members of the US foreign policy elite to infer the importance of their alma mater, or at least the connections they made there, in developing this interest.

Key to FDR's developing global awareness was his own extensive foreign travel. He grew up during the golden age of post–Civil War tourism when the number of Americans travelling abroad rose from 35,000 in 1870 to almost 250,000 by 1914. The increasing wealth of Americans, as their economy expanded, combined with improvements in rail connections and steamship travel to make foreign (particularly European) tourism a significant part of the popular imagination of the middle and upper classes.[4] FDR's mother Sara, commenting on her son's awareness of the wider world in 1933, indicated the importance of early travel when she recalled, "As time went on he acquired a remarkable flair for geography. This he attributed to his interest in stamp collecting...I think myself that his uncanny sense of direction may have resulted as much from the amount we travelled as it did from his absorption in stamps."[5] Between 1885 and 1905, he made no less than ten extended trips to Europe—first, annual trips with his parents for his ailing father to take the cures at the German spa-town of Bad Nauheim, then again with his widowed mother in 1901, followed by his own trip in the summer of 1903, and extended honeymoon with new wife Eleanor in 1905. He also knew the Caribbean well—his mother took him on a cruise of Puerto Rico and Cuba in 1904 and he made an extensive tour of Jamaica and Panama to see the canal construction in 1912.[6]

At a basic level, FDR appreciated how improvements in transportation and communication strengthened links between nations and their economies. People and goods were shipped with relative ease and a "cable" announcing the departure or arrival of travelers was now commonplace. The world seemed inextricably interconnected, interdependent, and smaller. The sentiments expressed by President William McKinley in his last public address affirming that "isolation is no longer possible or desirable" rang true with FDR's experience of the world.[7] FDR's basic knowledge of the world and how it was interconnected, although not unusual among members of his own class, was a characteristic and experience that made him different from the majority of Americans with a more parochial frame of reference.

A further factor breaking down FDR's vestigial Jeffersonianism was his precocious awareness of the military, particularly naval, technological and tactical revolution that was taking place during the late nineteenth and early twentieth century. By the 1880s, as the United States grew in size and strength, and as improvements in the armaments and sailing capacity of warships became more self-evident, there were increasing calls for the protection of her interests in a more forceful way. Naval theorists began to advocate a large battleship-based navy to assert the nation's will and withstand the ambitions of other nations on the world stage. The navy should have the capacity to operate unilaterally and meet the enemy on the high seas to protect the Western Hemisphere and American interests wherever they lay. These naval theorists fundamentally rejected Jeffersonian concepts of national defense, the geographic isolation of the United States and concerns about negative implications arising from a powerful federal government and military.

FDR was an immediate and enthusiastic believer in the new naval gospel and from an early age, he believed in the necessity of a large, battleship-based navy for the United States. At Groton, in 1897, he debated in favor of increasing the size of the navy and enthusiastically reported to his mother, "Over 30 votes were cast out of which our opponents received three! I think it is about the biggest beating that has been given this year. I expected we would win, but I did not think we would get as many votes as we did."[8] Theodore Roosevelt (TR) long advocated increasing the size and power of the navy and was a strong influence on his fifth cousin in this respect. His first book, *The Naval War of 1812* (1882), was highly critical of the Jeffersonian approach to naval strategy, and from the 1880s he continually argued for a large modern navy as a prerequisite of great power status and national defense. As president, he delivered on naval expansion and famously sent the 16 battleships of the "Great White Fleet" around the world in 1907 as a mark of US naval power and engagement with the world.

The naval theorist, Alfred Thayer Mahan, argued many of the same points and also formed a distinct influence on the young FDR. Mahan had close ties to Groton school, sending his son Lyle there and delivering a lecture on naval power the year before FDR joined the establishment.[9] FDR was also familiar with his writings—he was given *The Influence of Sea Power on History 1660–1773* (1890) for Christmas in 1897 and for his following birthday *The Interest of America in Sea Power, Present and Future* (1897). Sara Roosevelt reported that he "practically memorized the whole book."[10] Both TR and Mahan influenced FDR's youthful appreciation of the theory of power in international relations. Their knowledge and proselytizing of the naval military revolution helped condition the young FDR to perceive an expanded geography of US security that stretched way beyond the Western Hemisphere.

TR also introduced a Hamiltonian tension to FDR's conception of democracy long before promulgating his "New Nationalism" of 1910 and long before another important influence in FDR's life, Woodrow Wilson, made a similar transition to ideas of a powerful executive. This point of political philosophy dated back, in the American context, to *Federalist Papers* and the days of Jefferson and Hamilton's argument over the size and purpose of the Federal government, but it now took on crucial importance in a much larger, more powerful, and increasingly world orientated United Sates. Initially FDR's sensitivity toward the constitutional separation of powers had been fairly typical—writing to his mother from Harvard in 1902 on TR's intervention in a coal strike he thought that "his tendency to make the executive power stronger than the Houses of Congress...a bad thing."[11] In 1902, assertive executive power was still a very new phenomenon and was, no doubt, as shocking to FDR's sensibilities as it was for many others. FDR soon began to talk of his own presidential ambitions though. In his first job at the Wall Street legal firm of Carter, Ledyard, and Milburn in 1907, he announced candidly that he had no intention of following a career in law, but would rather enter politics and would run for office as soon as possible. His ultimate aim was the presidency and he planned to begin with a seat in the state assembly, then after some years win an appointment as Assistant Secretary of the Navy and then move to governor of New York before his final step—exactly the route to power taken by TR.[12]

Through his bold leadership and personal diplomacy as president, TR provided a vivid demonstration of the promise of power in world affairs. His mediation of disputes in Latin America, Europe, and Asia were regarded by many as stunning examples of both an executive lead and a personal ability to influence the course of history. This point was not lost on FDR—while

sea-ocea- as history not barrier

on honeymoon in 1905, news came of the president's role in the Japanese-Russian peace treaty prompting FDR to write: "Everyone is talking about Cousin Theodore saying that he is the most prominent figure of present day history, and adopting toward our country in general a most respectful and almost loving tone."[13] FDR, already a firm believer in the ability of humans to influence the course of history from his childhood reading of historians such as Thomas Carlyle, no doubt found it easy to picture his cousin as one of the "great men" of history.[14] For FDR, though, this did not imply unrestrained idealism—the individual could still influence history within a governing framework of world forces described by theorists such as Mahan.

FDR's appreciation of power on the world stage was less nuanced than that of his presidential cousin. The immaturity of FDR's diplomatic understandings is best demonstrated by his attitude toward the worsening relations between the United States and Japan during the early years of the twentieth century. The desire for cheap labor in the United States led to increasing numbers of Japanese immigrants, first to Hawaii and then California, breeding suspicion and causing racial tensions to erupt. TR, respectful toward the Japanese to a degree, had already maintained a policy of friendly accommodation as Japanese power grew in the Pacific. Wary of Japan's greater regional power, he compromised on matters such as the control of Korea, in return for accommodations in China and the Philippines. He was again conciliatory in finding a workable compromise in the "Gentleman's Agreement" of March 1907 and his direct appeals to Governor Johnson of California to halt racially inflammatory legislation in 1909. TR, in his diplomacy, was therefore at odds with a purely nationalist approach and he was clearly prepared to expend domestic credibility for the sake of America's strategic Pacific interests and wider security.

FDR's personal experience seems largely to mirror growing American uneasiness with the Japanese. In 1899, responding to a talk at Groton, he was dismissive of them and felt the speaker "thought too much of the Japs."[15] However, following the Japanese victory against the Russians in 1904–1905 suspicions of Japanese military capability began to develop as a significant public force. This change is reflected in FDR's account of a meeting with some Japanese naval officers on his honeymoon in 1905 where he found himself "giving out more information than I receive."[16] Sadly, there is little evidence of FDR's views toward the Japanese following this encounter until he joined the Wilson administration. During this time, FDR was not in a position of significant national power and it is unlikely that he appreciated TR's more nuanced diplomatic position. Indeed, FDR's party, the Democrats played the nationalist card and took full advantage of the exposed Republican position in California during the 1908 presidential campaign. William Jennings Bryan, clearly appealing to local sentiment, stated that the Japanese were not "assimiable [*sic*]", and thus set his party's stance on the issue through to the 1912 election.[17]

It is likely that FDR saw the Japanese, through their assertiveness and extensive immigration, as posing a physical threat to the United States. With hemispheric security taking precedence in his primitive strategic calculations, it would have been easy for FDR to adopt the more nationalist position of Bryan, but without the former's well-known pacifism. In stark contrast to both TR and Bryan, FDR more likely would have backed up arguments of exclusion and the prevention of miscegenation against Japanese protest with bellicose talk of war, as he did later in 1913. As these differences over Japan between TR and FDR demonstrate, the latter held, or could politically afford to hold, a much less nuanced appreciation of world diplomacy at this stage. International relations for FDR were a question of basic military power protecting material interests and clearly defined spheres of influence among the Great Powers. Contrary to how he is often portrayed, TR saw more porous national boundaries and a host of other methods and concessions, in addition to military power, to protect US interest and exert global influence.

FDR's youthful attraction to assertive power on the world stage as a strategy for the United States does raise the question of whether he held any deeper, underlying psychological motivations for his position. Historians have used gender as a category of historical analysis to explain the aggressive and often acquisitive imperial approach to world affairs as a product of the insecurities men felt during the late nineteenth and early twentieth century. These insecurities, particularly among the middle and upper classes, originated in fears of decadence due to increasing industrialization and associated material wealth. They were reinforced by increasingly activist women challenging the traditionally male dominance of political life and Darwinian-based fears that the tough manly vigor needed for the struggle of life was being dangerously dissipated. In this explanation, an assertive foreign policy becomes a way of recovering, confirming and reinforcing men's sense of masculinity as a coping strategy for the challenges and strains of modern life.[18]

There are figures close to FDR that offer the potential of transferring such a coping strategy to him. Perhaps the most obvious is TR and in all FDR's exaggerated manly actions throughout his early life and political career he is often described as aping his fifth cousin who championed and exemplified the "strenuous life."[19] FDR was demonstrably proud of his connection to TR—as he got older, he even adopted some of TR's style and language by wearing a pince-nez and using phrases such as "bully" and "dee-lighted" in conversation. There was, of course, an even more direct connection to TR through Eleanor Roosevelt (TR's niece from his brother Elliott) whom FDR married in 1905.

The difficult fact remains, that although FDR may have read TR's speeches, heard him speak at Groton and even been inspired to enter politics by his example, he only had very rare and occasional contact with TR prior to entering politics—the first volume of FDR's personal letters records only three occasions between 1897 and 1901 when FDR either attended a lecture by his cousin or met him in person.[20] An equally likely candidate for influencing FDR to take an assertive approach, and one who does not receive such a great deal of attention, is TR's friend the Rev. Endicott Peabody at Groton. Indeed, FDR said himself that "as long as I live, the influence of Dr. Peabody means and will mean more to me than that of any [person] next to my father and mother."[21]

FDR joined the private male boarding school at Groton in 1896 and remained there for four years until he went to Harvard in 1900 with only short holidays at Christmas, Easter, and during the summer months. The boarding school was kept small, not much more than 100 pupils, deliberately by Peabody who took his role of in loco parentis literally. He treated his pupils as a family and himself as Paterfamilias with his wife presiding over the school as mother. Peabody was in near daily contact with FDR for four of his most formative years and carefully guided the development of his character. Among the characteristics Peabody emphasized at Groton were the aggressive manly virtues of pluck and fighting spirit. War and martial combat were the most obvious opportunities to display such spirit and an enthusiasm for such activities developed in private schools across the Atlantic world during the period. This often took on a romantic, chivalric quality that refused to acknowledge the technological horror of modern war. The peace lover was often seen as a poltroon and fool, lacking in manly spirit and a pacific boy had great difficulty justifying his position.[22]

Whereas more intellectually effusive men such as TR have, perhaps, provided better candidates for tracing the links between societal insecurities and foreign policy, such links are extremely difficult to discern in FDR. There is certainly much circumstantial evidence that FDR experienced some of the insecurities common to middle and upper-class men at this time. In his own family there were direct examples of the results of wealth without discretion—"society" viewed FDR's half-brother James "Rosy" Roosevelt with some disdain for leading a dissolute and pleasure seeking life, while the Roosevelt family ostracized his son "Taddy" after he made an "unsuitable" marital match. Taddy's waywardness at Groton caused FDR a great deal of embarrassment and he felt little sympathy for him—his only comment on the marriage was, "It will be well for him...to go to parts unknown...and begin life anew."[23] There were also frequent negative assessments of FDR's own manliness—TR's niece, Corinne Robinson Alsop, and her friends referred to him as "the feather duster," while TR's daughter Alice referred to him as "a good little mother's boy."[24] As a cosseted, and slightly English-sounding boy arriving at Groton two years later than normal, he was also never quite accepted as one of the "boys" and longed to be seen as having "school spirit."[25] This theme continued as he grew older and FDR's rejection at Harvard by the exclusive Porcellian Club, to which both his father and TR belonged, cut him deeply and was, he told a relative, the "greatest disappointment of my life."[26]

The evidential obstacles facing any attempt to extend such gender or class-based causative explanations to FDR's views on international relations in his early life appear insurmountable. At no point did he expressly discuss his insecurities—we can only guess at them from his personal circumstances and the comments of others. Furthermore, he gives no extended discussion of foreign affairs at this time in a way that convincingly links his position to any masculine insecurity he experienced. So, while such explanations have shed some light on turn of the century US international relations, at present, they can tell us little about FDR's personal views.

The difficulties of evidence continue with how FDR perceived himself as an American. National feeling at this time contained a strong strain of ideological separation from the rest of the world, particularly Europe. Americans saw themselves as a people set apart from the old world and unconnected to its power politics, secret diplomacy, and aristocratic wars. FDR's extensive travel and cosmopolitan experience affected his perception of the ideological divisions in the world. Travel was a process through which people made sense of the wider world and tested their views.[27] Analyzing the impact of travel on TR, Frank Ninkovich traces a "thoroughgoing cosmopolitan cast of mind" that set him apart from a provincial mindset and enabled him to see civilization as a world movement. Ninkovich continues that "his perception of the globe's unity in space and time was crucial, for it obliterated the geographical, cultural and temporal distinctions between the old and new worlds."[28] Although TR is known for advocating the protection of American vital interests with his famous "big stick," the president also clearly operated on an idealistic plane. For TR, world order and civilization were vital to preserving American global interests.

It is tempting, given the similarities in class and background, to assume that FDR drew the same lessons from his foreign travel. As president, however, TR held very different concerns and priorities to the younger Roosevelt. FDR saw the United States as part of a global whole and inextricably linked to it by modern technology, but there is no evidence that he made an intellectual connection or moral investment in a more idealistic concern for order and civilization as a function of national security in his early years. Neither is there evidence that he shared TR's more idealistic investment in a duty toward a particular type of civilization, namely "English-speaking" as vital to US security. Yet FDR's clear and connected view of the world shows he did not espouse a traditional hemispheric Americanism. It seems more accurate to describe an international awareness in FDR that gave his country unavoidable material and physical interests rather than political or idealistic connections. For FDR, the Western Hemisphere remained off-limits to European ambitions while the United States should robustly and unilaterally defend against any challenge to its global interests and security.

FDR's Dutch heritage, his extensive travel, foreign tutors, schooling at Groton, French and German language lessons, and even some public schooling in Germany all added to his cosmopolitan frame of mind. FDR positioned the United States at the pinnacle of civilization, but there is no contemporary evidence to suggest that he held a particular preference or dislike for any other European country or people. Perhaps, FDR's cosmopolitanism and lack of reflection meant that he was less inclined than others to see particular nations as a threat or particularly friendly to the United States. There is little evidence, for instance, that FDR had in his youth a "habit," widespread in the "Anglo-Saxon world" of employing tropes of pathology and gender to denigrate the French.[29] Indeed, FDR travelled often in France; spending some of his honeymoon there in 1905 and his mother continued to visit her sister who made her permanent home in Paris.[30] Similarly, there was no deep-seated antipathy to the Germany of his youth despite some anecdotal evidence of irritation at German boorishness and officialdom.[31]

Neither was there a special affinity with the British. James Roosevelt did affect the lifestyle of an English country squire at Springwood. He also introduced his son to upper-class British friends and acquaintances and supplied him with English reading matter in an attempt to develop similar interests in his son.[32] This has led to suggestions that FDR's father gave him an early bias toward the English; if so, his firm countervailing strand of American nationalism prevented this from taking root. At Groton the *Spectator* became known as the "Speckeled Tater" and along with *Punch* was "hardly appreciated by others, as they are so English you know."[33] Alongside the English magazines his father sent him, he was also an avid reader of native magazines such as the *Scientific American*.[34] There is little evidence to suggest FDR's cosmopolitanism contained the same degree of partiality to Anglo-Saxon order and civilization that TR, Mahan, or even his father, expressed. Likewise, there is no evidence to suggest that FDR, unlike TR and Mahan, advocated early formal alliance with the British or anyone else to restore the European or world balance of power.

It is, of course, possible to speculate on the source of FDR's unwillingness or inability to develop his thoughts to any great extent with regard to links to the rest of the world at this time. The contrast with TR, who was able to pursue vigorous assertive nationalism while at the same time developing ideological connections to other nations, is all the more stark and illuminating because FDR is so often compared to him. The most that can be inferred is that his failure to appreciate ideological connections was possibly due to a combination of FDR's youth, his character and personality, the retarding nature of aspects of his Americanism, and perhaps the wider ethos of anti-intellectualism he would have encountered in society and particularly at Groton.

Peabody did encourage a virulent anti-intellectualism in his pupils at Groton. He stressed action over thought—the wholesome fellow did not think too much and there was no place for the sensitive, intellectual child at his school. Groton was supposed to prepare its students for Ivy League university entrance and the lack of intellectual stimulation was eventually noticed by an inspection team from Harvard. Criticizing the school badly, their report said Groton provided mediocre instruction, but an excellent education.[35] FDR became obsessed with a broad range of sporting activity at school and university, but it would be mere speculation to argue that by embracing the sporting ethic, he eschewed intellectual depth and thus set the course for a nonreflective approach to international relations throughout his life. It could equally be argued that his youth or basic personality led to such characteristics at this time. The evidence for any pivotal impact of Peabody and Groton in this respect is insufficient.

However, FDR did reflect on his youthful views towards European countries on at least one occasion during his presidency. In a memo FDR produced for his press secretary Steve Early in October 1939 refuting claims made by journalist Ernest K. Lindley that he was an internationalist with a preference for the Allies, he wrote:

> The statement... "in later years he made it plain by his comments that he did not look back upon Germany with the same friendliness that he felt for Great Britain and France" is deliberate falsification. As a matter of simple fact, I did not know Great Britain and France as a boy but I did know Germany. If anything, I looked upon the Germany that I knew with far more friendliness than I did on Great Britain or France.[36]

Taken at face value this would seem to support a claim of FDR's ambivalence toward European nations and provide evidence of a more long term and deep-seated nationalistic "Europhobic-Hemispherism" in the mature president that originated in his youth.[37]

Yet this picture of strong American nationalism is far from convincing. It does not explain, for instance, why FDR became such an early and ardent supporter of the Allied nations in World War I—heartily advocating intervention even before Britain had declared war. It also ignores the important context of the memo written at a time when FDR was deeply involved in managing the revision of the Neutrality Act. The president had spent months carefully moving forward behind the scenes with revision to include a "cash and carry" provision as part of his "aid short of war" policy to the Allies. Publicly he felt it was necessary to maintain the appearance of strict neutrality—the last thing that he wanted was to appear partial in character at such a crucial time. Thus, he downplayed his links with the Allies and exaggerated his links to Germany because, by then, he perceived the latter as a threat to civilization that needed to be countered by an achievable revision to the Neutrality Act. The memo was clearly part of the campaign to secure revision that the Senate passed on October 27, the House on November 2, and which FDR signed into law on November 4.

FDR's early ambivalence and sense of impartiality toward all European nations was, in essence, superficial and vulnerable in an era of decline for the world order underwritten by the *Pax Britannica*. As Germany built up its navy, surpassing the United States in the number of battleships by 1907, and appeared more aggressive in its intentions on the world stage, FDR's primitive strategic calculations of power would have governed his response. The British and their large navy stationed in the Atlantic could help mitigate the German threat to US security and FDR was increasingly drawn to them as another power feeling threatened by Germany. TR, of course, was in the vanguard of increasing rapprochement with the British, but FDR watched only as an outsider. While the older TR understood early on the importance of other nations to US security, in FDR's case, his youthful Americanism acted as a brake on his acceptance of this idea. Only toward the end of the period did FDR begin to develop his appreciation that nations of the world could share strategic and ideological interests. Thus, a great deal of the complex subtlety of international diplomacy was lost on him at this time. FDR's Americanism continued to work against making ideological connections with other nations until it was increasingly challenged by the rise of a powerful German navy in the years before the outbreak of World War I.

FDR's nationalism was firmly grounded in an idealistic veneration of the American way of life. He believed deeply in his country's republican government and felt that its citizens should have regular and free democratic choice of their representatives. He also held that equality and the broadest universal male suffrage were the best conditions for democracy. This Jeffersonian faith in the majority placed liberty securely in the hands of the people rather than any intermediary aristocratic elite. While there is no direct evidence that FDR held these values during his early life, as the Democrats nominated less radical presidential candidates, FDR followed his father politically by becoming a member of the party of Jefferson. He also had a fierce pride in the Revolutionary War heritage and tradition of resistance to British monarchical oppression displayed on both sides of his family. FDR's fondly recalled that his ancestor Isaac "the patriot" hated British trade laws and was forced to flee his Dutchess County home for the duration of the war after voting for independence in 1776. On the Delano side, the British imprisoned FDR's great-grandfather for a time during the war of 1812 and FDR's grandfather remembered experiencing as a child the threatened shelling of Fairhaven by the British.[38]

Wider US culture and society challenged and subverted FDR's democratic views. For many Americans in the late nineteenth and early twentieth century the color of a person's skin denoted levels of physical, moral, and mental development in a hierarchy of race that ranked white as superior and black as the lowest condition with yellow and Latino brown somewhere in the middle. FDR accepted this without questioning the inherent contradiction—the American system proclaimed liberty and equality for all citizens, but at the same time applied strict rules of racial prejudice that excluded blacks from participation in such a system. Faced with a domestic racial dilemma, FDR resorted to a casual form of racism, endemic throughout white society, to exclude blacks. He frequently used the pejorative terms "nigger" and "darky" in his private correspondence during this period, though these were later changed to "colored" in more sensitive times by the editor of his letters.[39]

The evolutionary thought of Charles Darwin as interpreted by Herbert Spencer in his inaccurate, though popular, concept of "survival of the fittest" became a powerful transnational rationale for racial domination at this time. Social Darwinism provided white Americans, who identified themselves as superior, with the biological justification to enslave or sweep aside other peoples (in the case of the American South and West) or indulge in imperialism (in the case of the Caribbean and Philippines). There is no evidence to suggest that FDR ever took such a biologically determinist view on race. Instead, he believed that over time even those races he viewed as presently deficient could progress to civilized status. It is unlikely that FDR was aware of the ultimate philosophical origins of his rejection of Spencer's interpretation of Darwin, but it probably owed something to the popular evolutionary theory of Jean-Baptiste Lamarck. This Lamarckian perspective rejected the search for "anthropometric" differences between races and held that society progressed by the transmission of culturally acquired characteristics. Thus, an acquired capacity for "law and order", "self-restraint," and "self-control" could define both a race and its level of development. It could also justify imperial interventions on developmental grounds.

Politicians such as TR urged such a role for the United States using Lamarckian theories to broaden the Anglo-Saxon racial construct that was so popular at this time. Blood no longer mattered in their assumptions of superiority—identity coalesced around ideals and institutions, the creed, custom, laws, and language of peoples. Constructs such as "the English speaking peoples," as TR titled one of the chapters in his book *The Winning of the West* (1889), relied on terms such as "culture" and "civilization" as markers of a more inclusive identity still described as Anglo-Saxon, but increasingly as "Anglo-American," "European," or simply "white."[40] This latter description was closer to FDR's experience of race in the world. Although there is no direct evidence from the period under consideration, he did describe in a 1912 speech a thousand-year struggle by "the Aryan races...to obtain individual freedom...in almost every European and American country."[41] Though this suggests a northern European focus, there is no evidence of him ever indulging in either more narrow racial or cultural Anglo-Saxon rhetoric. This places him distinctly at odds with politicians like Henry Cabot Lodge and theorists such as Mahan who emphasized the necessary expansion of the Anglo-Saxon race as a justification for imperialist expansion and strategic alliances with the British. FDR, of Dutch heritage, did not consider himself an Anglo-Saxon and rejected such racial and cultural definitions, preferring instead the broader white identity. As Harper notes, FDR consciously avoided joining the anglophile Pilgrim Society, preferring instead lifelong membership of the Holland Society. FDR did later become a vice president of the English Speaking Union, but the American arm of this organization was not set up until 1920 (two years after the British arm) and had its roots in the experience of World War I. The founder of the American arm, Sir Evelyn Wrench, also claimed the organization held "no narrow attitude of race pride [and] no spirit of hostility to any peoples."[42]

When FDR's outlook on race combined with his democratic views it resulted in an early and deep antipathy to the colonialism practiced by European powers. He followed, in the case of the Anglo-Boer war, the majority of Americans rather than the minority pro-British stance of the Vice President TR, Secretary of State John Hay, and even Mahan. On the outbreak of war in October 1899, most of the American public and Congress instinctively sympathized with the underdog Boers and cheered their initial successes. As the Boers besieged Ladysmith, FDR wrote to his parents, "Hurrah for the Boers! I entirely sympathise with them."[43] He followed the war avidly and when challenged by his mother that the Boers "were not a race to do good in the world" he felt strongly enough to disagree with her more Anglophile sentiments arguing, "I cannot help feeling convinced that the Boers have the side of right and that for the past ten years they have been *forced* into this war. I am sure you will feel this if you only read up the Boer case."[44] At Harvard, he continued his support of the Boers by organizing a postwar relief fund that raised $336 from his classmates. He sent the money to TR who was able to forward support from sympathetic bodies in the

United States via the State Department. It seems that once the war was over and civilized British rule assured the president was more willing to acknowledge his own Dutch heritage.[45]

The debate over imperialism in the late nineteenth and early twentieth century did not merely involve taking a position on the actions of other world powers—the United States was increasingly implicated, following the annexation of Hawaii and the Philippines after the Spanish-American war of 1898. Economic, racial, and strategic arguments prompted an increasingly vocal imperialist movement to advocate that the United States join in the scramble for colonies. TR justified the acquisitions largely through claims of American cultural superiority, arguing that the United States had the right to bring order to the chaos and misrule in Spanish colonies.[46] Mahan, though he used more direct Anglo-Saxon explanations, pushed for the strategic needs of empire—expanding trade required bases and coaling stations in colonies, particularly the Pacific, so that the navy could protect American interests. For both men there was also the lurking presence of the Germans and possibly the Japanese ready to take advantage of US inaction.

Unlike TR and Mahan, FDR was not an imperialist of any stripe outside the Western Hemisphere. His knowledge of Mahan's work does not automatically mean that he subscribed to all of his arguments for geographic expansion. He may well have appreciated Mahan's claims for the application of naval power, but did not see an immediate US strategic benefit from imperialism. FDR failed to support Mahan's call for direct control in the Hawaiian Islands that Democratic president Grover Cleveland refused to annex in 1893. In a debate at Groton in January 1898, FDR did not see the necessary link to colonialism as the United States "already own Pearl Harbor without annexation." Neither did he agree with the proposed economic benefits stating, "Captain Mahan himself says it is nonsense to think of annexation unless we decide to spend an enormous sum for fortifications." As an afterthought to the debate and perhaps indicative of his true feeling on the feeble economic argument, he scrawled on his notes "Mr. P. [likely Harold Peabody, a participant] Says our trade will double in ten years, I do not see why this should be so as he had not proved it." FDR appears to have fashioned his response to imperialism via a primitive strategic assessment—thus it offended his moral and nationalist sensibilities. In the Groton Hawaiian debate, he asked rhetorically, "Why should we soil our hands with Colonies?...Why annex them without their consent?...Why take away the nationality of a free people?" He went on to ask, "Why meddle with this land thousands of miles away whose inhabitants are so different from us in every way? Why...spend millions in a foolish cause?"[47] Pupils were given the positions to argue in Groton debates, but FDR's impassioned pleas demonstrate he was at least aware of anti-imperialistic positions and was attempting to reconcile his adherence to aspects of TR and Mahan's thinking with them.

There is little contemporary evidence on FDR's opinion towards possession of the Philippines. He did take the position favoring independence in a Groton debate of January 1900—writing to his parents, "We...are pros...in favor of independence...Our opponents are pretty strong but I hope we can win."[48] Again, this demonstrated at least a clear knowledge of the arguments that at some future date the Filipinos would reach a sufficient level of civilization to allow them self-determination. The only comment he made after he lost was that "our opponents were all fair, and had the entire sympathy of the audience & made the American eagle crow as loud as he could." This perhaps indicates a cynicism toward cultural justifications for expansion that may have grown after February 1899 when full-scale war erupted against the insurgent nationalist forces of Emilio Aguinaldo.[49] After the bitter conflict and with the Philippines such a difficult possession for the Americans to defend, even TR ceased to support retention by 1907 and had by this time largely retracted all his overt imperialistic positions. In contrast, at no point did FDR feel any sense of racial superiority or clear-cut strategic advantage important enough outside the Western Hemisphere to compromise his Americanism by welcoming European or American-style imperialism. His anti-imperialism was more homegrown. For FDR, the Hamiltonian emphasis on executive-led action he acquired from TR did not transform into support for expansionary imperialist schemes. Indeed, he probably agreed with the Jeffersonian anti-imperialist sentiment centered in the Democratic Party that prioritized the threat posed by imperialism to the democratic institutions of the United States.

Anti-imperialism was bound to cause positional difficulties in any area of the world in which FDR could see a clear strategic interest for the United States. Here FDR developed a deep humanitarian and paternalistic concern for the welfare of his fellow man as a justification for intervention. Although it sounds a thoroughly cynical move, this was an almost unconscious response that had its origins in the broad influences FDR encountered in his family, schooling, and wider society. FDR's father provided an important role model with his concerned patrician service to the community and expected his son to instinctively follow his virtues of honor, fairness, love of God and country, and sense of noblesse oblige. For James Roosevelt, the latter meant running many aspects of life for the inhabitants of Hyde Park—he was a dominant voice in the management of village affairs, was senior vestryman at St James' Episcopal Church and an unpaid manager at the nearby Mount Hope hospital. Sara Roosevelt's stated ambition for her son was for him "to grow up to be like his father, straight and honourable, just and kind, an upstanding American."[50] The family ethos was a powerful force that FDR kept in mind even with the distractions of Harvard. The Roosevelts, he argued in a sophomore paper, felt that "being born in a good position, there was no excuse for them if they did not do their duty by the community, and it is because this idea was instilled into them from their birth that they have in every case proved good citizens."[51]

There were, of course, other possible sources of FDR's concern for the welfare of members of society. TR and Jacob Riis, the social reformer, visited Groton to give inspiring talks to the boys that FDR attended, while TR's presidency provided a dramatic example of domestic reform. FDR's future wife Eleanor was also a member of the New York Junior League, a voluntary women's body conducting civic charitable work, and reputedly took FDR on a tour of the squalid New York tenements. His wife, it is suggested, opened up a world previously unknown to the young patrician.[52] Another possible source of FDR's concern for the welfare of his fellow man was his religion. FDR was firm in his Episcopalian beliefs throughout his life and held an unquestioning acceptance of a beneficent God, belief in the Ten Commandments, the Sermon on the Mount, and the direct teachings of the Bible as an ethical guide for life. This is in stark contrast to FDR's later reputation as a supreme casuist. H. L. Mencken once joked about FDR as president that if he "became convinced tomorrow that coming out for cannibalism would get him the votes he so sorely needs, he would begin fattening up a missionary in the White House backyard come Wednesday."[53] Raymond Moley, no friend of FDR after leaving his position as presidential adviser, was perhaps the more perceptive observer when he noted, "Roosevelt was no cold-blooded opportunist. In fact, he felt so intensely the need to do right that he had to believe that he did right. Those that said otherwise 'do not know their man.'"[54] The right thing during FDR's youth meant showing a humanitarian concern for those Americans less fortunate than he was.

The influence of FDR's family and upbringing was clearly important and Groton's Episcopalian head, Endicott Peabody, reinforced many of the same values. As late as 1941, FDR dutifully wrote to his 84-year-old former master, "I count it among the blessings of my life that it was given to me in my formative years to have the privilege of your guiding hand and the benefit of your inspiring example."[55] Peabody had read a biography of Charles Kingsley, one of the founders of the Christian Socialist movement, while at Trinity College, Cambridge. Kingsley's scheme to Christianize capitalism and remove the stigma of individual responsibility from poverty and poor conditions profoundly moved him. On his return to the United States, he threw himself into missionary work and this became the later model of service for Groton boys.[56] Peabody derided the private life of gain and aimed to inculcate in the boys in his care an ideal of service to their fellow men. This perhaps resonated with FDR who had already reputedly been made aware of the tenets of social Christianity by a Swiss tutor Mlle Jeanne Sandoz before he arrived at Groton.[57] While at the school, FDR joined the school missionary society and helped aid the local needy and disadvantaged boys from nearby Boston.[58] Whether genuine or not, FDR's humanitarian concern for fellow Americans had a distinctly European flavor, though it no doubt flourished in the moral climate created by ministers of the Social Gospel such as Walter Rauschenbusch and Washington Gladden.

The ultimate point to FDR's humanitarian concern was a belief in human progress that, in truth, contained both secular and religious influences and was relatively common among Americans at the time. FDR's sense of history was also crucial—his mother noted, "He loved history in any form."[59] The journalist and early FDR biographer Ernest Lindley felt that he was "historically minded more than philosophically minded" and "well rooted in the past, by reading as well as by family tradition."[60] This was partly down to Enlightenment concepts on the perfectibility of man and linear, irreversible views of history that stretched back to Kant, Rousseau, and through the historical schemes of Hegel and Comte. Of course it is unlikely that the nonintellectual FDR was a student of Enlightenment thought; his liberal view of history was acquired via popular Romantic historians—particularly Thomas Macaulay, the British Whig, who emphasized the inevitable growth of constitutional government, democracy, personal fairness, and scientific progress. FDR absorbed this historical outlook throughout his childhood reading and education.[61]

To FDR history was also the unveiling of God's plan and in this, like many Americans, his Protestantism was truly liberal in the developmental sense. FDR confirmed this was the outlook at Groton during his time there when he recounted, "I well remember my old schoolmaster, Mr Peabody, teaching us that material and spiritual progress has had its periodic ups and downs, but that the up-curves are always the longer, and that the net advance is certain in the end." FDR therefore, like many others of his time, adopted a moral rather than intellectual stance toward the past—the lesson history provided gave it purpose. As his son Elliott noted, his father was "a firm advocate of the cause-and-effect theory of history."[62] While FDR did not reject the determinism of theorists such as Mahan completely, he maintained a deep faith in the ability of people to learn from the past and create their own future within God's plan. Individuals who understood the framework of world forces in which they operated could still direct history.

This belief in the historical progress of humanity was also the source of FDR's famous optimism—humanity had the ability to learn from mistakes and what Peabody described as the "upward curve" would always become apparent. Optimism was a truly significant historical force for FDR; the pessimism manifest in determinism offended his sensibilities, which were common to his class and background. Thus in his view, the cynic, the pessimist, and the man of little faith were a truly subversive danger to humanity. Travelling to Europe on the *George Washington* in 1919, FDR and his wife read "Henry Adams" prompting Eleanor to comment that it was "very interesting but sad to have had so much and yet find so little." To Eleanor, Adams' pessimism was a betrayal of his class, but it was also evidence that the ramifications of vast impersonal forces still had to penetrate the Roosevelt clan, despite the fact that they were travelling to the scene of four years of seemingly unstoppable human carnage.[63]

By the 1890s, conceptions of progress that lacked an intellectual basis, such as FDR's, were under determined philosophical attack. The American pragmatic philosophers were questioning whether the past could ever act as a reliable guide—William James and later John Dewey, among others, had a distinctly radical sense of history. They treated ideas as historical (including their own), rejected static models of reality and all schemes of knowledge that idealists and empiricists advanced—in Dewey's words "progress is not automatic."[64] Such relativistic notions that admitted the contingency of truth were alien to FDR and he remained blissfully ignorant of the radical changes in philosophy of the time. William James taught at Harvard while FDR was a student there, but he did not sign up for his course. Neither is there any evidence of a wider awareness or interest in what Morton White described as the "revolt against formalism." Thorstein Veblen's economic theories that shifted the focus from laws to institutions and from profit to need failed to penetrate FDR's traditional reliance on Mill, Malthus, Ricard, and Say. Similarly, the innovative jurisprudence of Oliver Wendell Holmes, Louis Brandeis, and Roscoe Pound that shifted from absolute truth to a truth found in experience made no visible impact on FDR who retained his faith in Newtonian legal concepts.[65] Holmes's famous judgment on FDR as "a first class temperament, but a second class intellect" therefore sums up the nonintellectual and nonrelativist moralist succinctly. Pragmatism could well have provided FDR with a justification for imperialism had he devoted the intellectual resource to gathering the empirical evidence to support it, but such an endeavor would have been fundamentally out of character.[66]

In less esoteric circles by the 1890s, there was also a growing level of concern about the negative impact on society created by worst excesses of laissez-faire capitalism and its attendant industrialization, immigration, and urbanization. Concerned citizens, often described as Progressive, attempted planned solutions in problem areas such as politics, crime, poverty, inequality, slums, hygiene, and child labor. While FDR sympathized with many progressive positions during his early life and adopted increasingly a progressive language as he entered the political world, it is difficult to prove whether this constituted an actual progressive outlook. What is certain is that there is no evidence to suggest he took a philosophical approach to progressivism.

This was particularly true with progressivism on the international stage. It is difficult to argue that FDR was a progressive imperialist when he demonstrated such ambivalence to the United States expanding the territory under its control. Similarly, more ethical ideas for international exchanges and cooperative movements failed to grab his attention. Mirroring his later position during the Wilson administration, he appears to have completely ignored the international peace movement's activism at this time. The same was true with more formal governmental schemes even though FDR was a trained lawyer. At no point does the evidence show he demonstrated an interest in the Hague Conferences, despite TR's prominent role in calling the second, or in Taft's arbitration treaties. Neither was there any precursor evident in FDR's early life of his later support for the World Court. These and more general movements for international arbitration and law that attracted a great deal of support during the early twentieth century appear to have failed to spark his interest at this time.

It was a similar story with international economics where FDR's education was largely traditional. His opinions probably amounted to little more than advocating free trade and support for John Hay's "open door" in China.[67] Debating the fate of Hawaii in 1898, he saw no harm in English annexation as "we should have free trade with the islands, for England stands for free trade."[68] There is no evidence that he subscribed to the "glut" thesis that linked internal stability to the sale of surpluses in foreign markets or believed that overseas development was integral to US security. Thus much of Emily Rosenberg's "Liberal Developmentalism"—a conviction that other countries should replicate the experience of the United States and that government activity should promote private enterprise—did not register with FDR at this time.[69]

FDR followed a paternalistic humanitarianism founded on his need to do the "right thing," on his deep belief in human progress and on his optimism. It was equally founded on the rejection of determinism, ignorance of pragmatism, and lack of curiosity toward sophisticated progressivism. This had very clear and important implications for FDR's early views on international relations. FDR, like many of his contemporaries at Groton, was caught up in the martial excitement when war broke out between the United States and Spain in April 1898. When the *Maine* exploded in February of that year, he wrote to his parents that "everyone is much excited. If the accident turns out to have been done by Spaniards, I think the whole school [will] take up arms and sail to Spain."[70] Yet even this close to the United States he also had his doubts grounded in a lingering Jeffersonian pacifism and anxiousness over foreign adventures. This inner struggle became manifest in a letter to his parents in early April in which he wrote, "I feel every moment of delay is in the interests of peace, and that the President is doing all he can to prevent war."[71] President McKinley was under intense pressure from the prowar lobby to open hostilities and was vilified publicly as a weak president by the Spanish while TR famously declared he "had no more backbone than a chocolate éclair."[72]

After McKinley acquiesced to war, there was little chance that FDR's slight retention of pacific ideals could withstand such an onslaught of public and Grotonian opinion. It became a formative point in FDR's attitude to hemispheric intervention and he negotiated his personal difficulties by viewing the conflict as geographical. By concentrating on the expulsion of the Spanish from Cuba, FDR defined the dispute as an exercise of chivalric humanitarianism and paternalism that drew on all his sense of duty toward the Cuban people. He glossed over difficult questions such as the Cuban desires and role in the conflict. In a later letter to his parents, he advised, "[Spain] will of course refuse to leave Cuba and on Saturday our army is to cross over and invade Cuba. I think by the time this reaches you that Cuba will have been rid of Spaniards and Spain will be soon ready to give in."[73] Thus reconciled, he could fully support the war and when fighting broke out he was "wildly excited" and itched to join the conflict himself—both he and his friends were allegedly only prevented from enlisting by an outbreak of scarlet fever at Groton.[74]

There were further strategic challenges to FDR's sense of Americanism at this time. Naval theorists had long identified the need to concentrate naval power effectively and argued the United States, with coasts facing the Atlantic and Pacific, had a desperate need for an isthmian canal. Both TR and Mahan advocated early construction. A canal would link the Atlantic to the Pacific and drastically cut the time it would take the US fleet to gather in either ocean without a trip around Cape Horn. FDR was intensely interested in the issue and, given his knowledge of naval theory, clearly appreciated the strategic need for a canal. In any case, he seems to have supported such a venture—he followed the Nicaragua Canal Bill debate in Congress from at least February 1897 hoping by 1899 that "there won't be much opposition now."[75]

TR eventually set the canal location in 1903 with the controversial Panama Canal Treaty. Unsubtle intervention and heavy handedness secured a canal and US interests. TR then augmented US claims with his corollary to the Monroe Doctrine that declared a US right to exercise "an international police power" in the area.[76] Later this would become less direct control of customs houses and finances of Caribbean and Latin American countries and the "dollar diplomacy" that flowered fully during the Taft administration. Even so, TR felt little need as president to justify applying a "big-stick" or "dollar diplomacy" in the Western Hemisphere.

In contrast, the presence of perceived overriding strategic need by FDR triggered his belief in doing the "right thing" and human progress that set him on the road to paternal and humanitarian justifications for intervention. TR was, at the very least, ambivalent toward more developmental justifications having "scant... patience with those who make a pretense of humanitarianism to hide and cover their timidity, and who cant about 'liberty' and the 'consent of the governed' in order to excuse themselves for their unwillingness to play the part of men."[77] Although FDR saw the strategic importance of the Caribbean and Latin America, there is no evidence that he ever stated a belief in heavy-handed imperialism or dollar diplomacy. In the absence of comment, it does not seem an unreasonable assertion that his position mirrored that of his paternalistic humanitarianism during the Spanish war and his clearly stated view when he entered public life. Progress, paternalistic uplift, and humanitarianism for less civilized races were FDR's key justifications to accommodate imperialism in the Western Hemisphere with his Americanism. Indeed, it is no surprise that throughout his youth, as well as in later life, FDR's favorite author was Rudyard Kipling, the great panegyrist of empire and the romantic white man's "burden."[78]

FDR's early international outlook was the result of a complex mixture of family influence, schooling at Groton and Harvard, extensive foreign travel, and developments in transport and communication technology. Key individuals, such as TR and Mahan, by communicating theories of power, the revolution in naval weaponry and tactics and (in TR's case) the need of a strong lead by the Federal executive also played a vital role. Although FDR was sensitive to more traditional hemispheric viewpoints founded on geographic isolation, he was able to appreciate both the increasing interconnectedness of the United States to the world, the threat posed by powers outside the Western Hemisphere, and from instability within it. Thus from an early age, he held an expansive geographic conception of US security. This required assertive military protection not only of US territory and borders from external threat but also of property and interests wherever they lay in the world.

Yet this was never just a simple lifting of the ideas of TR and Mahan by FDR—his youth, inexperience, and Jeffersonian American nationalism combined to shape the way he interpreted their thinking. FDR saw primitive calculations of power operating in national spheres of influence, where TR saw more porous national boundaries and flexible diplomacy operating on the international stage. There was little of TR's nuance or subtlety visible in FDR's appreciation of diplomacy at this time. Similarly, where TR made an intellectual connection and moral investment in world civilization as a function of US security, FDR's Americanism led him to initially eschew identifying with other nations in ideological terms—particularly European ones with their old-world politics, diplomacy, and wars. There is no convincing evidence to suggest he favored a particular European nation in his youth. This though proved to be a somewhat superficial and transitory position for FDR. It dissolved not so much after an intellectual communion with TR, but with the rise of a powerful and threatening Germany that enhanced the attractiveness of other nations, particularly Britain, as potential allies to support his primitive strategic calculus of US security.

FDR's Americanism also led him to emphasize republican government, democratic choice, and equality underpinned by a Jeffersonian faith in the majority. When these views combined with his Lamarckian racial perspective that rejected biological determinism it caused FDR, unlike both TR and Mahan, to reject imperialism in the wider world. Unable to perceive strategic need, there was to be no following of TR's presidential project to expand US power territorially around the globe. This was a more difficult position for FDR to justify in areas like Panama where the United States had clear strategic interests. Rather than follow deterministic implications of TR's heavy-handed "big stick" and rejection of humanitarianism, FDR adopted a position of paternalistic concern for the advancement of the colonized. In the Western Hemisphere, he drew on the family ethos of noblesse oblige and notions of progress originating in both his religion and popular articulations of Enlightenment thought to override his concerns about conforming to his more traditional American ideals. Again, his position lacked a certain intellectual depth—FDR was no pragmatic or progressive from any philosophical perspective. Though FDR personally held a deep conviction and optimism about the progress of humanity, he focused largely on the domestic scene and did not yet have an idealistic international reforming streak as a function of US world security.

The linking of domestic and global reform to notions of national security was not yet part of FDR's relatively unsophisticated worldview. He clearly rejected the strict determinism of a realist approach to world affairs, but did not yet apply his idealism outside of the Western Hemisphere. His realism was reserved for dealing with the old world, his idealism for applying in the new. This highlights a significant gap in FDR's view of international relations that did not exist by the time he became president. The factors that brought such a fundamental change, how he communicated those changes to the American public and the story of how and why they came to influence him are the important questions addressed in the following chapters.

CHAPTER 2

THE CHALLENGES OF PUBLIC OFFICE, 1910–1917

THE YEARS 1910–1917 WERE A TIME OF GREAT change for FDR, as he left the private world of a Hudson Valley patrician and businessman for the public life of a politician. Initial success as a Democrat in New York led to service in the Wilson administration and relocation to Washington. Although his wife Eleanor brooded about the amount she and the children saw of FDR, the excitement of a political career and ambitions of public power increasingly drew him away from family contentment and responsibilities. FDR's move into the public and political sphere also brought new experiences and challenges that had the potential to transform his views on international relations.

The old families of the Hudson Valley did not traditionally engage in politics, viewing it with a mixture of revulsion, fear, and contempt.[1] Competing for votes was deemed unseemly, unprincipled, and vulgar—unworthy of a gentleman and against every ideal they held dear. The distaste for the grubby world of electoral politics was still strong when FDR entered public life and he experienced the first slurs of a lifelong accusation that he was a "traitor to his class." His mother recalled that she was one of the few in her milieu who encouraged and supported her son's political ambitions.[2] Social mores were changing, however, and entering the struggle of politics and leadership was increasingly accepted, provided the right posture was adopted. TR, in his presidential career, was an important model of form for FDR in this respect.[3]

FDR's upbringing and background was hardly an appealing "log cabin" heritage guaranteed to attract the electorate. The Republican Poughkeepsie *Eagle* noted his patrician origins on his nomination as state senate candidate in

1910, commenting: "Presumably his contribution to the campaign funds goes well above four figures—hence the value of his discovery."[4] Josephus Daniels viewed FDR's schooling at Groton as "one of the worst things that could happen to a man who wants to be a Democratic candidate" and graduation from Harvard, "that bastion of conservative and Republican ideas," as the second worst. The difficulties arising from FDR's later contraction of polio was rated a poor fourth in Daniels' analysis of his assistant's prospects.[5] FDR was well aware of the political handicap arising from his background; it proved a sore point and a source of constant worry to him. In a letter to Daniels about a proposed naval training cruise for members of the public in 1916 he wrote:

> I fear you have some kind of an idea that the cruise will be taken advantage of only by college boys, rich young men, well-to-do yachtmen [sic], etc. I want to remind you of the fact that I have twice been elected to office in a fairly large and cosmopolitan kind of district and that I can rightly claim to be in touch with every element in the community.[6]

Both Daniels and FDR were heavily involved in programs to eliminate class prejudice against enlisted men in the navy and the improvement of living standards, education, and promotion prospects for them. Yet even after serving in the administration for three years, FDR still felt it necessary to restate his democratic credentials to his boss.[7]

A desire to counteract the handicap of his background may have influenced FDR's choice of political party at a time when the Republicans were commonly perceived as the party of special privilege. FDR's partisan sympathies are often portrayed as somewhat amorphous and unprincipled in his youth. His allegiances did seem to flit from side to side as if trying to find a safe home at this time and TR, it is argued, proved an irresistible draw for his fifth cousin. In October 1900, FDR joined the Harvard Republican Club and supported the McKinley-Roosevelt ticket in a torchlight parade. He even placed his first vote in a presidential election for TR and attended his inaugural in March 1905.[8]

Yet FDR's very first vote was as a Democrat in the off-year election of 1903.[9] Historian Frank Freidel has argued that FDR chose, like many of his generation, to follow the politics of his father and there is probably much truth in this, though FDR erroneously claimed that his father had always been a Democrat and the family had long been that way.[10] It is unlikely that FDR's father James, a Democrat, could have supported Williams Jennings Bryan, considered a dangerous radical by many, in 1896, and he even campaigned for TR as governor of New York in 1898.[11] TR was more likely an acceptable temporary alternative to Bryan for FDR and his father until a more suitable candidate was chosen by the Democrats.

In his politics, FDR identified with reform interests in both the Republican and Democrat parties. In the Republican Party conservative forces seemed to be gaining the upper hand against "insurgent" reformers from 1909 onward. With the Democrats, however, as David Sarasohn has convincingly argued, a distinct reform identity was emerging. Whereas historians have seen the Democrats of this era as supporters of weak government, local autonomy, the preservation of individual liberties, and an ineffective reform force, the truth was actually revealed in their voting for William Jennings Bryan, not their quoting of Thomas Jefferson. Woodrow Wilson, in effect, inherited from Bryan a reformist Democratic Party that he refined, solidified, and made more palatable to more conservative Democrats.[12] FDR's firm choice of political party seen in this light was therefore compatible with both the politics of his father and the moral outlook provided by his family and schooling.

In his early political career, FDR was possibly inspired by the antiparty activities of Republican "insurgents" during the Taft administration. His fight against the Tammany candidate for the New York US Senate seat, William "Blue Eyed Billy" Sheehan, in 1911, was strongly reminiscent of their tactics and brought FDR national renown at a time when state politics was much more prominent on the national stage. In the immediate term, however, FDR was politically astute enough to become part of the extended Wilson machine before the latter was nominated as his party's presidential candidate for 1912. TR's storming out of the Republican convention to found the Progressive "Bull Moose" Party helped ensure Wilson's victory that year. The defeat of TR also perhaps confirmed FDR's agreement with the new Democratic president's stress on the importance of party structure and organization. Wilson supported the existence of the two main parties and believed the president should provide principled leadership for a party, rather than just inspiring partisan loyalty through the offer of patronage.[13]

Luckily, FDR won his own race for reelection to the state senate, thanks to the efforts of Louis Howe who began his pivotal political and public relations association with FDR at this time. Howe would always be ready to give advice and opinion on the domestic political implications of any policy or position. As his reward for service to the Wilson campaign, FDR was made Assistant Secretary of the Navy. This was at the request of the new secretary, Josephus Daniels, the pacifist ally of William Jennings Bryan and owner of the respected Raleigh *News and Observer*. FDR had met Daniels at the Democrat's 1912 Baltimore convention and, when he had a chance second meeting with him in the lobby of the Willard Hotel, Daniels offered him the post.[14] It was the beginning of an important association for FDR. Although they did not always see eye to eye, and FDR often chafed under

Figure 2.1   FDR and his "chief" Secretary of the Navy Josephus Daniels in May 1918. They had a difficult relationship at times, but the forbearing Daniels enabled FDR to learn a great deal about Washington politics. (National Archives 19-N-3147).

his leadership, Daniels was an immensely skilled and knowledgeable political practitioner from whom his assistant could and did learn a great deal.

FDR's journey to Washington and public office via "insurgent" style tactics and support for reform measures was not made without gaining his share of enemies and the laying down of a political reputation. His involvement in the attempt to block the nomination of Tammany candidate William Sheehan for US senator in 1911 isolated him in party circles. Frances Perkins, progressive campaigner and FDR's future labor secretary, said: "He won the battle, but it did not leave him with many friends in the Senate or Democratic Party of the state."[15] Joseph M. Proskauer, an adviser to Alfred Smith, noted that "none of us took him very seriously. At that time there was a tendency to laugh at Roosevelt a little . . . it accounted a little bit for the lack of seriousness with which Mr. Roosevelt was regarded in those days."[16] It did not get much better when FDR reached Washington; Republican Henry Cabot Lodge said, "he did exactly what Daniels wished him to do. He is a well-meaning, nice young fellow, but light."[17] Added to this was

FDR's ill-advised attempt to gain his party's nomination for US senator for New York in 1914. Louis Howe was furious at FDR and considered it a big mistake, as did Daniels who also counseled against the move. After FDR's defeat in the primary, Daniels commented, "everyone said that was the end of Franklin Roosevelt" and rated it the third worst obstacle to a successful political career for his assistant.[18]

The distaste for politics of the old families, public suspicions of a patrician together with the enemies FDR made on his way to Washington, and his reputation as a "light" and not very serious politician combined to give him reason enough to take a combative stance in public life. He desperately needed a strategy to counteract these negative forces if he was to succeed in politics and legitimate his public position. Yet contained in his career thus far was also the potential answer to his problem—his identification with reform interests and the exaggerated dogmatic positions he had taken seemed to work. They got him noticed and had taken his career as far as Washington and the same office his famous cousin had occupied. They might take him further up the political ladder and so there was no immediate reason to abandon his successful methods as he settled into his new role as Assistant Secretary of the Navy.

Political ambition aside, FDR position as Assistant Secretary of the Navy required that he take public positions on international relations. His strategic vision at this stage was defined and circumscribed geographically. The national ideals he professed applied within the continental United States, but he saw the military defense of a much wider territory as essential to the physical protection of those ideals and interests. His awareness of the naval technological and tactical revolution, acquired via TR and Mahan, meant he appreciated the importance of defending the Western Hemisphere from both external intervention and attack at points often far from his country's coasts. There was now the added responsibility, as Assistant Secretary of the Navy, of defending overseas possessions. In a speech in 1916, FDR emphasized the geographically expanded interests of his country:

> I asked that this map should be put up here to give you an idea of distance...if we believe in the maintenance of the Monroe Doctrine—America has very distinct interests inside of a line which I will draw very roughly. Starting up here at the North Pole...and coming on down through to the North Atlantic ocean, and around Cape Horn, and up this way around America Samoa, and then up here and around Guam...then around the Philippines, then up here past the Aleutian Islands and back to the Pole—that is some territory.[19]

The speech offers a striking parallel to FDR's 1942 "Fireside chat" in which he invited listeners to take out their maps to appreciate the strategic nature of the globe, but also highlights differences with his later thinking. In 1942, FDR's strategic vision encompassed the globe; in 1916 his vision, while it appreciated the world's vastness, was more closely defined than 1942 when the US was fighting a world war. Neither was FDR necessarily uncommon in his early outlook among the nations leaders—Wilson demonstrated a similar appreciation of the relation of geography to security and of the increasing need to communicate this to the public. In his 1913 Mobile speech, Wilson said:

> The great bulk of South America, if you will look at your globes (not at your Mercator's projection), lies eastward of the continent of North America. You will realize that when you realize that the canal will run southeast, not southwest, and that when you get into the Pacific, you will be farther east than you were when you left the Gulf of Mexico. (I am reciting these things because I recently discovered them, by myself, renewing my study of geography.)[20]

FDR's defensive assessment of threats was not radically different, apart from the addition of colonial possessions, from the view he held before entering political life. The Panama Canal remained vital to bringing the fleet to battle and he still maintained the need for a battleship-based "sea going fleet [that could] ... overcome an enemy before he gets to our shore or before he can establish a base near us."[21] FDR now advocated a similar conception applied to US territories:

> If they [the American people] want to be in a position at any time to defend successfully their possessions and their interests that lie beyond the limits of the continental United States, they can only do so by obtaining and maintaining what has been called ... "The Control of the Seas."[22]

In this case FDR was directly quoting Mahan, but he also quoted TR when he railed against thinking that saw the defense of the United States as solely about its borders. Such people were ignorant with "an inability to visualize our position in the world" and also hopelessly stuck in the past in calling for a "Chinese wall kind of defense."[23] Unsurprisingly TR, as one of the key progenitors of FDR's thinking in this respect, held almost identical views, though he had abandoned any wish to defend the Philippines by this time.[24] FDR may also have privately felt the same given the closeness of his thinking to TR in naval matters, but would not be able to express an opinion on such a sensitive matter until the Wilson administration began its own tentative moves toward independence for the Philippines. Instead he borrowed TR's rhetoric to defend a position that TR was clearly not in agreement with and had not been since at least 1907.

FDR continued to believe in the importance of defending US merchants and their right to trade around the globe. The problems over neutrality after the war erupted in Europe were a big spur to his concern, but he already had an appreciation of the interconnectedness of the modern world. The opening of Panama Canal in August 1914 and his service as one of three National Commissioners to the Panama Pacific Exposition held in San Francisco during 1915 reinforced this viewpoint. The exposition attracted 39 foreign nations, 37 states, and 3 territories highlighting the increasing importance of world trade links to the US economy.[25]

FDR thought trade should be protected because it was essential to the maintenance of the American way of life. This created a defensive problem of how to protect "merchant ships in time of war, no matter where they go."[26] This defense became an immensely strong theme for him and he returned repeatedly to it in speeches and articles. In 1915, he wrote: "If you cut off the United States from all trade and intercourse with the rest of the world you would have economic death in this country before long."[27] Economic isolationism was no longer desirable in the modern world, as he further explained in early 1917:

> [The] most important of all, control of the sea means that our exports and imports would continue. If we were attacked tomorrow by a nation with a stronger navy than ours not one bale of cotton, not one pound of tobacco, for instance, could leave our shores. We could survive a year or so of that, but not much longer, and the enemy could keep up an indefinite blockade at comparatively little cost even if it did not seek eventually to land.[28]

This defensive outlook should not be confused with schemes of economic expansion and the domination of markets. TR had never shown a great interest in economic matters, but had gone along with schemes to control the market of the Philippines and gain easier access to the market in China as a justification for imperialism at the start of the century. With Wilson, particularly in his attitude toward foreign oil concessions in Mexico and the capture of Latin America markets after the outbreak of World War I, there is a greater case to answer. FDR certainly did not speak a language of economic expansionism and never publicly mentioned the necessity of capturing markets during this period. In contrast, from the start of the war in Europe, Wilson continually pressed for a Federal Shipping Board to empower a commission to build and purchase a merchant marine and eventually got the requisite bill in 1916. Although this was a strategy to avoid some of the complications of neutrality, it can also be seen as a bold attempt to develop a strong American trading position. This was particularly evident in Latin America where the United States virtually replaced Europe as the major trading partner during World War I. Surprisingly, given his interest in all things maritime, FDR demonstrated no public interest in Wilson's scheme. This was not because of a desire to protect the dominant British trading position, but rather because FDR's economic thinking simply did not follow Wilson's ideological direction at this stage.

FDR still did not subjugate domestic concerns to world diplomatic considerations. This is clearly demonstrated by his attitude to relations with Japan where he still failed to connect domestic security issues to wider diplomacy. The festering Californian landholding crisis erupted once more in the spring of 1913 when Progressive and Democratic politicians in California, attempting to attract the farm and labor vote, promoted legislation prohibiting Japanese ownership of land. This resulted in the Alien Land Bill of May 1913 despite the appeals of Wilson and Secretary of State Bryan who now favored a less provocative approach.[29] Domestic opinion in Japan was outraged and the Japanese ambassador lodged a formal protest with State Department. As president, TR had expended a great deal of domestic political capital for the sake of wider strategic concerns in the Pacific and, now in power, Wilson and Bryan reversed their previous inflammatory position for similar reasons. All three men now appreciated domestic concerns could impact on other areas of the world important to the United States.

In stark contrast, FDR perceived a real threat from the Japanese and was confrontational from the start of the crisis, presenting himself as the unheeded naval expert pushing necessary preparations for war. His unreflective exaggerated aggression in international relations led him to join with the bellicose Rear Admiral Bradley A. Fiske in calling for redeployment of naval forces from the Yangtze river to the Philippines—a sure indicator of war. FDR appreciated the need to gather forces and the danger of splitting the fleet both from his knowledge of Mahan and of the Russian defeat of 1905. Though TR wrote to him to advise the same, the two men clearly felt very differently on relations with the Japanese and it would be an error to view them as acting in concert. Despite abandoning his commitment to protecting the Philippines, TR continued to hold conciliatory views in 1913 toward the Japanese. This was presumably because the Americans had not left the Philippines and still had interests there and in China. Writing to FDR, he said: "I do not anticipate trouble with Japan, but it may come."[30] FDR by contrast clearly favored a firm stance by the government, but the move to relocate the Yangtze forces was headed off by Secretary Daniels and the administration succeeded in further easing tensions with the promise of negotiations.[31] FDR was left to declare there was no Japanese crisis and temper his disappointment by arguing that it was an excellent campaign of education conducted by the "jingoes" on the preparedness of the navy.

New tensions erupted in early 1915 when the Japanese presented China with "twenty-one demands." The United States sent a long note on April 27, advising that they would not recognize a treaty impairing the rights of their or Chinese citizens, Chinese political integrity, or the Open door. There is no further comment from FDR on Japanese relations, but perhaps the 1913 disturbance was a peak in his assertiveness as attention turned toward European problems. Indeed, it could be argued that the US note of April 27 was an early precursor to FDR's more conciliatory view toward the Japanese during the 1920s and his eventual acceptance of the Stimson Doctrine in 1933. Wilson subsequently abandoned this early version of a nonrecognition policy at Versailles when he controversially acquiesced to Japanese agreements with the Allies granting them concessions in the former German province of Shantung.[32]

In Mexico, the situation was somewhat different for FDR because it was not immediately clear to him that a military threat to the United States existed. After a military coup by General Victoriano Huerta in February 1913 Wilson instituted a policy of "watchful waiting" to see how the situation would play out.[33] At this stage FDR was interested, but had no immediate cause to justify intervention. Mexico was the "only place just now where there is real action" but he felt the situation would either "get better or explode."[34] His view quickly changed in February 1914 when some US sailors were accidentally arrested by Mexican police at Tampico. The local naval commander demanded a 21 gun salute by way of apology and Wilson used this as a pretext to land American troops at Vera Cruz on April 21. To FDR, the arrests were a direct assault on US forces and he bristled for intervention to defend his country's forces against attack and uphold its honor. This formed his only stated justification for intervention and was markedly less ideological than TR. The former president publicly called for intervention to save "outraged" nuns and countless priests from murder. He also claimed that the United States had a moral obligation to protect American citizens and wider humanity from endemic serious crime and disorder.[35]

The intervention quickly became an embarrassment to Wilson as Huerta's government refused to crumble and resistance to the Americans mounted. Wilson agreed to an offer of mediation by Argentina, Brazil, and Chile and, through this, eventually obtained the abdication of Huerta on July 15. Even after Wilson had already agreed to negotiations, FDR wrote: "I do not want war, but I do not see how we can avoid it. Sooner or later, it seems, the United States must go down there and clean up the Mexican political mess. I believe that the best time is right now."[36] FDR's thinking remained clear on the need to intervene in what he saw as a location of persistent trouble and a direct threat to US security, particularly after the Villa raids on the United States during 1916. In the summer of that year, he wrote: "The Mexican situation is going through one of its periodically peaceful revivals, but the pendulum will swing back to intervention in a week or a month or a year. I don't care much which as it is sure to come."[37] His position was out of step with public opinion that was not inclined to support full-scale intervention. Instead, Americans endorsed Wilson's 1916 election slogan of "He kept us out of war" that applied as equally to Mexico as it did to Europe.

Wilson's reasons for intervening in Mexico divide historians—some see US economic interests as key, others emphasize Wilson's idealistic desire to assert the democratic rights of Mexicans. Either way Huerta's declaration of a military dictatorship on October 10, 1913, was an affront to the administration's policy and prompted a formal demand for Huerta's resignation from Wilson who declared in his annual address to Congress: "We are the friends of constitutional government in America; we are more than its friends, we are its champions."[38] Huerta's stubborn retention of power, eventually forced the president to make good on his private claims to "teach the South American Republics to elect good men" with military action. To underline this Wilson used the law as a coercive weapon in Mexico by attempting to change the regime through the principle of recognition. The US Jeffersonian tradition had always previously given de facto recognition to governments whatever their composition. Wilson overturned this in Mexico by making de jure status a condition of its recognition by the United States. The point here is not that his action was ill-judged and of dubious effect, but that he was prepared to justify meddling both militarily and diplomatically in another country's affairs for democratic ideals—an argument that FDR simply did not deploy at this time. FDR saw the restoration of order in the country as purely a question of applying force and did not articulate any agreement with more ideological approaches at this time.

Beyond the borders and immediate contiguous neighbors of the United States, FDR's Americanism often collided with what he viewed as strategic necessity. This was particularly true in the Western Hemisphere following the completion of the Panama Canal in August 1914. The United States was at pains to prevent outside interference in an area that it considered of key importance. Unfortunately for this policy, the countries surrounding the canal were wracked by violence and political instability that in turn created concern that European powers, claiming interests and historic links, would intervene. Since TR's corollary to the Monroe Doctrine of 1904, a series of interventions and Taft's "dollar diplomacy" had kept outside interference to a minimum. The Wilson administration may have talked of friendlier policies, but it was just as guilty of forcefully meddling in the affairs of a string of countries in the region.

The most notable of Wilson's interventions in this area was Haiti where once more FDR indulged in a combative rhetoric supporting US involvement.

This was not, on its own, sufficient for FDR to justify forcefully depriving the Haitians of their liberty and freedom—Haiti clearly did not pose an immediate threat to the honor or physical security of the United States. In response, FDR drew on the strong sense of paternalism and humanitarianism grounded in the chivalric noblesse oblige, Christian duty, and racial experience of his youth. As a co-opting force this enabled him to smooth over the contradictions of intervention both in Haiti and the other territories previous imperial ventures had given his country.

When revolutions in the nations of Haiti and contiguous Santo Domingo, situated on the strategic approaches to the Panama Canal, threatened to get out of hand, intervention seemed the logical option for the United States. Predictably FDR was enthusiastic for a military solution—the prospect of military action placed him in his element and allowed him to display his patriotic qualities of vigor and fighting spirit much as he had done with the Japanese land crisis and Mexico. As the situation worsened in Haiti during the summer of 1914, Wilson decided to dispatch a precautionary force of Marines to Cuba. In his letters FDR portrayed himself as in the center of the action, advising the president and sending the regiment of Marines himself.[39] Sadly for the enthusiastic Assistant Secretary, the Marines were not immediately required to go on to the troubled island and in reality FDR's influence was limited.

As the administration tried to pursue more idealistic policies, FDR portrayed himself again as the unheeded military expert operating in the company of poltroons. Privately FDR joked about Secretary Bryan's inability to differentiate a "battleship" from a "gunboat" in attempts to quell the troubles in Haiti.[40] Frustratingly for FDR the decision to send Marines to Haiti finally came while he was at his summer retreat in Campobello. His exasperation was evident in a letter to Daniels when he wrote: "It is certainly a curious coincidence that as soon as I go away we seem to land marines somewhere."[41] Due to a continuing series of revolutions Marines had landed on July 28, 1915, after the latest president, Guillaume Sam, was literally torn to pieces by a mob. Over the following months the Americans established complete control over the government of Haiti by imposing Wilson's choice of a new president and a treaty gaining control of customs houses, financial affairs, and law enforcement. So complete was the assumption of power by the Marines that Daniels was jokingly referred to as the "King of Haiti" in cabinet meetings.[42] By this time FDR was back in Washington and playing the role of military expert once more, deciding to "stay 'on the job' over Sunday as Haiti is not a calm spot and there might be important dispatches from Admiral Caperton."[43] There was indeed a "ticklish" situation that resulted from a revolt by the northern *cacos* who opposed the American intervention and proclaimed a patriotic uprising against the foreign invaders on August 24. The Americans responded in force sending Marines led by Major Smedley Butler north to crush the resistance that was accomplished with a final climatic storming of Fort Rivere on the November 17, 1915.

FDR, captivated by such martial excitement, managed to wangle a tour to the island in late January 1917 taking along his Harvard friend Livingston Davis and former Groton tutor George Marvin. Daniels was probably aware that the occupation might become an issue in the coming midterm and future presidential election and so authorized the junket to get some first-hand knowledge to fight future political battles. For FDR, however, the trip turned into an adventure with "rifle shots from the hills and an occa-sional bullet going overhead." He reveled in the activities of the Marines and counted a personal guided tour of Fort Rivere by Butler as the high-light of his trip.[44] The urgent summons from Daniels requesting FDR to return to the United States following resumption of submarine warfare by the Germans added to the drama of the tour. FDR felt he was in the thick of the action—exactly where he wanted to be.

FDR was aware of the contradictions the actions in Haiti highlighted within his wider frame of Americanism. By intervening, the United States appeared heavy handed and seemed far away from its Revolutionary War ideals and democratic principles. TR had experienced no such qualms with his "big-stick" approach to the region, arguing it was both his right and duty to uphold the law and protect American interests and its citizens. When this became unpopular he initiated the "dollar diplomacy" that flourished under Taft. FDR never demonstrated such blatant self-interested thinking despite the Caribbean being such an important strategic area, perhaps viewing it as inimical to his sense of Americanism.

In many ways Wilson faced the same dilemmas as FDR in trying to reconcile strategic interventions with his strong sense of American ideals. For Wilson, naked self-interest in the Western Hemisphere could be clothed in a diplomatic language of friendship. In a speech in Mobile, Alabama, on October 27, 1913, he famously pledged that the United States "will never again seek one additional foot of territory by conquest" and made a further call for a "spiritual union" with Latin America.[45] This policy took actual form when Wilson attempted to make a treaty with Columbia in 1913–1914 to repair the harm he perceived done to Latin American relations by TR's aggressive seizing of the Canal Zone. Wilson also attempted to set up a Pan American alliance offering a "mutual guarantee" of territorial integrity and political independence under a republican form of government principally aimed at the "ABC" powers (Argentina, Brazil, and Chile). The plan was clearly a forerunner of Wilson's League of Nations, but it is more difficult to directly connect it to FDR's later "Good Neighbor" policy. There is no evidence that he paid it any attention at the time other than by attend-ing obligatory administration dinners in honor of various South American politicians. Wilson's policy of extolling friendship and community of spirit held no interest for FDR who at this time ignored Wilson's Mobile speech and all attempts at Pan Americanism.

Similarly FDR failed to show an interest in Wilson's more ethical economic activities in the wider world. Almost immediately on taking power the president set the tone of his administration by withdrawal from a six power consortium formed in 1911 to loan $125 million to China. The consortium, he claimed, affected the administrative independence of China. Nor was this moral position restricted to developing countries. In October 1912, the British lodged a protest that free use of the Panama Canal by US shipping violated the Hay-Pauncefote Treaty of 1901. Wilson agreed and, claiming it also violated national honor, forced his decision on Congress, causing much outrage among those wanting special favors for American shippers. While FDR's position as Assistant Secretary of the Navy would not necessitate opinions on the use of economics as a diplomatic tool, as a member of the administration it is surprising that he did not celebrate any of these major policies in speeches—particularly China that he claimed to have a family sympathy toward. He failed to mention them once, even during the 1916 election campaign, and it would appear that another more idealistic part of Wilsonian economics passed him by.

Wilson's New Freedom may have claimed to be the antithesis of paternalism and the president did attempt to remove racial allusions from his rhetoric, but when security needs demanded it Wilson operated according to an underlying Southern racism that viewed nonwhite races as inferior and in need of guardianship. This resulted in a paternalism that justified intervention publicly in the name of friendship, but privately in the racial terms of his Southern background. At home Wilson had systematically excluded blacks from the Post Office, Treasury, and Navy Departments with the cooperation of Southerners like William Gibbs McAdoo and Daniels and against the protests of activists like William Monroe Trotter who spotted the flaws in the president's liberal rhetoric. By advocating friendship, democracy, and republican government while avoiding a paternalistic language allowed Wilson to appear responsive to domestic US sensibilities. Despite the public rhetoric, however, Americans in Haiti adopted conceptions of racial hierarchy and a concern for black welfare similar to that shown toward slaves or tenants on Southern plantations. Josephus Daniels, when he ordered Admiral Caperton to cease hostile operations against the *cacos* in November 1915 "to prevent further loss of life," was not just responding as a pacifist, but as a concerned Southerner who felt he had a duty of care toward blacks. This Southern duty of care had a timeless quality and firmly eschewed any notion of progress for blacks.

FDR, in contrast, was from the North that had crushed the South during Civil War—there was no "lost cause" for him and, while he was still racist in much of his outlook, he held a very different view on race to Wilson that affected the way he justified strategic interventions. To FDR, Southern racism was something of a joke. In a letter to his wife he took great delight in the scandal that would have resulted among the predominantly Southern administration in Washington when he reported: "I dined with the Lansings to meet the same dusky gentleman [Mr. Cardoso, the Brazilian minister to Mexico] and his duskier wife and daughter."[46] His trip to Haiti armed him with many stories of John McIlhenny, a Civil Service commissioner from the South, who "speculatively" valued one of the Haitian cabinet at $1,500 "for stud purposes."[47] FDR viewed races as developmentally, rather than biologically, inferior. This was similar to the thinking of TR except that, unlike TR, he did not use progress as an excuse for intervention unless there was a clear strategic need apparent to him. All races could ultimately achieve a high level of civilization and there was no urge to retard black progress as there was in the Southern outlook. If whites were to meddle in the affairs of tropical countries they needed a strong set of ideals and guiding principles to justify their interventions.

FDR found these ideals not in the democracy of Wilson, or the strict right of maintenance of order or imperialism of TR, but in the ideals of his youth. Noblesse oblige, Christian duty and a firm belief in human progress combined with his sense of masculinity to produce a humanitarian paternalism underwritten by military power and the use of force for the good of the people concerned. FDR shared a sense of noblesse oblige with TR but it was a product of his upbringing, not the predominant influence of his cousin. In any event, TR viewed interventions quite differently by linking them to the good of civilization as a whole and thus the security of the United States rather than on the level of individual compassion that was a rather pointless activity to his mind. FDR, like both Wilson and TR, had a strong sense of Christian duty, but again this was a product of his own faith and upbringing—there is no reason to connect such a personal matter to the influence of either man.

In 1916, FDR penned a proposed article on the Marine actions in Haiti that succinctly summarized his paternalistic view of interventions at this time:

> People are very apt to think of the marines only as a fighting force...but it is right to call attention to the way they have gone about the task of helping the people of Haiti along the highroad of order and progress. This has been a work more of peace than of war and the spirit of fairness and cooperation has already been recognized almost unanimously by the Haitians themselves.[48]

The Marines had, for FDR, become agents of order and progress by helping the Haitian people in their basic needs as a duty of humanitarian and compassionate service. FDR further underlined the nonimperialistic nature of the American presence in Haiti in two stories he recalled in his account of his 1917 trip. The first was of an old classmate from Groton, Preston Davie, he found in a deplorable state after the latter had spent months attempting to set up a plantation in the country. The second was a story of Mrs. Kanes, wife of a Marine commander, who thought FDR's last night summons to return to the United States "due to political conditions" must mean a coup by Charles Evans Hughes against the president. FDR felt she had obviously "been in the tropics too long!"[49] Both stories indicate FDR's view that the unsuitable climate meant that whites might stay a while as guardians and educators, but in the longer term there was no future in ruling over the natives. This was a fairly common anti-imperialist argument throughout the period that did not necessarily indicate biological or geographical determinism—natives could still eventually achieve "civilization" and whites could avoid degradation because of their essential racial equality by choosing to avoid colonial schemes.

Here was the alternative compassionate side of FDR's thinking on international relations that offered to be a father and protector to less developed nations. His paternalism existed only where the United States held strategic interest that was not supported by a direct threat to security. FDR demonstrated no interest, for instance, in the humanitarian crisis in Armenia that erupted in 1915. There was also still an underlying factor of force and compulsion provided by the Marines—FDR did not discuss, for instance, the harsh system of corvée labor that they reintroduced to build the roads, bridges, and sanitation that he had witnessed firsthand on his Haitian trip. His humanitarianism followed strategic need and ultimately it could be enforced at the point of a gun.

As Wilson gained more experience in office he increasingly resorted to an expansive democratic vision to justify US involvement in the wider world rather than paternalistic humanitarianism. In early 1916, he embarked on a speaking tour to rally support for his stance on the preparedness issue. As it turned out, he rarely mentioned preparedness, concentrating instead on the importance of democratic ideals to world security in what appeared to be a test run of his justifications for taking the United States into the war over a year later.[50] The tour was fully publicized, but none of Wilson's themes appear in any of FDR's speeches despite his keen interest in the preparedness issue. The only occasion FDR did take up the presidential theme was in a proposed speech (it is not clear if it was ever delivered) in May 1916 where he described:

> The people of the United States have, through their Congress and their Administration, repeatedly sought to encourage the principles of

representative government and of enlightened civilization and to discourage anarchy and despotism... We have definitely accepted the responsibilities of a world power, not because we seek increased territories or military glory, but because we believe that we can be a factor in bringing about higher standards of civilization and usefulness.[51]

One could argue that this is the seed of a much later Wilsonian flowering, but this interpretation does not fit the form of his arguments. In the speech he does not make a bold declaration of personal belief in the principles of worldwide democracy as the basis for US security, but offers instead a paternalistic and humanitarian concern as his justification for such a policy. Later in the speech he also reaches his purpose that was to request that supporters of international idealism better provide a navy to underwrite their dreams. FDR was effectively hijacking calls for democratic peace and reducing them to a fairly convoluted justification for a bigger navy. Even he must have thought the logic somewhat tenuous as he did not return to the theme in future speeches.

Wilson continued to travel in the opposite direction with a major speech to the League to Enforce Peace (LEP) on May 27, 1916, in which he declared "that every people has a right to choose the sovereignty under which they shall live." He did temporarily drop the theme of exporting democracy in favor of peace and progressivism from September to November 1916 for the presidential election campaign, but he returned to it once more after he had won the election. His famous "Peace without Victory" speech on January 22, 1917, explicitly linked democracy to peace.[52] The absence of the idea of democratic peace in FDR's rhetoric was not just a following of Wilson's policy turns however—there was no parallel let up in FDR's preparedness campaigning during the autumn of 1916 and he continued to privately favor entering the war. Thus, it seems clear that a major strand of Wilsonian foreign policy failed to penetrate FDR's internationalism during this period.

When war broke out in Europe in August 1914, the danger of US involvement seemed to multiply almost daily. Growing numbers of concerned Americans began to campaign for an increase in defensive military forces. Most of the chief spokesmen advocating preparedness were Republicans associated with financial and industrial interests, but included TR who became the leading advocate of the movement from November 1914. At first glance FDR does appear to follow his cousin's lead in advocating preparedness as a popular issue—he shared many of TR's friends in Washington and even passed government information on the navy to the son-in-law of Henry Cabot Lodge, Representative Augustus P. Gardner, who chaired the House Military Affairs Committee.[53] Yet FDR fully realized the political dimension of the issue, writing to Daniels in 1915 that "I have felt for quite a long time that a good many people...in the Republican and Progressive parties are going to take advantage of the national preparedness issue in the Fall and also next year."[54] He was also more than willing to disagree with TR over his preparedness record. In a speech to the Navy League in May 1916, FDR said that it had been necessary to strip all other ships in the navy of men and supplies to send the "Great White Fleet" around the world in 1907. TR sent him an indignant two-page letter pointing out that his memory "was not in accordance with the statement as you made it" and added that a "Naval officer of high standing" believed "Mr. Roosevelt is wholly mistaken." FDR offered to withdraw his statement "cheerfully" when he realized the increase in ships personnel had been due to increased enlistments, but insisted that what he said had been true about a naval review organized for President Taft in 1912. Even so, FDR likely did not want to escalate the dispute and attract an unwanted kind of attention on the Navy Department from TR's careful eye.[55]

FDR's pacifist chief, Josephus Daniels, was a controversial enough appointment to the Navy Department for exactly that reason. The Secretary of the Navy was also a ponderous and deliberative character in contrast to his lively young assistant. Throughout the period FDR made many private insinuations and remarks on Daniels' competence, his slowness, and even implied that he was actually running the department at times.[56] In truth, there was nothing unusual about this—assistant secretaries were often picked for being young and enthusiastic, so they could be given the bulk of the administrative chores. Fortunately, for FDR, Daniels was a patient and forgiving man reluctant to take offence or reprimand his junior.[57]

Daniels' forbearance also benefitted FDR in another way. The fact that Daniels let him keep his job, despite numerous provocations let him learn from his chief's broad political experience. The Secretary of the Navy's handling of the legislative arm of government and particularly his careful negotiations during the 1916 Naval Appropriations Bill debate was a lesson for FDR on how to get things done. He also gave FDR careful advice on his various appearances before Congressional committees that was invaluable training for him.[58] This cooperative spirit with the legislature was part of a more general feature of Wilson's first term of office. Wilson viewed himself as an interlocutor and coordinator who guided legislation through Congress paying close attention to the use of patronage, the party caucus, and the egos of Congressmen. As a result the 63rd congress passed an impressive set of reform measures. FDR's service in the administration together with his association with Daniels and friendship with other cabinet members, such as Secretary of the Interior Franklin K. Lane, was extremely useful in learning how government functioned.

Wilson initially denied that any increase in military spending was required despite the growing preparedness campaign. This changed during the submarine crisis of 1915 and particularly following the sinking of the *Lusitania* when pressure for a review of military preparedness became intense. On July 21, 1915, Wilson asked Secretary of War Garrison and Daniels to recommend a program and, following their submissions, he approved a plan for $500m spending in the first five years announced on November 4. When Congress assembled in December 1915, Wilson made patriotism, preparedness, and a new shipping bill the keynote of his annual message. Congressional debate centered on the proposed continental army and the potential for increased federal power. There was a strong Jeffersonian tradition of antimilitarism and antifederalism in Congress and when the bills were introduced they went nowhere, blocked by a mixture of states' rights southerners opposed to expansion of the federal military and assorted Bryanite pacifists.

FDR opposed both positions—to begin with he had long argued that the Jeffersonian outlook on security was no longer appropriate to modern conditions. In a 1914 speech, he stated "I am a great admirer of Jefferson—but that good and great gentleman had about as much knowledge of sound naval protection as did the people of Portland, Maine, in 1898 when their fears of attack by the Spanish fleets were alaid [*sic*] by the arrival of a Civil War monitor."[59] FDR was drawing attention to the danger posed by outdated weapons and conceptions of defense. In a later speech he also linked his position directly to the preparedness issue:

> People are beginning to realize more and more—especially since the general European conflict—that the mere valor of an overnight "spring to arms" not only cannot save a people from defeat and possible loss of liberty, but it will result in the reckless sacrifice of human lives and of material well-being.[60]

As his position developed he also discounted the Jeffersonian focus on unobtrusive government and antimilitarism. He argued that federal government should have recourse to strong military power. The "policing" duty that sometimes falls to the lot of a nation should be carried out by the regular army and navy.[61] This, of course, sounds like TR, but FDR's definition of "policing" duty was much more tightly circumscribed.

Given the strong public sentiment against intervention in the war at this time, it was difficult for any politician to advocate a tougher position on Germany without arousing harmful accusations of militarism and warmongering. This led FDR and others to a strategy of promoting the physical and moral health benefits military training would provide for the nation's manhood. FDR was heavily involved with plans for a "Naval Plattsburg" training cruise similar to that run by the army and he had high hopes for its democratic credentials. He also emphasized the benefits of military training for citizenship and creating a "clean cut body of young men."[62] Compulsory universal training, he argued, could bring a host of benefits to the individual and society and produced "physically stronger, mentally more alert...cleaner...firmer specimens of American manhood."[63] The moral protection of young men entering military service also became something of a minor obsession for FDR. To counter claims that service brought moral degeneracy he stressed continually the benefits of service and the important work of Christian organizations such as the Young Men's Christian Association (YMCA) in safeguarding the purity of young sailors.[64] All this was, of course, military preparedness by the back door and these strategies enabled him to promote it without directly mentioning the war in Europe and the possible involvement of the United States.

With strong positions on both sides of the preparedness issue Wilson could see danger in mounting Congressional and public criticism. In the absence of a majority he decided on a compromise to neutralize the issue in an election year. Following a speaking tour on preparedness in late January the president capitulated on the issue of a continental army and let Secretary Garrison resign on February 10, to be replaced by Newton D. Baker. The compromise finally agreed on May 13 allowed for an increased army and National Guard integration into the federal defense structure. Through this pragmatic approach the president salvaged a reasonable preparedness program. FDR's main interest was expansion of the navy and there was less controversy over this as naval forces did not threaten states' rights in the obvious way that a standing army did. The Senate voted for the administration's plans within three years instead of five and the House accepted the bill on August 15.[65]

Wilson's approach and tactics in 1916 provided FDR with an important example of the importance of public opinion to national leadership and how to secure it. In the presidential campaign, Wilson focused on the twin issues of progressivism and peace to finally achieve Bryan's goal of attracting a "Great Crescent" of voters across the West and the South. The result was a close but no less stunning victory for Wilson that took him to the White House for a second time. The importance of the victory was not lost on FDR—here was a successful plan to win a Democratic electoral majority that would prove pivotal to the 1920 campaign and his subsequent election strategies to at least 1936.

The war in Europe clearly brought domestic challenges, but it also crystallized many international issues for FDR. In August 1914, Wilson had proclaimed American neutrality and aimed to maintain the US right to trade with all parties for as long as it was possible to do so with honor. He sensed public opinion on the matter, but also felt that participation in the war was the greatest threat to American democratic values and institu-tions. Wilson saw no moral significance in the conflict stating that "with its [the war's] causes and its objects we are not concerned" and calling for Americans to be "neutral in thought and deed."[66] Yet his call for neutrality toward the war did not involve an abandonment of neutral rights. Wilson made various attempts to refine his position, such as efforts to persuade the British to adhere to the nonratified Declaration of London, the withhold-ing of loans, and issuing a note of "strict accountability" to the Germans on February 10, 1915. Without risking war in defense of those rights, however, the United States was placed in a passive, reactive position that left it open to the naval strategy decisions of the belligerents.

In his private life, FDR was fundamentally opposed to neutrality and immediately argued for intervention by the United States in the war. He regarded the allied nations as involved in a defensive struggle and aggressive German militarism as the root cause of the conflict. Even before Britain declared war he wanted to see "England...join in and with France and Russia force peace *at Berlin!*"[67] In a letter to Eleanor from Washington a few days later FDR reported: "Everybody here feels that this country as a whole sympathizes with the allies against Germany."[68] FDR perceived a threat to US security from German ambitions. This had become apparent to him as her naval power overtook that of the United States to become the second largest navy in the world during the first decade of the twentieth century. As Assistant Secretary of the Navy he was even more aware of comparative naval strength and the weakened position of his country.[69] TR, Mahan, and the author Homer Lea all viewed Britain and her navy as the outer line of defense for the United States. FDR, who was given a copy of Lea's *The Day of the Saxon* (1912) with its dire warnings of Teutonic world ambition in April 1914, held similar, if less firm views, toward the *Pax Britannica*. There was also evidence of FDR's growing appreciation of an ideological connection between the United States and the Allies. He enthusiastically reported that the "Belgians are putting up a glorious and unexpected resistance" and that their defense was "magnificent."[70] In a letter to family friend Bob Ferguson, he declared: "Even I long to go over into the thick of it & do something to help right the wrong. England's course has been magnificent."[71]

With opinion so divided on the war it was difficult for FDR the politician to state his true position in public. Even the usually forthright TR dithered, declaring in his first public statement on the war that he was "not taking sides one way or the other" and that Belgium's plight merely reflected the weakness of international law.[72] Only later in 1914 would TR call for inter-vention because of the threat to civilization, a moral duty toward Belgium and the need for an alliance with the British.[73] The importance of civiliza-tion and order among nations would develop into a major justification of intervention for TR. His idealistic emphasis on duty, service, and republican virtue as the key to maintaining peace was a practical cover for the clear US interests he saw in Europe. This strategy, however, was not something that appealed to his fifth cousin constrained as he was by his position in the Wilson administration.

FDR chose instead to criticize peace efforts and pacifists viewing diplomatic attempts to avoid or mediate the war as a wasted effort. In 1913, Bryan had attempted to set up a series of "Cooling Off" treaties that proved worthless to the United States because the aggressive power, Germany, had refused to sign. The repeated mediation attempts by Wilson and his envoy Colonel House in early 1915, February 1916, and a final note to all parties in December 1916 also ended in failure. With this record there is, perhaps, little wonder that FDR chose to exclude diplomatic alternatives from comments in 1915 when he explained, "this sounds brutal, but war is a contest and a fact, no matter how much we may theorize... it is only by beating the enemy—i.e. hurting him more than he hurts you—that a nation can win a war."[74]

FDR also saw broader pacifist schemes for world peace as "idealistic nonsense" in the face of such a vast conflict.[75] In his speeches and writings, FDR continually criticized the peace movement, pacifists, and idealistic hopes for a pacific settlement in general:

> Dr. David Starr Jordan...has some excellent ideas; he believes in the Brotherhood of Man, So do I. He believes that this country should be the Big Brother to Mankind; that we will never have war... but unfortunately in the present state of civilization, nobody is able to give that guarantee.[76]

Adopting a skeptical stance toward all such schemes he wrote in 1914: "I look for the time that war will cease, but it is not likely to be in my age, nor that of my children."[77] He also displayed an uncharacteristically pessimistic note, writing on another occasion "one cannot help feeling that these national forces are going to continue to line up against other national forces which are hostile to them for many generations to come."[78] The political situation and reality of the war was clearly pushing FDR further toward the strict determinism of the realist interpretation of international relations. His idealism, which he rarely applied outside the Western Hemisphere above the level of a general anti-imperialism, was notable only by its absence from his rhetoric toward the situation in Europe during this period.

FDR's position contrasted dramatically with what was expected of him as a member of the Wilson administration. The need to toe the Wilsonian line meant he described the war as "due to no person or persons," ascribing it to "the outcome of national forces."[79] Underneath the public persona, however, he chafed at the "abandonment of the interests and the honor of America" and the lack of "military and economic steps" by Wilson.[80] This was always a difficult balance to maintain and he feared he would "do some awful unneutral [*sic*] things before I get through!"[81] At heart FDR believed a position of neutrality hopelessly misunderstood the conditions of modern war that was infinitely complex. It was therefore foolhardy and impractical to expect to remain impartial toward the European conflict. Much of FDR's wrath, in this respect, fell on the Secretary of State, Bryan, and his own chief, Josephus Daniels.[82]

Wilson's declaration that "there is such a thing as a man being too proud to fight" underlined the president's neutral position after a German submarine torpedoed the liner *Lusitania* on May 7, 1915, with the loss of 128 American lives. The president's first note of protest on May 13 asserted the technical rights of Americans to travel as passengers on merchant ships. His second note on June 9 refuted charges that the British blockade was illegal while his third on July 21 stated that the United States would consider further sinking an unfriendly act. TR took a more direct moral position on the tragic event by condemning Wilson and clamoring for war. FDR was less clear on points of morality and international law, but was rapidly losing patience. After the sinking, he complained that "we go on negotiating by notes and more notes—but of this there is a limit—witness the war of 1812."[83] Wilson's second note also proved too much in a different way for Bryan who was willing to sacrifice neutral rights for peace and resigned. FDR was "disgusted clear through" with the Secretary of State.[84] When the *Arabic* was sunk on August 19 with the loss of two American lives and Wilson requested a German account, FDR commented, "I personally doubt if I should be quite so polite."[85]

Underlying Bryan's disagreement with Wilson was the president's conception of executive power that placed control of foreign policy in his hands rather than his Secretary of State or anyone else for that matter. As an academic Wilson had specialized in government and one of his main concerns was the problems brought about by the separation of powers in the constitution, in particular the lack of a dominant, coherent, guiding power. Initially impressed by the British cabinet system, from the 1890s he was drawn to the strength demonstrated by Grover Cleveland in his second term and subsequently by TR's performance in office. Wilson began to see power and leadership centered on the presidency rather than a cabinet and detailed the transformation of his thinking in his book *Constitutional Government* (1908).

Once in the White House, Wilson applied his theories on a strong presidential lead to government. This was most evident in foreign policy which, like TR, he viewed as solely his domain. Wilson largely sidelined the State Department and further tarnished its image with blatant political appointments—the inexperienced William Jennings Bryan as Secretary of State being a prime example of political necessity. After Bryan's resignation, Wilson wanted a more compliant administrative secretary. He chose Robert Lansing on this basis and to enable Wilson and his adviser, Colonel Edward House, to run foreign policy directly. This has similarities to FDR's treatment of his Secretary of State Cordell Hull, often described as a political appointment because of his extensive congressional connections. Wilson also used personal envoys, usually Colonel House, rather than his Secretary of State for most of his diplomatic missions—a practice again similar to FDR's with the famous Welles mission prior to World War II and the various diplomatic trips of Harry Hopkins.

FDR appreciated Wilson's direct control of foreign policy, but likely did not follow the president's more intellectual route to executive power. The "New Freedom" of the 1912 political campaign and Wilson's emphasis on free and open competition as the route to liberty served to conceal his thinking and make TR's active example the more profound influence on FDR. Wilson may have seen the president as the powerful centre, but he did not yet make the connection to the powerful executive agencies. FDR was ahead of him in this respect—in the summer of 1915, FDR took a plan for a "Council of National Defense" to oversee industrial mobilization (similar in concept to the War Industries Board eventually headed by Bernard Baruch when the United States entered the war) directly to Wilson. A disinterested president put him off this time because he did not "want to 'rattle the sword' while Germany seems anxious to meet us half way" during the tense summer after the *Lusitania* was sunk.[86] Wilson would subsequently provide, through the Overman Act of 1918, a vivid example of the efficacy of executive agencies for public policy, but for now he remained reluctant to allow power to slip from his grasp. FDR would file Wilson's wartime example away and recall it to good effect during the New Deal and World War II.

In late 1916, Wilson made one further diplomatic effort at mediation among the belligerents, but his position on neutrality meant the military initiative always lay in German hands and their notification to the United States on January 31, 1917, of their intention to resume unrestricted submarine warfare made war seem certain. By this stage FDR, like many others, had completely rejected neutrality and was conferring with prointervention members within Wilson's cabinet and even his close adviser Colonel House who lent a sympathetic ear to many cabinet members.[87] FDR's position was clear—on the evening of Wilson's inauguration on March 4, 1917, he dined at the Metropolitan Club with TR and assorted militant Republican interventionists to plan a strategy to support entering the war as soon as possible.

As FDR entered public life for the first time he faced many challenges. His background and upbringing was often a handicap and the dogmatic insurgent style he often used alienated him from party circles. Yet he was politically astute enough to tie himself to Wilson and amply demonstrated his skilled ability to respond to the political climate. His flexibility in differences with Wilson over neutrality demonstrates a pragmatic assessment of his need to accommodate his views with the president's if he was to retain his job. Similarly, his realization that he could not use the European war as a direct justification for preparedness shows an equal regard for public opinion—few people directly linked preparedness to potential intervention, but FDR's attacks on the Jeffersonian conception of defense and promotion of the physical and moral benefits of military service represent a masterful dissimulation of his true beliefs.

FDR was heavily influenced by both TR and Wilson during the period 1910–1917, but often in areas of form rather than substance. They taught him important lessons about how to run presidential foreign policy and he was already using both TR and Wilson's rhetoric to argue positions that neither supported. The influence of TR on FDR's thinking was more limited than sometimes stated. FDR was guarded in his acceptance of TR's more forthright ideological views on protecting European civilization as a function of US security and nonhumanitarian interventions in the Western Hemisphere based on power and duty. Neither did FDR adopt much of Wilson's thinking on either democracy or friendship cloaking racism at this stage. The president clearly did not have the impact on FDR that is so often ascribed to him before 1917 and this logically pushes FDR's discovery of the ideological aspects of Wilson's thinking to a later date, or serves to reduce their overall importance to FDR as a whole. However, it should be noted that Wilson still had the majority of his second term to serve and this would include leading the United States into the war and attempting to establish a global system of collective security.

In many ways FDR's international view was clearly his own and not cloned from TR or Wilson. It retained much that was remarkably personal and was still deeply intertwined with his background, upbringing, character, and beliefs. The years 1910–1917 see FDR becoming his own man. This is particularly evident in his response to the war in Europe where his clear recognition of the threat to US security from German aggression directed his thinking. Unable to accept Wilson's neutrality and unwilling to adopt TR's moral justifications for war, FDR was drawn into an increasingly realist and deterministic assessment of world forces. In public, he toed the Wilsonian line while strenuously advocating preparedness and attacking the position of pacifists and neutrals. In private, he felt there was little the United States could do except acknowledge participation in war was inevitable and prosecute it with all vigor. This position would become his dominant approach to world affairs in the months following April 1917. American participation in World War I would test FDR's international views to their limits. How he responded to continued service in the Wilson administration during the war and the massive upheavals it brought to both his personal life and American society are the focus of the next chapter.

CHAPTER 3

WAR AND PEACE, 1917–1919

WHEN WOODROW WILSON TOOK HIS COUNTRY TO WAR ON April 6, 1917, few could imagine the profound implications his decision would have for the position of the United States in the world. FDR had heard the president's speech to Congress a few days earlier, but showed little interest in any of his more idealistic reasons for entering the European war. He had long believed that German aggressive militarism was a threat to the country's security interests and he now threw himself into the war effort with a fierce energy and enthusiasm. Yet the war did not turn out as he imagined—the practical accommodations it required, the disruptions in his personal life it brought, and the arguments of the peace settlement would all combine to transform FDR's international viewpoint dramatically.

For a long time FDR, like Mahan, TR, and the Navy General Board, had called for preponderant naval power centered on a battleship-based fleet so that the United States could assert its rights and interests around the globe. Entry into the war served to heighten and exaggerate this assertiveness in FDR, but it also aroused doubts in turn about the battleship as the central pillar of US foreign policy. Many of these doubts originated with the way that the reality of naval warfare failed to conform to Mahan's theory. To start with, FDR's hopes for a full-scale naval conflict had been "disappointed" early in the war by England's inability to "force a naval action" on the German fleet.[1] Indeed, after the inconclusive battle of Jutland in May 1916, the German surface fleet remained bottled up in its home ports for the remainder of the war—hardly the decisive encounter of grand fleets on the high seas FDR expected. This reluctance of the powers to engage their fleets extended beyond the British and the Germans; FDR made a trip to Rome, as part of his European trip in the summer of 1918, in a desperate, and ultimately unsuccessful, attempt to prod the Italians into using their navy more aggressively. At a speech at the Harvard Union earlier that same year, FDR was already attempting to reconcile naval theory with his experience of the war arguing:

> It is a pity to have to hold them [the navy] on defensive terms only...authorities like Mahan...have always maintained that an offensive can consist of two methods of war; first, to seek the enemy and destroy him in his own "rat hole"; Secondly, so to place yourself about "the mouth of the rat hole" that the rat cannot come out. That is practically what has happened.[2]

His emphasis on fleet actions centered upon the battleship was being transformed by the practical requirements of the Allied blockade and the reluctance of the Germans to join in a direct engagement.

The entry of the United States into the war saw the demise of the battleship as the centre of naval strategy due to the immediate tactical need to counteract the submarine as a weapon of war. Britain kept her shipping losses from German submarines a closely guarded secret, but then quickly revealed their devastating extent to the Americans when they entered the war—over one million tons lost in February and March 1917 alone. At that rate the Allies were staring at defeat long before the United States could make any substantial contribution to the war effort. FDR seems to have had a talent for quickly appreciating the impact of new weapons technology and saw earlier than many Navy Board members the need to defeat the submarine. In a 1915 article analyzing the submarine's impact, he acknowledged his own limitations, writing, "I had a theory that I knew much about naval strategy and warfare. But I have come very quickly to realise that I did not."[3] By July 1917, he feared that if the rate of destruction of shipping continued, the United States would find itself with a trained army and no way to move it to Europe.[4] Later that year he wrote directly to Wilson arguing: "The elimination of all submarines from the waters between the United States and Europe must of necessity be a vital factor in winning the war."[5]

One solution pushed by FDR was a plan to create a North Sea mine barrage between Orkney and Norway to block off that route to German submarines. Despite technical difficulties and a good deal of skepticism, the scheme was implemented toward the end of the war. The major threat from German submarines, however, came from those operating at short range in British waters at the points where transatlantic shipping routes converged. To counter this, the Allies requested that the Americans send as many destroyers as they could to Europe as a matter of urgency. The US naval representative in London, Admiral William S. Sims, became an early supporter of the need for destroyers and FDR followed his lead, even claiming to have taken the matter of gathering destroyers up with the president, who rejected the suggestion, before the US declaration of war. FDR later recollected that Wilson would not allow him to gather the destroyers prior to the declaration of war as he did not want anybody "rattling the sword."[6]

There were several other obstacles to supplying the destroyers. Daniels maintained his circumspect and considered approach to naval affairs, much to the chagrin of FDR. Indeed, so frustrated was FDR that at one point he even cooperated with the American author, Winston Churchill, on a damning report concerning naval efficiency submitted to the president in August 1917.[7] Daniels could count, however, on sympathy within the Navy General Board. The Allied request required a complete reversal of the US naval strategy of never splitting the fleet and the Board were particularly reluctant to drop its adherence to this Mahanian doctrine. Apart from an ability to meet the enemy in force they worried, in a similar fashion to the debate on sending troops to Europe, about piecemeal commitment of forces to the struggle and Allied command over US forces.[8]

Entrance into the war and the enormous Allied shipping losses proved a great lesson for all concerned and the navy eventually appreciated the need to give up outdated doctrines and send the destroyers to Europe. The change in strategy was dramatic—Wilson's "Big Navy" Act of July 1916 had originally called for an accelerated construction program of ten battleships and six battle cruisers in the first year, but by July the following year Secretary Daniels had shifted the naval construction plan away from battleships to concentrate on destroyers. This was augmented by the Urgent Deficiencies Act signed by Wilson on October 6, allowing Daniels to order a further 265 destroyers. The first contingent of 6 American destroyers arrived in European waters by May 1917 and 79 were operational by the end of the war.[9]

FDR visited the European base of the destroyers at Queenstown in Ireland on his inspection trip during the summer of 1918 and was suitably impressed by the local British commander Admiral Sir Lewis Bayly. Knowledge of the US Navy's effective record under local British command and of "the principle of unity of command" no doubt paid dividends for the forging of a military alliance with the British during World War II.[10] The other product of FDR's extensive involvement with naval affairs and the Atlantic shipping battles was that it gave him a detailed understanding of the issues of submarine and destroyer warfare (such as convoying, operational range, and targeting areas) that was particularly useful in 1941 in managing his policy of undeclared naval warfare against Germany.

One further aspect of the FDR's wartime experience also told him that the central role of the battleship, while not superseded, was at least being challenged. Aircraft were beginning to play an increasingly important role in naval warfare. There were men in the navy who argued that aviation had revolutionized naval warfare—most notably Admirals William Fulham, William E. Sims, and Bradley Fiske. Fulham argued for what he called a "three-plane navy" giving equal roles to surface craft, submarines, and aircraft, while Sims predicted the aircraft carrier would become the mainstay of the future fleet and Fiske pioneered experiments with aerial torpedoes.[11] Despite the tactical use of destroyers, the dominant opinion in the navy still privileged the battleship to the detriment of aviation. Indeed, in August 1919, the Chief of Naval Operations Admiral William Benson disbanded the Division of Naval Aeronautics thus removing any definite status for naval aviation.[12]

Again FDR was not slow in appreciating the new weapon's implications and was inclined to accept arguments for the growing importance of aviation for the navy. On his European trip during the summer of 1918, it was a prominent theme. While visiting the naval air station at Pauillac, France on August 14, he was shown a bombing trial on a mock submarine and even managed a flight himself.[13] More ominously, crossing the English Channel a few days later by destroyer the ship was twice bombed en route by enemy aircraft.[14] Once back in England FDR's party drove to Firth of Forth to visit the American battleship squadron, then under the command of the British Grand Fleet. Here he was treated to a practice attack display by British aircraft on the US flagship *New York*.[15] Thus he could argue with

Figure 3.1   FDR had an early interest in the potential of all types of aircraft. Here he investigates a Navy dirigible in 1917. (National Archives 80-G-48929).

some authority in the summer of 1919 that "[i]t would be probable that a great fleet action of the future would be preceded by a determined effort of one side to obtain mastery of the air."[16] He also accepted Admiral Fulham's tactical view—noting in a speech to Brooklyn Chamber of Commerce in January 1920 that "there is very little difference today in the basic principles [of war] from what they were in the time of Nelson" though he added "we have new weapons, we have new dimensions—downwards and upwards."[17] Evolving naval theory at this time made a strong impression on FDR and stayed with him when he became president. In his May 1940 "Fireside chat," he sounded very much like Admiral Fulham when he stated "the airplane is just as much an integral part of the unity of operations as the submarine, the destroyer and the battleship."[18]

FDR's emerging position on aviation was later complicated in the summer of 1919 when he became the first administration member to publicly attack General William "Billy" Mitchell, the prominent campaigner for an independent air force. FDR actually agreed with Mitchell's view on the potential for airpower, but rejected his denigration of the naval air arm and plans to take away its aviation capabilities.[19] This certainly did not represent a return to the doctrine of battleship-centered navy for FDR. Even as

Figure 3.2   On August 29, 1918, FDR visited the US main battle fleet in the Firth of Forth where he witnessed a simulated attack by British aircraft on the US flagship *New York*. His early appreciation of airpower contributed to his move away from a belief that the battleship was central to US power. (FDR Library 09-2607a).

president, although he backed naval expansion under his enthusiastic secretary Claude Swanson, no battleship was laid down until the *North Carolina* in 1937 and this only after Japan had abrogated the 1922 Washington Treaty. In contrast, he emphasized the importance of naval aviation—before US entry into World War II FDR worked on designs to improve defenses of ships against aerial attack. He was also personally responsible for dreaming up the improvised *Independence* class carriers in August 1941. With no new fleet carriers scheduled to arrive until 1944, these nine converted cruisers provided a valuable aviation capability for the US Navy much earlier in the war than they could have otherwise expected.

FDR's experience of aviation in Europe had further important implications for his view of US security. He was able to see, first hand, the destructive power of aerial bombing at Calais and later Dunkirk where he observed: "There is not a whole house left in this place. It may truthfully be said it has been bombed every night that flying was possible for three years."[20] When he later toured the most easterly American bomber bases in France he caught a glimpse of the future of strategic bombing. Here he learned the effects of destructive German 1200lb bombs, but was able to rejoice that new US Navy bombers would carry 1750lb bombs.[21] This gave him an appreciation of the offensive capabilities of aircraft very different from the typical American view that saw them as essentially defensive weapons that enhanced the value of Atlantic hemispheric isolation. This was an extension of America's Jeffersonian hemispheric smugness into a further dimension of war—aircraft patrols could range out from the coast to smash an enemy before it ever reached the United States.[22]

While there is no evidence that FDR made the connection to a strategic bombing threat to the continental United States, at this point it would be unsurprising if he did. During the summer of 1919, he first followed the failed attempts of the Navy C-5 dirigible to cross the Atlantic and then was closely involved in the planning of the successful attempt by the US Navy NC-4 plane to fly from Long Island to the Azores in May. Though the flight was overshadowed by the first successful nonstop flight by British aviators Alcock and Brown on June 15, FDR remained "warm friends" with the flight planner and aviation pioneer Lieutenant Commander Richard E. Byrd.[23] Thus FDR had an early appreciation of both the offensive capabilities of aircraft and their potential ability to cross the Atlantic long before the Munich crisis of 1938 and this possibly explains his acute perception of the direct physical threat from the "recrudescence" of German airpower at that time. His involvement with the NC-4 aircraft crossing also, perhaps, provided the origin of his deep concern with the Azores and western Africa as a staging post for hostile aircraft in the run up to World War II. In his "Fireside chat" of May 29, 1940, he famously warned the American people that "the distance [between Africa and Brazil] ... is less than five hours for the latest type of bomber." The threat of German bombers and submarines based in the Azores was even enough for FDR to call for active planning for the occupation of the neutral islands during 1941. Planning for this only ceased when it became apparent the German invasion of the Soviet Union had made moves on the Portuguese territory unlikely.[24]

The powerful lesson of the 1938 Munich crisis was that airpower was a formidable diplomatic tool, but it is clear that FDR appreciated this point much earlier. He had long been an enthusiast for the military use of aircraft, particularly during the preparedness debate of 1915–1916.[25] Military aviation went on to become something of an embarrassment during the war with much money spent and little in the way of aircraft produced. Wilson had originally called for a program for 100,000 planes, but this was subsequently revised downward several times as a result of poor planning until eventually most of the aircraft used by the United States during the war were supplied by the French.[26] Thus when FDR called for a program of 10,000 aircraft per year in 1938 he was fully aware of the dangers of delay and the obstacles his request would face having learnt from Wilson and, Secretary of War Newton Baker's previous experience.

Figure 3.3 Josephus Daniels and FDR (seated second left) with the crews of the Navy NC-4 flight across the Atlantic July 2, 1919. FDR was involved in the planning for the flight and this contributed to his understanding of the relationship of airpower and the Azores to US hemispheric security. (National Archives 80-G-464938).

While FDR's anxieties about the threat to US security from German aircraft were new, his concerns about airpower generally were not. Early in 1919, FDR became aware of British plans to develop commercial flights between Constantinople, India, and elsewhere and a "feverish effort to expand her airforces [sic] to a point so far in excess of any other nation that she can virtually control the air in the face of all opposition."[27] The answer for FDR was to match the British, in this case, but clearly also any other rival or hostile nation. Speaking from the cockpit of a British Handley-Page night bomber at the Aeronautical Exposition in Madison Square Garden, New York, on March 18, 1919, FDR claimed he had recently returned from Europe where he had investigated "the aircraft situation." It is not clear whether the irony of sitting in a British bomber was intended or missed by FDR, but he called for the United States to remain in the "van" of aircraft production and adopt "definite policy for control of the air." This control was absolutely necessary for "commercial purposes, for travel, and for defense in future possible wars."[28] This sense of competition with the British in aviation would never entirely leave him as the negotiations over the post–World War II civil aviation regime amply demonstrate.[29] Thus, when the Munich Crisis erupted, it is clear FDR already had an appreciation of both the threat of aircraft to the Western Hemisphere and of the need to match the airpower of other nations as both a defensive and diplomatic strategy. The "Munich Analogy" and lesson of history that Ernest May so clearly perceived does not apply to FDR who experienced a valuable education of military aviation as a diplomatic tool during the years 1917–1919.[30]

FDR matched his sophisticated awareness of airpower with a new and equally subtle appreciation of naval power. Ironically, at the very time FDR was losing interest in the battleship both Wilson and Daniels were gaining in theirs. The second of Wilson's Fourteen Points affirmed the need for freedom of the seas, but the British insisted that they had the right to defend their imperial trade. Colonel House was anxious not to disrupt the peace negotiations and bypassed the issue in late 1918, but not before he threatened to start a naval building program to challenge British naval dominance. With the Peace Conference rapidly approaching, Wilson wanted to pressure the Allies into accepting his plans for the League of Nations and discovered that a threatened naval arms race was a good way to twist the arm of the British. To this end he got Daniels to endorse a three-year building program for the Navy in early December 1918 with the aim of forcing the British to adopt his plans for a league, and in particular his amendment in March 1919 to include in its covenant a provision for the Monroe Doctrine.[31] A compromise was reached in early April only after Daniels went to Paris and agreed with the British representatives to postpone the new naval program until after the peace treaty had been signed and offered to consult on any future plans.

FDR was no doubt appraised by Daniels of the diplomatic schemes and put his own mischievous oar into affairs by talking to reporters about plans to build new "super-battle-cruiser" that would make the battleship "obsolete."[32] Though the British might be naval rivals, following the experience of the war they were not perceived by FDR as a threat to be seriously countered. There were some in navy circles who were against naval expansion at this time as a pro-British measure. Admiral Sims was one such person, but it is unlikely that FDR was following his lead at this point as relations between the two had cooled distinctly. Sims had vigorously opposed FDR's scheme for the North Sea barrage and made it known he took a dim view of political junkets such as FDR's trips to Europe. Indeed, the Admiral gave the FDR a particularly frosty reception after the Assistant Secretary announced he had come over to see there was nothing the Republicans could pick up in an investigating committee. Overall, therefore, FDR remained firm in his move away from the battleship as the centre of US strategy while gaining a further education in diplomatic brinkmanship from Wilson and Daniels.[33]

In the immediate term, emotional responses to the war took precedence over intellectual ones for FDR; the German enemy focused his aggression and exaggerated his assertive nationalism. Throughout the conflict he called for the total defeat of Germany and the Central Powers and continued calling for harsh peace terms after the Armistice. On viewing the destruction in France and Belgium on his trip to Europe in summer 1918, he reported to Daniels that "a drastic lesson against the Germans themselves on German soil will be necessary before any understanding can be hammered into the German mind." Later when he revisited the Rhineland area he knew from his youth he insisted that a Stars and Stripes be raised over a German fortress despite concerns of the local American occupation authorities that it would unnecessarily humiliate the Germans.[34] FDR was not unusual in that he clearly perceived a threat to US security in German militarism and aggression. Although a large segment of liberal opinion called for a peace of justice for the Germans, FDR saw no reason to sacrifice security for such notions. A broad spectrum of politicians from TR, Lodge, and even Wilson agreed with the need to deal with the threat and also advocated harsh peace terms.[35] FDR's assertive internationalism was, however, coming under increasing pressure from aspects of his public political and personal life.

TR had resigned his position as Assistant Secretary in 1898 to organize the Rough Riders and tried desperately to launch a similar volunteer scheme in this war. As a keen believer in the benefits of military experience, TR pressured FDR to enlist in the forces on several occasions after his own ambitions to volunteer were scotched by Wilson. A mixture of a genuine desire to serve and the manifest benefits of a glorious war record to a political career encouraged FDR to try. Wilson and Daniels promptly put a stop to his ambitions because they viewed his role in Washington as too important and he was never able to serve in the armed forces.[36] Instead, FDR would have to resort to compensatory claims that "as a father" he looked "forward to the day when my boys will be able to render service to their country."[37] Insecurity on this point perhaps encouraged FDR to increase his public emphasis on the moral and physical benefits of military service for others. In a 1917 article, he told his readers that if they could see the men (in this case those who had served on the Mexican border) they would "understand what a short course of military training has done for the bodies and minds of young Americans." Neither did he merely write about such physical schemes, he gave an active demonstration by joining the well-publicized morning calisthenics routine organized in Washington by Yale's renowned football strategist, Walter Camp.[38]

To FDR, military service also continued to be an effective political strategy to counteract slurs on his class origin. It had a "broadening effect" and counteracted the "danger" of "sectionalism and class feeling" by teaching "the true kind of equality—the equality that gives every individual a fair chance to recognize individual endeavor and ability."[39] In reality, as his career progressed, class origin was becoming less of a problem for FDR and he actually needed his emphasis on the military ethos less as a political strategy than before. The publicity he received as wartime Assistant Secretary of the Navy meant he began to be talked about as candidate for New York State senator or even governor and proved he was finally shaking off the image of the privileged patrician. As his political star rose the politicos of Tammany Hall also realized his worth and there was a mutual peace made in July 1917, each realizing how much they needed the other.[40]

The next best thing to military service and actual combat was arranging exciting junkets to Europe to gawp at the war—FDR managed two, the first in the summer of 1918 to inspect navy units and report on general conditions, the second to aid the demobilization of the navy in early 1919 following the Armistice. FDR took along his crony "Livy" Davis and loved every minute of the adventure—even designing his own "destroyer costume," making sure he toured all the forward battle areas to collect souvenirs and reveling in the exploits of "one of [my] Marine regiments" at Château Thierry and Belleau Wood. Eleanor came along on the second European trip in the hope of a second honeymoon and quickly sized up the malign influence of Livy who was "lazy, selfish and self-seeking to an extraordinary degree."[41] Friction between his wife and male friends aside, FDR's trips to Europe in 1918 and 1919 meant his speech at Chautauqua in 1936 in which he declared "I have seen war" was literally true, even if he had not taken an active combat role.

The other important development to come out of FDR's first trip to Europe was the discovery by Eleanor of his affair with her former social secretary Lucy Mercer. Neither FDR nor his wife ever directly confirmed the affair happened, but it seems most likely that Eleanor discovered letters from Lucy to FDR in his luggage while he recovered from a bad case of influenza and pneumonia upon returning from Europe in September 1918. In practical terms, given social mores at the time, a divorce would be the end of FDR's political career. There is a debate as to whether Eleanor refused to grant him his freedom, but in any event FDR's mother Sara refused to countenance the idea and threatened to cut him off from all his family inheritance should a divorce go ahead. FDR's entire political future was in the balance. He had little choice but to follow Sara Roosevelt's direction if he wanted to continue his political career and enjoy a degree of financial security. Thus, in the years that followed, he attempted to be a more family orientated, dutiful, and contrite husband and abandoned many of his more youthful excesses even before the ravages of polio made them impossible.

FDR was not normally a reflective man, but with everything that had happened to his conceptions of naval theory, the application of US power and the disruptions in his personal and political life it would be unsurprising if he did not, as he grew older, ponder some of his major positions. In the immediate term not having served in the forces would have made it increasingly difficult to talk publicly of assertive nationalism when there were now many veterans to question his approach. TR had also died on January 6, 1919, leaving exponents of military service and application of power without a major pillar of public support, though FDR's comments were muted on his cousin's death—he merely said it was "a great shock."[42] FDR's recognition of the changed circumstances was demonstrated by a speech he gave at Syracuse, New York, in the summer of 1919 in which he said: "I would have preferred to have been in action at the front, to have stood side by side with you, now home; to have met the enemy in physical death grapple rather than coldly plotted his destruction from an office chair. Men from the front, I welcome and I envy you." Later in 1921, when a war memorial was planned at Groton, FDR pleaded, "though I did not serve in uniform, I believe that my name should go in the first division of those who were 'in the service,' especially as I saw service on the other side, was missed by torpedoes and shell, and had actual command over 'material' navy matters in Europe while I was there."[43] FDR's personal motivations are hard to gauge, but he clearly felt the need to associate himself with those who served for political reasons.

The horrors of the Western Front do not appear to have had much impact on FDR personally who complained at Verdun that "it didn't look like a battlefield, for there was little or nothing to see but a series of depressions and ridges, bare and brown and dead" though he did acknowledge that "probably over a hundred thousand men were killed in this little stretch of valley." That was as philosophic and poignant as it got with FDR at the scene of one of the great tragic battles of the war, but if anything the war made him step back from the determinism of world forces he had been drawn toward in recent years. For FDR it was the living he encountered who had the more profound impact upon him and who, he believed, still held the ability to progress humanity. During the summer of 1918, he reported to his chief Daniels: "One of the things that has struck me particularly this week in England has been the absolute unanimity among all the Government people here to see this thing through to more than what they call 'a patched-up peace.'"[44] The thought stayed with FDR over the winter until, at the start of March, he reported to a meeting of the League of Free Nations Association (LFNA) in New York that he had received a letter from a college student asking whether he favored a bigger navy. "We get hundreds of such letters," FDR said "but this letter I held and thought about. And for the first time in my life I dictated a letter in which I did not advocate a larger navy." FDR then went on to describe the process of this change in thinking:

> Last Spring I thought the League of Nations merely a beautiful dream, a utopia. But in June I went abroad, in those critical days. I found in Europe... a growing demand that out of it all must come something else. When our glorious offensive began this demand for something greater than peace grew larger.[45]

After such a tragic and costly war, the public mood, and that of the troops, was naturally focusing on peace. FDR the politician realized that there was no longer any enthusiasm among the American public for large military expenditure following the effort and sacrifices of the war and he was forced to cut his cloth accordingly. Yet it was not just rhetoric convenient to the debate opening up in March of 1919—it fits with FDR's report to Daniels the previous summer and confirms that he had indeed dwelt on the feelings of the people he had encountered on his European trip. Thus, with all the other pressures FDR encountered at this time, there was a rare opening for a change in his thinking toward alternative approaches to international relations.

The major alternative approach to international relations discussed at the time was, of course, the League of Nations. Wilson had first publicly spoken in favor of a league at a League to Enforce Peace (LEP) rally in 1916, but it was not until his Fourteen Points were delivered on January 8, 1918, that he gave a specific pledge for "a general association of nations... under specific covenants." Since then he had failed to provide much in the way of

Figure 3.4   On August 6, 1918, FDR visited the scene of one of the great tragic battles of World War I at Verdun. He was disappointed that "it didn't look like a battlefield" and was more influenced by the living he met on his European trip than the memory of the dead. (National Archives 80-G-48939).

further detail. Wilson's absence from the United States at the conference in Paris from December 4, 1918, until February 24, 1919, meant he had little time or contact with his administration to direct policy toward the League and he made no attempt to engage with the press or public to educate them or develop a base of support. Nor had he attempted to court Congress or any public bodies, such as the LEP, to build an organized support movement. Until the release of the Covenant to the Paris Peace Conference on February 14, 1919, supporters and opponents alike only had the vaguest of statements to go on. Even then, Wilson retained the initiative by claiming any discussion of the Covenant would be premature until he held a meeting with the Senate Foreign Relations Committee (FRC) and House Committee on Foreign Affairs at the White House on February 26. In this situation, it would be difficult for any minor administration official, let alone a keen Assistant Secretary of the Navy, to talk with any authority on the subject.

Historian Frank Freidel argued that FDR experienced a "conversion" in favor of Wilson's League when both men returned to the United States from France on board the *George Washington* in February 1919.[46] President Wilson was certainly a persuasive orator—his physician, Dr. Grayson, left a diary account of a shipboard luncheon, attended by FDR, at which the president made the first recorded use of his dramatic argument that failure of the United States to back the League would "break the heart of the world."[47] In reality, however, FDR's only direct knowledge of the League came from this lunch with the president and a hasty reading of a copy of the League Covenant given to him by a journalist while travelling to Brest by train en route to the United States.[48] While in Europe he did visit Paris, but had no official role at the Peace Conference and was unable to gain any great insight into the secretive Peace or League negotiations.[49]

There was also a distinct lack of clear alternatives to the League. The "Atlanticist" viewpoint that called for a separate peace treaty, consultation with the Allies over future threats to security, and for eventual ratification of a French security treaty was one. Implicit in this was the belief that the domination of Europe by an aggressive military power was also a menace to US security. TR did most to push proposals for a balance of power alliance against the resurgence of a powerful Germany, but he died in January 1919 and the only other serious public proponent was Senator Philander Knox with his "New American Doctrine."[50] Lodge, of course, agreed with Knox's position, but was pursuing a more calculated strategy to challenge Wilson's

Figure 3.5   FDR jokes with Wilson on board the USS George Washington returning to the United States in February 1919 following the publication of the League of Nations Covenant. FDR did not experience a full conversion to Wilsonianism on the voyage. (National Archives 127-PR-FDR-519053).

proposals for a league.[51] Thus, the position never really emerged as a rallying point for opposition to Wilson. Instead, Republican opponents chose to question the ultimate wisdom of the League through Lodge's strategy of reservations, a decision that crucially limited the debate. Given his background, FDR was probably sympathetic to the Atlanticists, but his experiences during the war, his liberal inclinations, and, of course, membership of the Wilson administration made him crucially aware of its limitations.

Isolationism emerged as an alternative political position during the neutrality period and opposed the commitment of troops or military and political alliances outside the Western Hemisphere. As a cross-party phenomenon it provided some of the most dynamic, even demagogic, rhetoric of the League Fight. Democratic senator for Missouri, James A. Reed said of the League just before Wilson left for Paris, "it is the old Holy Alliance again."[52] Other popular isolationist themes at this time were that the league was alternately a "triumph" or "Trojan Horse" of British imperial diplomacy, that the United States would be forced to become the policeman of the World and that a League threatened a world superstate. Indicating that it was Wilson's personal vain scheme, Democratic senator James K. Vardaman of Mississippi referred to his "little golden rattle," that risked the destruction of the Monroe Doctrine, the Constitution and flew in the face of advice against entangling and permanent alliances. Another Republican senator William Borah of Idaho felt it was against "the national spirit" as an example to the world of "freedom to do as our own people think wise and just."[53]

Hardcore isolationists, though vocal, were small in number, but FDR would still feel compelled to reject their position wholeheartedly in the coming months.[54] FDR maintained a firm belief that it was impossible for the United States to avoid contact with the world and that it should play an active role to assert its interests. Even during the height of the League controversy in June 1919 he argued:

> It is clear as the sun that the United States would commit a grievous wrong to itself and to all mankind if it were even to attempt to go backwards towards an old Chinese wall policy of isolation...there will be many crises in international affairs for many years to come. In them the US cannot escape an important, perhaps, even a controlling voice.[55]

In this instance FDR was using TR's "Chinese wall" allusion to support the idea of the League of Nations—hardly something TR would have done. FDR's old understanding of an interdependent world brought about by technological developments in communications and transportation, and the increasing economic links the United States had with the world remained intact. To explain his position in public he no longer had to rely solely on his favorite historical example of Jefferson's failed embargo or dire warnings of "economic suicide" to describe the harm hemispheric isolation could do, he now had a practical example. In the period immediately prior to US entry into the war merchant ships had been confined to port causing enormous nationwide disruption. The lesson that the United States should defend its trading ability was not lost on FDR who noted that "the effect of this tie-up spreads quickly back to the interior parts of the nation...causing general confusion throughout the land."[56] The war thus reinforced his existing appreciation of the importance of US contacts with the world.

Despite this clichéd picture of deep divisions over international relations during the League Fight, it is remarkable how much general agreement there actually was regarding an international role for the United States at the end of the war. Wilson, though not enthusiastic for some of the measures, also made an effort to incorporate many suggestions originating from both domestic and international sources into the League Covenant. FDR, as someone deeply interested in international relations and who was politically astute, no doubt would have sensed the general consensus on many of the ideas floating around at the time that included proposals for disarmament, judicial and arbitral settlement of disputes, international progressivism, and collective security.

Calls for disarmament had an extensive heritage, particularly in the Democratic Party, but they gained new strength and wider respectability from the war. Although nationalists such as TR and Lodge were fiercely opposed, there was a significant interest within the Republican Party centered on key figures such as Elihu Root, former secretary of state and first president of the Carnegie Endowment for Peace. Their influence grew in response to the public mood and, beginning with the Washington Conference of 1921–1922, disarmament became a major element of Republican policy during the 1920s. Wilson, too, was sensitive to interest in disarmament among the public and made provision for it, albeit vaguely, in Article VII of the Covenant of the League of Nations. Given FDR's previous belligerent record, it is unsurprising that disarmament was not a prominent theme for him during the League Fight. He did occasionally use it in a negative sense to justify the League, claiming at one stage that if the League was not ratified military spending could reach "at least $600,000,000" per year.[57] FDR held a deep skepticism toward unilateral disarmament, but the League offered a structure for multilateral arrangements and discussions that encouraged his interest.

Legal internationalists drew on a long heritage of calls for law to form the basis for international involvement. The LEP, founded in 1915 and with ex-president Taft at its head, called for a judicial tribunal, council of conciliation, and regular conferences to codify international law. Importantly they also called for their world regime in which decisions were ultimately backed up by military force. Wilson, perhaps because of the reliance on force, was not keen on judicial settlement and certainly kept his distance from the LEP, but again made provision for judicial settlement in Article XII of the covenant while Article XIV called for a permanent court of international justice.

The Permanent Court of International Justice was eventually set up at The Hague in 1921 with key Republicans such as Elihu Root and John Bassett Moore playing pivotal roles. The Senate refused to ratify US membership, however, fearing that it was too close to the League of Nations.[58] FDR, though he showed no expressed interest in a legalist approach to world order at this time, had no quarrel with it. It was an acceptable regime for FDR because it promised to set the moral boundaries for potential conflict, but without requiring US political commitments to other countries. FDR had contact with many key LEP members during the League Fight and international law would become an important theme for him in the future—supporting calls for a codification of international law during the 1920s and unsuccessfully attempting to achieve Senate ratification of the World Court in 1935.

FDR's tentative support for legal solutions did not extend to support for arbitration as a basis for world peace and US security. Arbitration had a long pedigree and was again closely linked to the Republican Party. Both John Hay and Elihu Root arranged numerous bilateral arbitration treaties as secretary of state and more recently President Taft pursued his own treaty schemes. On the Democratic side, Wilson had also supported William Jennings Bryan in his attempts to set up arbitration treaties and included provision for them in Article XII of the League Covenant. FDR never demonstrated any interest in arbitration treaties, particularly Bryan's, and probably remained skeptical because his appreciation of power suggested that nations would always fight to protect matters of vital national interest or honor. Many nationalists such as TR opposed such approaches outright and it is unlikely that the qualification FDR's notions of power received during the war engendered any conversion to support of the arbitration idea. Unlike the legalist solution, arbitration had a political, rather than moral, foundation and was much more open to challenge by disputing parties.

Liberal internationalist opinion in contrast with the more conservative LEP was slow to organize, but eventually coalesced around the League of Free Nations Association (LFNA) in late 1918. This organization brought together a mixture of Republican and Democratic liberal opinion and included many members of the progressive elite such as Jane Addams, Frederic C Howe, Felix Frankfurter, Learned Hand, John Dewey, Charles Beard, Herbert Croly, and Paul Kellogg.[59] In contrast to the LEP, the LFNA argued that it was not enough to establish the machinery of arbitration, law, and coercion if the old order of international relations existed unchanged. It damned imperialism as the cause of war and called for the "liberty, progress and fair economic opportunity of all nations" and for the "orderly development of the world."[60] The LFNA also emphasized the need for "democratic principles" to shoot through the peace settlement to make it tolerable. This was in tune with Wilson's wider progressive credentials and, though the provision of mandates under Article XXII was cause for concern, he did attempt to speak to progressive liberal opinion through Article X with its protection of self-determination, Article XXIII with its call for fair and humane conditions of labor, and Article XXV with its call for the promotion of health and control of disease.

The LFNA was predominantly centered in New York and FDR's first public comments on the League were at one of their meetings in the city on March 1, 1919. In the absence of Wilson, or much comment from him, the LFNA impressed FDR with its articulation of general liberal opinion in support of the League. They demonstrated a broader appeal by avoiding the specifics upon which there was less agreement and focusing on the idealism of the League. FDR's speeches are often attributed to the intellectual influence of Wilson, but it seems more likely that he was adopting the language of the LFNA to make a similarly broad appeal. On March 1, FDR argued the success of the League depended on the "spirit with which it was accepted." He also claimed that the League would lead to an internationalism of "goodwill, honor, and service among nations, [and would] prevent the horrors of war."[61] FDR's next public comments on the League were in a speech on March 6, in Baltimore, Maryland, where he made a vague call to aid the "civilization of the future" and added that younger nations now looked to the United States for their "justice," "liberty," and "safety." At a time when Wilson was not very forthcoming with arguments supporting a league FDR looked to the LFNA's arguments to articulate his position.[62]

Proposals for world collective security were also surprisingly, given the tone of much of the historiography, the focus of a great deal of agreement. In May 1910, TR had actually called for a "league of peace" to protect "by force if necessary" world order and a world "posse comitatus" in a series of articles in late 1914.[63] Henry Cabot Lodge also spoke in favor of a league to the LEP in June 1915 and continued to argue for a more tightly defined league that avoided the vagueness in Wilson's scheme.[64] There also remained a significant amount of support within the Republican Party for some form of world collective security organization. This was focused predominantly within the LEP, which, although it proposed a legal rather than political solution, supported Wilson's ideas for the League even after the Covenant was published. The LEP was a well connected and funded lobby group that had been pushing the idea of a League since 1915. It mounted a strong educational campaign of speaking tours and literature publication throughout the ensuing fight. Indeed, the LEP was the most important source of information for League supporters and FDR attended their sponsored events and shared platforms with its representatives.

The future of the League and the form of its acceptance by FDR was also affected by the immediate political context. In the period immediately preceding the League Fight, partisan conflict had abated. The defeat of the Republicans in the 1916 presidential election prompted a period of reorganization and reflection within the party that was not conducive to vigorous political offensives. The war also united Americans in a common task and fostered a cooperative spirit that often relegated "politics" to the realms of the unpatriotic. Wilson's silence on the key foreign policy issues stifled debate, but he had also consciously shared administration appointments among Democrats and Republicans to encourage broad support for the war effort. This was something he notably failed to do in selecting his delegation for the Peace Conference at Versailles. In contrast, FDR as president made a point of appointing two Republicans to his cabinet, Henry Stimson as Secretary of War and Frank Knox as Secretary of the Navy in 1940, as well as many other Grand Old Party (GOP) members to lesser government posts to garner cross-party support for his foreign policy.

The early summer of 1918 saw the cooperative political atmosphere falter. The Republicans, with the November Congressional elections in sight, racked up political pressure. In foreign affairs this meant some Republicans adopting stronger, more definite, positions to attack administration policies. If Wilson succeeded in getting American and world acceptance for "his" League of Nations it would become a ticket for reelection in 1920 and four more years of Democratic administration. This resurgence of partisan activity combined with the disappointments of liberals over the coercive aspects of the war on the home front, Westerners' annoyance with the administration's failure to support farm prices, and a seemingly arrogant appeal to the electorate by Wilson. The result was a Republican victory that gave the majority leadership and chairmanship of the Foreign Relations Committee in the Senate to Lodge and provided an ideal position for Wilson's opponents to attack him.

Once the Draft Covenant was published on February 14, 1919, and the Senate Foreign Relations Committee met with the president at White House on February 26, the real political fight erupted. In the Senate, Lodge called the covenant a product of haste and full of crudeness and looseness of expression. He then launched a scathing point by point criticism of it and highlighting particularly the threat of Article X to the Monroe Doctrine. Just as Wilson was leaving to return to Paris, the Senate also released the so-called Round Robin signed by 37 Senators stating that the United States should not accept the League constitution and that peace negotiations should be limited to settlement with Germany. It was a clear signal that Wilson's opponents in the Senate had enough power to prevent ratification of the Peace Treaty.[65] Wilson's initial reaction was bitter—at a pro-League rally in New York, just before he left, he claimed that his opponents showed "comprehensive ignorance of the state of the world" and asserted that the Covenant could not be "dissected" from the treaty without destroying its vital structure.[66]

Despite Wilson's apparently intransigent stance toward partisan opposition and the increasing polarization of debate there was still a great deal of underlying unity. Both the LEP and LFNA supported the covenant, the former embarking on a huge publicity campaign to publicize its benefits. Taft also joined Wilson on his farewell platform in New York and dealt with points of opposition in a much more placatory manner.[67] By mid-March, the president was back in Paris also endeavoring to be more conciliatory toward his US opponents by seriously considering suggestions for amendments to the League Covenant. He corresponded with Taft and had indirect communication with Elihu Root via Henry White on the Peace Commission. This was in the hope of finding a formula for amendments to bring senators with milder opinions back into the fold. Two suggestions for amendments, that of the right to withdraw from the League after two years notice and a requirement for unanimity in the League Council passed through the League Commission without problem. Specific protection of the Monroe Doctrine was covered under regional understandings detailed in Article XXI while the exclusion of domestic issues such as tariff and immigration was also included. Discussion of Article X was limited, however, because of the central role Wilson attached to it. The president had constructed a comprehensive document of progressive measures for the world, but it was the commitment to collective security that he deemed central. This was where Wilson and FDR differed—FDR had absorbed the necessity for liberal reform, but never subscribed to collective security as a doctrine. Throughout the fierce debate centered on Article X's provision for collective security FDR rarely mentioned or alluded to it and never attempted a stout defense of Wilson's central concern.[68]

Given the broad areas of agreement and Wilson's own attempts at modifying the Covenant, FDR believed that the League was actually well suited for compromise and probably initially assumed that this was what Wilson intended. He began to use a language of compromise toward different internationalist approaches almost immediately. In a March 7 speech, FDR talked about "a" league, clearly indicating some flexibility and argued: "We can honestly differ in details, but we must come out for the principle itself, and that is where our opponents fall down."[69] The following day he again showed a willingness to compromise when he stated "whatever the result of these negotiations may be...I am a sincere and outspoken advocate of some form of league of nations." After Wilson's return to Paris, FDR made a more definite proposal of compromise. In his speech on March 29, FDR argued it would be "very nice" if the Covenant had amendments added to recognize the Monroe Doctrine and give the assurance that the United States would not be called to interfere with European questions unless there was an absolute need to prevent world war. This last point was in response to Root's call for the exclusion of the Monroe Doctrine and the allocation of a temporary, limited status to Article X's undertaking to "respect and preserve...the territorial integrity and existing political independence" of League members.[70] To aid compromise FDR made a mild criticism of Lodge's points and gave his only hint at a positive view toward collective security throughout the entire period stating: "We must be willing to give up something, even if it be a sovereign right of our nation."[71] The point here is that FDR probably did not think he was doing anything outrageous—he accepted the broad liberal nature of the League Covenant and, while he did not accept the notion of collective security wholeheartedly, everything Wilson was doing suggested compromise. Like Lawrence Lowell of the LEP, FDR was "willing to make a try on the present instrument" and placed the emphasis very clearly now on a compromise position.[72]

Wilson's changes to the covenant were made public on the April 26, but they did little to calm the political conflict in the United States. The 66th Congress coming to session from May 19 added to his difficulties. Here Lodge quickly took advantage of the new pulpit by announcing on May 23 that Wilson's amendments had made the treaty worse. The League gave Lodge a strong issue with which to forge party unity and reach out to the more independently minded Republicans like senators William Borah and Hiram Johnson. All the new seats on the FRC went to League opponents including Johnson, which cemented Republican control and facilitated Lodge's strategy of resistance to the League.[73] On June 28, the Peace Treaty including the League Covenant was finally signed in Paris and Wilson immediately left for the United States, arriving back on July 8. On July 10, he went to Congress to formally present the treaty. Given the mounting hostility to his plans in the United States it was clear that Wilson and his supporters now needed to work very hard if he was to have any hope of seeing the Treaty and League ratified.

Strangely, given Wilson's obvious need for assistance, FDR made only four further speeches directly supporting the League during June and July, and then ceased to speak directly on the subject at all. Of these summer 1919 speeches, only one, at Poughkeepsie on July 18, can be described as a major attempt to state his position.[74] Indeed, it was not until a year later in July 1920 that he made another speech on the topic. FDR was experiencing an enormously busy period and this, no doubt, restricted the time he was able to give to making public speeches or producing articles. Secretary of the Navy Josephus Daniels was away in Europe in connection with the peace negotiations and FDR was regularly working 16-hour days. There were also persistent rumors that he had plans to run for the US Senate, which hardly made it a time to rock the boat politically. All this contributed to FDR keeping a lower profile, but his absence from the League debate just at the time it reached its height is intriguing.

FDR set out an idealistic theme throughout the speeches to keep his comments general rather than focusing on specifics. On July 18, FDR argued that "all of the struggling nations felt that something more than the signing of a peace treaty would be needed to put an end to war. We still feel that same way today." He added: "a great step has been made through our intervention and the injection of American ideals into the conference."[75] Idealistic rhetoric aside, the important point here is to note that FDR was urging liberal support of the League without subscribing to Wilson's central notion of collective security that was shaping up as the contentious issue of the fight. That FDR did not hold a strong commitment to collective security and felt Wilson should compromise to save a more general liberal approach is a compelling reason why he chose to avoid involvement in the League Fight. Like many people at the time, and historians since, it seems very likely that FDR was unable to understand why Wilson did not compromise. The individual meetings Wilson held with senators to plead his case, the public FRC hearings and even Wilson's ambitious tour to take his case to the nation beginning September 3 passed without comment from FDR as did the final defeat of ratification attempts in the Senate on November 19, 1919, and March 19, 1920. This was clearly because FDR did not adhere to strict Wilsonian internationalism and from May 1919 had been developing his own strategy to appeal to liberal opinion. FDR was learning from Wilson's mistakes and beginning to construct his own liberal approach to international relations.

The crucial point, where FDR parted company with Wilson, came with the leaking of the summary Peace Treaty on May 8, 1919, and what many liberals saw as an unworthy peace. The harsh treatment of Germany and the naked imperialism of the Allies and other powers such as Japan evident in this document crushed the ideals for which many had acquiesced to war. Key reforming journals that had previously supported Wilson now turned against him. Oswald Garrison Villard's *Nation* attacked the "intrigue, selfish aggression and naked imperialism" of the peace, while the formerly proadministration *New Republic* called for a peace of "fairness, unselfishness, and non-punitiveness."[76] Neither was all well at the Paris peace conference—on May 17, William Bullitt, a staff-member, resigned publicly declaring his disillusionment with Wilson and the president's failure to follow his stated ideals.[77] This common feeling of disillusionment among liberals was further fuelled by the publishing of the actual Peace Treaty text on the June 9. By mid-July there were at least four "liberal" views on the Peace Treaty and League in stark contrast to their former unity after the Armistice. There were now those that called for complete rejection of the Treaty; those calling for ratification with reservations to the League Covenant; those calling for ratification with a pledge confirming adherence to liberal policy; and those calling for straight ratification.[78]

FDR's speeches clearly indicate that a crucial change occurred in his thinking after the leaking of the Peace Treaty in May and over the course of the summer that followed. The period is important because it saw two key developments in his international outlook where he took on aspects of a liberal world view as vital to US security. The first of these changes was his linking of a reactionary view on international affairs to a reactionary view on domestic affairs—as stated in a key speech given at the Democratic National Committee (DNC) on May 29, 1919. Here he made a clear attempt to take ownership of the progressive language of foreign affairs by stigmatizing opponents as reactionary. First he described a conflict over "fundamental principles" and between "safe conservatism" and "sane liberalism" within the Democratic and Republican parties during the last 20 years. This possibly drew on the idea of "sane radicalism" contained in one of TR's last public speeches of October 1918.[79] FDR defined sane liberalism as "common sense, idealism, constructiveness [and] progress" that served to draw attention away from his party's own conservatives and isolationists like Senator James Reed by making it appear the Republicans were achieving a monopoly in them. He then went on to describe the Republicans as the party of the "Old Guard" in which "the progressive movement...has been dying ever since 1916." The Republicans were "devoted to conservatism and reaction, to the principles of little Americanism and jingo bluff." In effect the Republicans, particularly isolationists such as Borah and Johnson, held a nonprogressive attitude to foreign affairs because they wanted to rely on an outdated view of America's ability to defend itself without regard to world conditions. More importantly because they held reactionary views on foreign affairs, FDR argued the same was true for their domestic views.

In essence, FDR was arguing that to maintain and preserve reform at home, it was necessary to pursue a liberal attitude toward international affairs—the two spheres were inseparably linked. In his Chicago speech, FDR argued that the broad principles had been settled in advance of the 1920 election; conservatism, special privilege, partisanship, destruction on the one hand—liberalism, common sense, idealism, and progress on the other. Over the course of the summer FDR talked this up into a sense of crisis to encourage liberals to rally in support of internationalism. In a speech at Worcester Polytechnic Institute on June 25 entitled "The National Emergency of Peace Times," his core argument was that the United States faced as big an emergency now as it had done during wartime, although it was not recognized: "The nation constantly is passing through national emergencies in the midst of piping times of peace—emergencies which mean the triumph of Right or Wrong, of Progress or Reaction. These crises have come throughout our history."[80]

FDR did stress the perils of Bolshevist or anarchist revolution by way of contrast to his "sane" liberalism. This was a standard LEP argument that FDR first used on March 1 when he warned against "the internationalism of the red flag or the black flag."[81] The unsettled times bred a call for order and if this was not listened to FDR feared "many...people will throw up their hands and say 'well, if the forms of government existing today cannot give us the answer, some kind of answer, why not try some other form?'" This was a clear reference to the threat of Bolshevism and anarchy already existing in parts of Europe and the growing "Red Scare" at home.[82] Not too much should be made of FDR's revolutionary theme as it was really specific to these months and he quickly dropped it when world conditions became more settled. The spring and early summer of 1919 was a period of growing fear of anarchy and revolution fanned by the enthusiasms of Attorney General A. Mitchell Palmer. FDR had had a very real and frightening personal experience of anarchy on June 2 when a bomb exploded outside the Attorney General's house on R Street in Washington blowing out the windows of FDR's home just across the street. Franklin and Eleanor returned home just after the explosion and rushed through the street strewn with parts of the former anarchist to rescue their son James who was in the house at the time but luckily unharmed.[83] The summer was also a period of growing racial tension throughout the nation and in Washington particularly. On July 20, Washington erupted into full-blown race riots that took the police and eventually the army several days to quell.[84]

The second key development in FDR's outlook was a belief that self-determination, social justice, and international law bred the kind of regimes that were less likely to act aggressively toward other nations. Democratically controlled governments would be more concerned with reform and less inclined to pay for foreign adventures. In the European context this would mean that the United States would face less chance of having to send an army overseas again to protect its interests and less chance of being directly attacked. As a late convert to international liberalism FDR viewed, until very recently, the defeat of Germany as the only purpose to the war and thus had suffered none of the general liberal disillusionment with the peace. Indeed, he could still state it was a great surprise to him "that anything at all came out of the Paris Conference." Every delegation had its own ideals and each was working for the interests of its own particular nation—to FDR "each nation was intent on getting as much as possible without giving up more than was absolutely necessary." He added: "My work [as Assistant Secretary of the Navy] ... has given me ample opportunity of seeing, at close range, the suspicions and jealousies which go hand in hand with international diplomacy and intrigue."[85] FDR, while not rejecting the old diplomacy out of hand, was empathizing and reaching out to aggrieved liberal opinion.

FDR was also offering an alternative to strict Wilsonianism that became evident in his speeches. Firstly, he stressed his belief in traditional American values such as democracy, equality, liberty, and republican government as beneficial to the world, though he offered no scheme for encouraging them other than the League itself. At a July 4 speech at Syracuse, New York, he stated, "the principles of equal rights of men, of justice toward the weak as well as the strong, of government by consent of the governed, as set forth in our constitution, are being recognized by all the great nations on earth as the most wonderful doctrine for the guidance of human conduct that had ever been devised. The world today is remaking its old laws and revising its old treaties with our Constitution as its text book."[86] A few weeks later he compared the League to "Magna Charta and the federal constitution" and argued it "will be a document which will make the world a safe place to live for ages to come."[87]

FDR's emphasis on international law would come later in 1920, but already visible was a strong commitment to measures for international social justice. At Baltimore on March 29, FDR hinted at the possibilities of a liberal foreign policy for the first time by arguing that the League "furnished an opportunity for putting forward one of the greatest progressive strides the world had ever undertaken" and that he had "faith that it will work out and that we and the other nations will use an unselfish effort to make it the best thing in the world, so that under it our relations with mankind will go from better to better."[88] After May 1919, however, he brought specific measures into the open. He supported the achievements of a social progressive nature coming from the peace, particularly for the "laboring classes" who benefitted from a "48-hour week, one day of rest each week and stringent anti-child labor laws."[89] To this end he supported the "International Labor Council," which was an enormously controversial body that attracted much criticism from American business leaders, but was highly popular among liberals. This interest stayed with him, however, and the United States finally joined the International Labor Organization during his first term as president.[90] FDR also stressed the importance of social bonds among the peoples of the world.

The people of Europe, even Germany, were clearly part of a worldwide desire for the progress he described. He now believed: "Among all the peoples of the Allies, and I believe in Germany, too, there is a demand that out of this war we should get something more than a mere treaty of peace." He declared "faith that the League of Nations will go through in the end with the support of the great majority of our nation to the unutterable delight of millions of the downtrodden in Europe."[91]

There were, of course, more familiar Wilsonian themes that FDR continued to use. He developed his ideas on nonpartisanship by calling for a return to the more cooperative, less political atmosphere of the war, where presumably a more inclusive internationalism would flourish. According to FDR, "there was not one case in any of the principal departments, where a question was asked of a man's politics" during the war.[92] He also noted that "Republicans [were] put into about 50% of the war positions by a Democratic Administration" and asked whether it was "necessary for us to go back to the old party narrowness and bickering?"[93] A heavy emphasis on the necessity for strong executive leadership also continued. This led to a general criticism of Congress on several occasions for its role in the demise of the Peace Treaty arguing it was "running…just about 100 years behind modern American conditions."[94]

FDR's basic position on international relations retained his old belief in the application of national power and continued to advocate unilateral protection of US interests and paternalistic humanitarianism in areas, such as the Western Hemisphere, where his country had a demonstrable strategic concern. His emerging liberal position applied only to Europe at this stage and there is no evidence that he had made a conceptual leap to apply developments in his thinking to the world as a whole. The encouragement of self-determination and republican government, adherence to international law and multilateral measures for social justice in Europe would augment US security. This would not only protect reform at home, but also make the world more settled and less likely to challenge US interests. FDR believed that the League was the body to encourage this, but stepped back from any rigorous enforcement regime, particularly collective security that he clearly divorced from other liberal multilateralist solutions. Nations in the new diplomacy may have equal rights, but for FDR they clearly still did not have equal power.

When FDR failed to give support in the League Fight he and Wilson became increasingly distant. This was not helped by the president's poor health—after his severe stroke on October 2, it was virtually impossible either to see him or obtain an opinion on any matter. FDR was also still out of favor with the president and his wife for entertaining the former British foreign minister, Viscount Grey, at his home in Washington on Christmas

Day 1919.[95] There was also some trouble regarding Admiral Sims and accusations of inefficiency in the navy during the war. In a speech in Brooklyn on February 1, FDR said that he was "opposed by the President who did not want an overt act of war" in his attempts at greater preparedness prior to hostilities. The speech was certainly noticed by Wilson—Secretary of the Navy, Josephus Daniels recorded in his diary "FDR Persona non grata with W."[96] In all this, FDR was perhaps distancing himself just enough from Wilson's increasingly unpopular presidency, but also registering his clearly different position on international relations to the president. FDR was never a believer in collective security and was therefore never strongly Wilsonian in his support of the League.

The years of 1917 to 1919 were a time of great change for FDR's international outlook. His traditional conceptions of power were challenged by his experiences of the war. Power still had a role in his view of international relations, but he now appreciated its limitations—new developments in weapons and tactics demonstrated how easily plans could be frustrated. If any further demonstration of this point were needed, Wilson's perceived failure to achieve his stated goals at Versailles, when the United States was supposedly in a preponderant position, provided a clear one. Part of the answer to these changed circumstances lay in greater military cooperation with Allies during wartime, but FDR also adopted for the first time a broader outlook that included progressive liberalism as an essential part of US foreign policy and security. Thus the period saw him step back from the determinism of world forces he had been drawn to during the recent years of war and reaffirm his belief in the possibility of human agency and progress.

Elements of FDR's progressive liberalism were evident from his childhood onward, but the experiences of war and of the peace augmented them and projected them onto the outside world as a vital part of US security. There were two essential aspects that came together finally in FDR's important speech to the DNC in May of 1919. The first was a linking of reform at home to a liberal approach to international relations—the two were now inseparable in FDR's eyes. In simple terms FDR believed that the reactionary politician abroad was a reactionary politician at home. The second aspect was the form of that liberal approach to international relations. From recent experience during the war FDR was beginning to appreciate that aggressive, illiberal military powers could create a situation corrosive to US democracy and reform. The answer was to encourage American ideals of equality, liberty, and republican government in Europe. Democracy, self-determination, and social justice measures there would provide an ideological framework for peaceful coexistence and thus in the longer term preserve domestic reform in the United States. The ideal vehicle to promote these measures was the League of Nations. This acceptance of a liberal ideological relationship with the outside world as a facet of US security represents a fundamental and important shift in FDR's thinking.

While Wilson certainly promoted a liberal approach to international relations, FDR's adoption of it was not down to any singular intellectual communion with the president. Wilson played a major role in FDR's ideological broadening, but he was not the only source of this change. The popular notion that Wilson was solely responsible has been qualified in two major ways. Firstly, due to Wilson's initial silence on the many aspects of the League, FDR gained a greater understanding of the issues involved from broader liberal opinion expressed by organizations such as the LFNA and LEP. Secondly, FDR always preferred compromise on collective security and did not view it as the "heart" of the Covenant as Wilson clearly did. As the president began to hemorrhage liberal support after May 1919, FDR was forced to think about how to retain that support. To do so he set about promoting his own approach to international relations that would remind liberals of the potential benefits of the Peace Treaty and would provide just the right amount of distance between himself and the president.

Wilson's tragic demise did ram home for FDR the dangers of not compromising politically and of leading without a careful reference to public opinion. FDR, of course, did not need a lesson in political compromise, but the consequences of not doing so illustrated by Wilson remained a powerful image to FDR for the rest of his life. As FDR once told his aide Sam Rosenman, "It's a terrible thing to look over your shoulder when you are trying to lead—and to find no one there."[97] There is another aspect of Wilson's performance that, perhaps, provided an equally powerful lesson for FDR. Wilson had discussed openly the qualities that peace should have and raised liberal expectations only to have them dashed by conditions dictated by other countries of the world and the Senate. It is perhaps no coincidence that FDR was reluctant to discuss the specifics of peace in the war he later faced as president and offered only vague generalities until hostilities were virtually concluded. It also, perhaps, suggests a further purpose in FDR's own calls for "unconditional surrender" as president. This promised to end World War II in a way that decoupled the peace making process from total victory. In doing so it provided less of a target for his opponents and helped mitigate acrimonious debate over the settlement among liberal internationalists. Linking the peace with victory, for FDR, was Wilson's other big mistake.

The new international outlook FDR developed requires some serious qualification. There were many aspects of a broad internationalist approach, such as any extended discussion of economics and international law, missing. It was also clearly still a rather regional approach to foreign relations. FDR's new outlook, because of the close attention to the peace, had a primarily

European focus at this time. He did not apply his liberal idealism to the rest of the world and continued to use paternalism as a justification for US involvement in some areas. Yet he had done enough to get himself noticed by liberals in the Democratic Party and in many ways his more coherent position on domestic and international affairs made him an ideal prospect for a leading position in his party and resulted in his 1920 nomination as candidate for vice president. Participation in the 1920 campaign would, however, expose many of the unanswered questions and contradictions existing in FDR's internationalism. His response to this and the further development of his thinking is the subject of the next chapter.

CHAPTER 4

THE PRESIDENTIAL ELECTION OF 1920

WOODROW WILSON STYLED THE 1920 PRESIDENTIAL ELECTION AS "a great and solemn referendum" and the high tide of his attempt to convince the people of the United States to follow his lead and engage with other nations in a scheme of collective security through the League of Nations. In reality, it was the ebb tide of Wilsonian internationalism that had already been rejected twice by the Senate and even the American public, which was once keen, seemed to have lost interest in face of the dislocations following the end of World War I. The issue of a League of Nations, however, remained an emotive one for many politicians—it crossed the ideological fault lines of both major parties and served as a rallying point for Wilson administration supporters and opponents, both in and outside the Democratic Party. Internationalism therefore was an important issue for the politicians, including FDR, in the 1920 campaign.

Most historians agree that the Democratic candidates, Governor James M. Cox of Ohio and FDR, were not keen to stress the League in the 1920 campaign—that they saw it as too divisive and controversial an issue to focus on. Both are seen as reluctant Wilsonians dragooned by the president, with FDR chosen by Cox more for his progressive credentials, geographic match, and famous name, than for his internationalism.[1] In fact, Cox was a mild supporter of the League on religious grounds and was firm in his intention to support some form of league as part of his proposals for US foreign policy. The League also fitted well with his election strategy that aimed to unite domestic and international progressivism in an appeal to western voters to return to Wilson's 1916 electoral coalition. Indeed, Cox spent over a month touring the West and made four separate tours of the Midwest during the campaign. Existing historical studies often downplay or miss this key geographic focus of the Democratic election strategy.[2] By advocating domestic and international progressivism in a way that was not too rigidly Wilsonian, Cox hoped to attract not only the powerful support of William Jennings Bryan, but also independent voters and disaffected progressive Republicans in the West.

Understanding Cox's strategy in this way sheds new light on his selection of FDR for his ticket. There were many personal qualities that attracted Cox to him, but the key reason was the internationalist language FDR displayed during the League Fight. Cox saw in FDR a progressive member of the administration, who could argue for the League and attract Wilsonians, while not being identified too strongly with the president or holding to his dogmatic position against reservations. Viewed in this light the crucial meeting held between Cox, FDR, and Wilson on July 18, 1920, can be seen as an attempt to force Wilson's support for the Cox campaign. It was also an attempt to head off a challenge from the Democratic National Committee (DNC) who were attempting to dictate a campaign focused purely on domestic issues, rather than acquiescence in the president's scheme. FDR was a vital part of this strategy as an administration insider and the ideal candidate to press the League in a vigorous campaign in the West.

In 1920, the political tide was running against the Democratic Party as the aftermath of the war brought massive upheaval to the social, economic, and political aspects of American life. The experience of military service for millions of Americans and the multitude of problems encountered upon returning to civilian life unsettled many people. A shrinking labor market and a retraction of wartime prosperity led to strikes as employers attempted to return to the open contract. The cost of living was more than double prewar levels by 1920 and a major recession began that year following drastic cuts in government spending. In rural areas, farmers, who had already suffered under price ceilings, now had to endure a reduced market for their produce. In the cities, ethnic and racial tensions increased with race riots in many cities and hostility to blacks who had moved North for jobs during the war.

From all this sprang a focus on the performance of Wilson and his administration. A series of cabinet resignations, a suspicion of government bungling emphasized by a number of congressional investigations, perceived failures in foreign policy, and doubt brought on by Wilson's poor health all left increasing numbers of Americans with a negative view of his administration.[3] The Democratic Party mirrored these fissures in society. With little direct leadership from Wilson it split into factional interest groups representing protestant and catholic, east and west, wet and dry, urban and rural, immigrant and native born, conservative and liberal. Overall there was a great deal of unease and disillusionment with reform and a yearning by Americans for a return to what Warren G. Harding called "normalcy."

Given the heavyweight political forces that squared up against one another during the summer of 1920 to decide the Democratic presidential ticket, the nomination of FDR by acclamation to the vice presidential candidacy seems, at first glance, an improbable outcome. As a minor member of the Wilson administration catapulted ahead of older and more experienced rivals, his place seems incongruous with the serious issues at hand. Ever the opportunist, FDR did nothing to harm his chances to gain an enhanced national political reputation—there had even been several presidential booms for him in the months prior to his nomination.[4] Crucially the Democratic presidential candidate recognized the importance of FDR's position and language on foreign affairs. Cox envisaged a vital role for FDR in an active campaign based on progressivism at home and abroad with the League playing a central role in his appeal to the West and Midwest of the United States.

Cox himself had beaten many powerful rivals to capture his party's presidential nomination on the 44th ballot at its San Francisco convention on July 6, including Secretary of the Treasury William G. McAdoo, Attorney General A. Mitchell Palmer, and even a rumored third nomination attempt by Wilson.[5] Announcing his candidacy on February 1, Cox was known as a careful reformer with "safe and sane" progressive credentials and as a mild "wet" with appeal to city bosses. Yet he was also strong on issues such as states' rights in the face of federal government encroachment and advocated leaving business to its own devices that gave him appeal to conservatives.[6] He also had no real connection with the Wilson administration and was only a distant supporter of the League of Nations—though Cox denied this and claimed to be in regular consultation with Wilson's White House during the war years. During the League Fight he offered only general support and had not endorsed Wilson's demand for unconditional ratification.[7] Indeed, in a major piece written for the *New York Times* in May 1920, he went as far as to suggest two reservations, the first declaring the cooperation of the United States was dependent on the League's "sole purpose" being "maintaining peace and comity among the nations of the earth" and the second that it be in "harmony with the terms and intent of the United States Constitution."[8] In choosing Cox as a compromise candidate, the Democratic Party had decided to place its hopes of unity and victory on a midwestern, boss-backed, nonadministration wet. All that remained for the convention to do was approve a running mate.

Cox faced early constraints in his stance as candidate because of the divisions that emerged in the fight over the Democratic Party platform. There were still plenty of Wilsonian supporters of the League strengthened by the president's January 8 call to make the 1920 election a "great and solemn referendum." The Democrats also had their own irreconcilables, the most audible of which was Senator James E. Reed of Missouri. The Chicago convention therefore witnessed long fights over the platform and particularly over the stance on the League making it seem at times as important as the candidacy nomination itself. The party platform was far from clear on the League. It offered a declaration of support, but the call for "ratification of the treaty without reservations" was made ambiguous by a further call for "any reservations making clearer or more specific the obligations of the United States."[9] Given the central importance of the League to the powerful Wilson wing of the party, however, Cox would have found it difficult to ignore it in his campaign strategy and choice of running mate. Yet in his autobiography written in 1946, Cox explained his selection of Roosevelt purely in terms of geography, progressive credentials, and a well-known name.[10]

Cox's first point was correct—FDR, an easterner from New York, balanced his ticket well. His second point was, however, more complex. FDR did have a reputation as an independent politician, but he had remained a loyal administration member through difficult times since 1913 and was still Assistant Secretary of the Navy under Secretary Daniels. FDR was skilled in appealing as an independent while maintaining the confidence and support of the administration. As such he could prove highly valuable as a bolster to unity by attracting Wilson and McAdoo supporters to the campaign.[11]

Cox's interest in the Roosevelt name was also understandable—the former president TR had died in January 1919, but his memory and popularity was still a powerful force in the country, particularly in the West. FDR was never shy of highlighting his connection and his shared name with his cousin. He started an interview with Frederick Boyd Stevenson printed on July 14 with TR's well-known phrase "That's Bully."[12] The newspapers often picked up on the parallels between the two men's careers, noting that he outstripped TR to the vice presidential nomination by four years. Republican opponents were also crucially aware of the appeal and assigned TR's son Colonel Theodore Roosevelt to the campaign trailing FDR through every western state and Maine. The Republican acknowledgment of the power of TR as a symbol of forceful persuasion demonstrated how important the right name was to Cox.[13]

Cox was impressed, as was everyone else, with FDR's positive headline grabbing ability at the convention and thought him a "very vigorous, upstanding, courageous and progressive Democrat."[14] The youthful and good looking FDR with his independent administration credentials and moderate "dry" position complemented Cox's more conservative "wet" position well. FDR was awarded the vice presidential candidacy by acclamation later on July 6. That day, however, Cox gave three reasons for his selection of his running mate that are very different to those in his autobiography, which are the ones usually accepted by historians. Speaking to reporters Cox claimed: "Mr Roosevelt's speech before the National Committee in Chicago…made a very strong impression,…his service in Washington has given him a wide acquaintanceship" and he was a good "stumper."[15]

Cox's comments downplaying the importance of his selection of FDR as running mate in his autobiography are more representative of his later association with the conservative wing of the Democratic Party when FDR became president.[16] In 1920, he was attracted by FDR's nondogmatically Wilsonian liberal position on domestic and international affairs—particularly his position on the League that he hoped to make a centre of his campaign. Key to this attraction was FDR's speech to the Democratic National Convention in Chicago on May 29, 1919, in which he began to describe a program of "sane liberalism" that saw domestic and foreign affairs as linked. To FDR, the reactionary at home was a reactionary abroad and thus failing to support international reform via the League would ultimately bring defeat of reform at home. Freidel argues that the speech placed him firmly at the head of the party's liberal wing, but he managed to do this without making a direct pledge of support for Wilson or dealing with any of the specific issues of the League Fight. FDR returned to this theme in his acceptance speech of August 9, 1920, when he stated that "the fundamental outlook on the associations between this Republic and other nations can never be very different in character from the principles which one applies to our own purely internal affairs. A man who opposes concrete reforms and improvements in international relations is of necessity a reactionary, or at least, a conservative in viewing his home problems."[17]

Cox clearly recognized FDR as somebody with the right liberal credentials, language, and rhetorical skills to aid him in uniting the divided factions of the party. They also agreed that liberal reform at home and abroad would be essential to uniting the party, winning the 1920 election and ensuring future US security. Both subscribed broadly to Wilsonian internationalism, but neither held any commitment to the rigid collective security. Cox hoped FDR could push the League as an issue in the campaign without becoming mired in either Wilson's shadow or the specifics of the debate.[18] In addition, Cox's observation that FDR's service in Washington also gave him a wide acquaintanceship was, of course, a nod to his national profile and his useful links with the Wilson administration. Cox's final comment that FDR was a good "stumper" indicated the kind of campaign he was planning. It was not to be centered on the "front porch" like that planned by Republican nominee Senator Warren G. Harding. Instead, it was to be one of active touring and FDR fitted well into that plan—all that remained to do was to confirm a campaign strategy. FDR arranged to meet Cox at Columbus, Ohio, on July 12—the first of at least five meetings

Figure 4.1   James M. Cox and FDR campaign in Dayton, Ohio, August 7, 1920. The 1920
Presidential Election was to have a profound impact on FDRs international outlook. (FDR
Library 09-2613a).

between the two men during the campaign.[19] This meeting was the start
of a delicate game to ensure Cox's strategy on the League was accepted by
the party hierarchy without the complete alienation of those wanting other
issues brought to the fore. To achieve party unity for the campaign it was
important that the two men meet. This would allow Cox to ensure FDR
was on message before the first big challenge at the meeting of the DNC at
Dayton on July 20.

Cox also knew it would be impossible to win the election without the
support or at least endorsement of Wilson—McAdoo's hopes had quickly
faded after his failure to obtain presidential approval. He also realized from
this that Wilson would not give his endorsement freely, Cox would have to
go and get it both literally and by genuflecting to the League issue in the
prescribed manner. Cox and FDR supported a league, but it would have
to be Wilson's League until the all-important endorsement was given. Cox
therefore began his courtship of Wilson by pushing the League as a major
issue soon after he was nominated by announcing that the keynote of his
campaign would be a Wilsonian appeal to the people for ratification of the
League "to keep the faith with the boys who went over there."[20] A few days
later in a major platform piece written by William H. Crawford in the *New
York Times* Cox again stressed the League as his primary issue, but was careful to discuss a whole host of other issues such as Ireland, prohibition, government reform, immigration, tariff reform, the high cost of living, radicalism,

progressivism, rural education, and the budget system to ensure he did not alienate Democrats uninterested in the League.[21] On July 13, Cox even went so far as to tell the press that he regarded President Wilson as beyond dispute the leader of his party and himself as leader of the fight to keep the Democrats in Federal administration.[22]

FDR was useful to Cox in several ways in this courting of Wilson's support. At their meeting they no doubt agreed to push the League as "the issue" until Wilson's support was assured and to prevent any attempt to crush it entirely at the forthcoming DNC meeting. Cox was confident enough to let his running mate handle the press following the conference. FDR announced to reporters that they regarded the League of Nations as the dominant issue of the campaign and it would be treated as such. This was especially important coming from FDR as a still active administration member.[23] He could also turn on the Wilsonian rhetoric when needed. On July 14, a major piece by Frederick Boyd Stevenson was printed in which FDR outlined Wilsonian arguments for the League in almost pure form. These included the necessity to maintain a huge army and navy financed by vast taxation if the United States did not join the League and the claim that the League was really very similar to the Monroe Doctrine, except on a world scale, which Wilson had first argued in his "Peace without Victory" speech.[24]

This all served to smooth the ground for the meeting with Wilson. Cox's political advisers disliked the idea—only too well aware of what a handicap association with Wilson could prove. Cox later related that his campaign manager at San Francisco, Edmond H. Moore, thought it would be unwise. He insisted that the defeat of McAdoo and Palmer had been construed by some elements as a victory over the administration, since they were both part of it and that Cox visiting Wilson might give offense. There was also the risk of being seen as a mere puppet of Wilson—a charge Harding made and FDR found himself having to counter a few days before the meeting. Cox appreciated just how important Wilson's endorsement was and prepared to meet him regardless of the consequences. In any case, he was already a firm supporter of a League and wrote curtly in his autobiography that the meeting "should completely refute the inaccuracies of two biographies who have written that until Mr. Roosevelt and I went to Washington we had been in doubt about making the League the issue." [25]

Cox arrived in Washington on July 17 and continued courting Wilson, announcing the president "knows more of international affairs than any man in this country that I know, at least. I'm here to counsel with him. That's the long and the short of it." He then went to meet Gilbert Hitchcock of Nebraska, the Democratic senatorial leader during the treaty fight, who said of Cox: "He possesses the ability to make the issue of the League of

Nations interesting and intelligent to the electorate. It's like a new hand taking up an old subject. His ideas are the same as many of ours, but his treatment is different." The hour-long meeting with Wilson took place on the morning of July 18 at the White House. Years later, FDR recalled the meeting with Wilson to Claude Bowers, then ambassador to Chile, who related that Cox said to the "very sick" Wilson "Mr. President, we are going to be a million per cent behind you, and your Administration, and that means the League of Nations." Wilson apparently approved of the visit saying "Governor Cox will have the vigorous support of an absolutely united party and, I am confident, also an absolutely united nation."[26] Cox, by going to see the president with a member of his administration and talking the right language, had effectively forced the president to deliver his approval—not to have done so would have been unthinkable. By visiting Wilson ahead of the DNC meeting in Dayton, Ohio, on July 20, Cox had also preempted forces aiming to have the League dropped as a campaign issue. With such publicity and public acceptance by the president he presented a fait accompli to the DNC.

The northern city political bosses who backed Cox were certainly not keen on the issue because of the peace treaty's unpopularity with immigrant constituencies. The major opposition Cox faced, however, was a desire by western Democrats to focus solely on domestic progressive issues. This was not only to echo Bryan's line; they were also all too aware of the deep unpopularity of Wilson in western states. FDR's point man for the campaign, Steve Early, reported to Louis Howe that "anything that sides with WW...catch[es] a lot of trouble" and in Seattle added there was "an evident belief...that Wilson controls Cox."[27] Cox and FDR faced a major obstacle to promoting the League as an issue in that the DNC selected was predominantly western in its makeup. Wilson supporter Homer S. Cummings retired as chair and was replaced by George H. White of Ohio, which was seen as a move away from the administration even though he was a friend of Wilson having been taught by him at Princeton.[28] It was usual for the DNC chair to go to the candidate's campaign manager, but Moore's negative stance on the League was unacceptable to Cox. The committee determined to make domestic reform issues the focus of the campaign. In press interviews, the League was not even mentioned by them. As these men were to be instrumental in gaining support for the campaign, the candidates had to bow to the inevitable to some degree and accept a more domestic emphasis. The visit to Wilson, however, meant that the DNC could not completely avoid the League as a campaign issue and they were forced by Cox to compromise on a plan to highlight domestic and international progressivism. The deal was sealed with Cox agreeing to highlight a progressive issue he had had running for several months—that of drawing attention to the Republicans possession of a campaign "fund sufficient in size to stagger the sensibilities of the nation."[29]

To unite the party around the twin issues of domestic and international progressivism it was now the time for the candidates to start to adopt their true position on the League that required some softening from the Wilsonian position of the previous week. On July 21, after the DNC meeting, Cox used FDR to announce this move. FDR, unattributed, probably in deference to Wilson and the delicate situation, told reporters that Cox and his advisers were well aware of the Republican strategy to make him appear tied to Wilson's foreign policies and for this reason he would leave setting forth his full position on the League until his forthcoming speech of acceptance. FDR continued to undermine the solid League position by informing reporters that at the White House meeting the previous Sunday the minute details of the treaty and reservations were not discussed, only the general principles. It was expected that Cox would make plain in his acceptance speech that his agreement with the president was on general principles rather than specific reservations. Any reservations would have to be submitted to Cox, but he was against any "nullifying" ones—though his concept of nullifying was different from the president's. FDR then added that Cox would have to derive his own foreign policy anyway after March 4. Interestingly, FDR did go on record regarding this last point, perhaps feeling that he needed to create flexibility for the campaign without infringing the sanctity of the private meeting at the White House, he added: "The Peace Treaty and the League of Nations can in no way be regarded as 'fixed issues' in the Presidential Campaign, inasmuch as their present status may be 'much changed' between now and March 4." FDR then suggested himself as a possible liaison between the new president and the Senate regarding reservations, though Cox rejected his suggestion.[30]

Cox may have felt his running mate had given away a little too much to opponents of the League on the DNC. When George White took possession of the campaign headquarters in New York, after conferring with FDR, the chairman was at pains to make clear that he was not worrying over the League of Nations matter. Neither was he at all concerned as to the various constructions put upon his remarks in Washington where it was reported he had said there had been no "iron clad" agreement between Cox and the president on the League. Meanwhile Cox had been doing his own softening of his stance on the League. On July 27, he met with Senator Pomerene of Ohio who was the first administration Democrat to come out in support of the Lodge reservations to the Treaty in November 1919. Then on July 30, he met with Democratic senator David I. Walsh of Massachusetts who had also bolted the party in League Fight and united with Republicans for reservations.[31]

Concurrent with these discussions was an attempt to decide how to campaign. If Cox chose to mount an active campaign, the question arose as to where its focus should be. In many ways the decision was made for them by circumstances beyond their control. The Democratic Party in 1920 suffered both organizationally and financially. The party had suffered a crippling blow to morale in the 1918 Congressional elections and had not yet recovered in many areas. Even some Democrats saw 1920 as clearly a Republican year and questioned whether any effort was worthwhile and campaigning, therefore, would often have to be driven by the candidates themselves. Similarly there was a desperate lack of cash—the total campaign spending for the Democrats of $2,237,770 was dwarfed by the Republican's $8,100,739.[32] This meant a distinct lack of funds to pay speakers and print campaign material. Senator Key Pittman, the head of the western campaign, was even forced to use his own money to finance the operation.

An increasingly important factor was the coverage of campaigns in the press. Cox as a newspaper editor and owner was fully cognizant of the fact that the majority of the newspapers in the United States were owned by those with Republican sympathies. Indeed, no Republican newspaper ever reported that he would accept reservations on the League Covenant. A week after the start of the campaign, FDR's point man Steve Early wrote to Louis Howe that there was "nothing approaching a Democratic newspaper in Seattle" and even Cox's acceptance speech given over a week earlier had "not been printed here." FDR himself was fully aware of the implications for their campaign strategy "it is only frankness to say that the great majority of newspapers throughout the country are owned or controlled by men affiliated with the Republican Party. It is therefore doubly necessary for us to present our views and our aims in person."[33]

It was certainly FDR's nature to mount an active campaign—he had done so from his earliest days in politics when he had won a state senate seat by driving around in a borrowed car talking to farmers. He was never shy of placing his name in the public eye, but he also enjoyed getting out into the country and holding counsel with the voters and getting a sense of their thoughts, feelings, and concerns. Wilson had made much of this in his tours and comparing tour itineraries, it is as if Wilson provided a manual on what cities were worth visiting and how to conduct a great swing around the circle. In a sense, they were copying him not just in method, but gaining a subtle connection to the president that no doubt aided them in attracting the support of the Wilson faction. Cox, sounding very much like Wilson, declared as he began his campaign "the shrine of government is in the communities of the land near to the homes that have given service and sacrifice."[34]

FDR also felt it was "the simple duty of the candidates to give to as many citizens as possible in as many states as possible an opportunity to see and hear and form their own impressions of the men they are to vote for."[35] Interestingly, the campaign saw FDR assemble a political team for the first time to guide and write many of his speeches. He hired Marvin McIntyre who had worked for George Creel's Committee for Public Information and had got to know FDR while working for the navy. FDR also obtained the services of a former Associated Press man and reporter Steve Early to act as his "point man." He developed an elaborate code to relay local conditions back to FDR and guide the focus of his speeches. Not to be left out, FDR's political adviser Louis Howe managed to join the party on the second western tour. Despite this new input, FDR retained ultimate control over the content and substance of his speeches, but the team were an important acquisition for FDR and all would go on to serve him as president.[36]

The second important question of campaign strategy was geographic focus. In *After Wilson*, Douglas Craig argues that Cox wished to use an updated version of the standard Democratic strategy of the Gilded Age by counting on the "solid south" and then gaining any northern states possible while completely ignoring the West.[37] Cox certainly did not feel any urgency to visit the South, stating: "I think it would be gracious to go into the South, even though it is not absolutely necessary." This explanation of strategy, however, pays insufficient attention to what the candidates actually said and did and their intention to use the League as a campaign issue. From their actions it appears that Cox and FDR aimed to rebuild Wilson's 1916 coalition of the South, West, and Midwest around liberalism applied to domestic and foreign affairs—in effect an updated version of Wilson's "progressivism and peace" campaign of 1916, hoping to attract independents and progressive Republicans. On this basis they planned an active campaign in the West and Midwest to get their issues across and maybe even in FDR's words "drag the enemy off the front porch."[38]

As early as July 10, the *New York Times* was reporting that Cox planned to open his campaign in the West, probably California. It also quoted an adviser of Cox as saying "the west is the logical ground for the first battles of the campaign." After his meeting with FDR on July 12, Cox called for an aggressive campaign covering every state of the union. In his report of the meeting, FDR explained the logic of focusing on the western states to attempt a repeat of the 1916 Democratic victory "Some of the western states have comparatively small electoral votes, but in the aggregate the votes figure up pretty big."[39] He also underlined the importance of the issues chosen for the region saying of the League "I know it will make a big hit in the west." Just before leaving on his first western tour he announced the purpose of his trip was "to go after the progressive votes."[40]

The DNC meeting on July 20, confirmed the strategy and by July 25, Cox was planning a speaking tour to "outdo" any presidential candidate in the past, aiming to spend the entire month of September in "California and other western states" together with a "comprehensive tour of middle west."[41] Even in the final month before the election, he largely concentrated on the Midwest with a few token visits to the South and Northeast. He clearly did not place much hope in obtaining any northeastern states. Similarly, FDR made two tours of the West, the first taking virtually the entire month of August with a shorter one in early October. He also spent ten days touring the Midwest. Interestingly, he did spend virtually the entire month of September touring New York and New England. New York was, of course, his home state and Cox perhaps thought he may contribute to a victory there. On balance, however, it is likely that Cox sent him through the region to "show the flag." He did not want to waste too much of his own time, while a tour by the personally popular local boy, but politically insignificant vice presidential candidate, could serve to refute charges that the area was being neglected.

To both Cox and FDR, the League, through its representation of a regime of liberal international relations, was both vital to US security and election victory. In many ways FDR's campaign was merely a restatement of views he had held for many years. Prominent was his belief that the United States could not avoid involvement with the world and live as a "hermit nation" with a "Chinese wall" surrounding it because of the complex "interdependence" that now existed.[42] FDR saw this interdependence as vital economically to the United States, but also argued it included broader issues of international social justice that he continued to emphasize as an indicator and route to human development.[43] As before there were also subjects he avoided—the controversial specifics of the League such as Article X received a wide berth.[44] He also avoided any discussion of arbitration because he likely did not believe it was a viable solution to world problems. The League was still clearly to be kept a vague, indefinite body on which to hang liberal international policies, but with no rigorous right of enforcement.

In an attempt to make the division between conservative and liberal principle clearer during the campaign, FDR constantly made negative comparisons between nations that had not joined the League and those that had. The League became a central organizing concept to divide the world into good liberal and bad reactionary or revolutionary nations. The United States would be "outside" and would be "partners" with Russia "the Turks" and Mexico if it did not join the League. For FDR the "charming company we are keeping" indicated that the United States risked being on the wrong side of the conceptual division that formed a basic aspect of his developing world view.[45] There is no single point at which this division of the world emerged, but what is clear is that since he had divided domestic opinion ideologically between liberal and conservatives in May 1919 a similar division of the world became a natural progression. To FDR a liberal outlook on the world would encourage liberal domestic policies while other liberal regimes in the world would pose less of a threat to the United States and thus also protect domestic reform by avoiding war. Though his definition was often flexible and politically motivated, FDR rhetorically divided the world into progressive liberal regimes and outside others who did not conform to that ideal and thus he laid the basic foundations of a major conceptualization of the world he held as president.

Closely linked to FDR's conceptual division of the world was his growing appreciation of international law as both an approach to world order and as a reinforcement of his attempt at broad appeal. He was aware of legalistic approaches to world order through his contact with the League to Enforce Peace (LEP), but he now appreciated more the need to appeal to independents and disaffected Republicans and this generated both greater clarity and more emphasis on law in his speeches. In Milwaukee, Wisconsin, he described his basic understanding of the development of international law as similar to that of community law in the western United States stating, "Gradually law and order among individuals asserted itself. The beginnings of community spirit came into existence...at last international law seems to be catching up to law of the individual or of the separate state." This allusion was pure TR and in another speech FDR continued to echo him arguing that "for the first time in history...the relation of one nation to another [is] on the same basis as one individual to another." Wilson had made similar allusions to individual morality, but FDR adopted a position that was a merging of viewpoints from both former presidents. For FDR the "League" became an "expression of the new law of nations...There can be no neutrality between right and wrong!" Although FDR had adopted conservative legal rhetoric, TR would never have countenanced Wilson's League as a body for enforcing international law. Yet FDR was also implicitly criticizing prewar Wilsonian neutrality for its lack of moral position. None of this was inconsistent with FDR's positive stance toward multilateralism and he even praised Elihu Root for his work in Europe to form a permanent court and for "helping [to] start one of the important factors in the league's machinery."[46] International law would remain an important criterion for dividing the world into liberal and reactionary regimes and would also provide a major crossing point for FDR's rhetorical appeal to non-Democrats throughout the 1920s and during his presidency.

Another important change was in FDR's position on disarmament and militarism. Despite his growing dissatisfaction with the balance of power as a sufficient system to maintain world peace, FDR had continued to insist on a harsh peace for Germany and universal military training (UMT) for US citizens to aid preparedness for future wars. The 1920 campaign, however, saw the complete disappearance of any calls for universal training by FDR and his development of a distinct antimilitarist peaceable stance. Throughout the campaign he hardly mentioned Germany at all and issued repeated statements that he was "not a militarist" and was "in favor of disarmament."[47] The harsh peace that came out of the Paris negotiations devastated many supporters of Wilson who were disappointed that the peace did not adhere more closely to his Fourteen Points. FDR was clearly aware of sensitive liberal opinion and therefore avoided Germany as a topic. There was, however, more than a political explanation to this move—FDR's own thinking had developed and cast off the final vestiges of the assertive militarism of his younger self.

The 1920 campaign saw the combination of two important changes affecting the way FDR legitimated his public position. The first was the ratification of the Nineteenth Amendment to the US Constitution on August 18, 1920, giving women the vote for the first time in the presidential election of that year. FDR, unlike Wilson, could claim a long history of support for female suffrage dating back to at least 1911. He also felt strongly that women, particularly mothers because of sons lost in the war, were a progressive force in politics and "they show[ed a] tendency to cast ballots in favor of a definite and permanent peace" and would "furnish a tremendous surprise in the League."[48] This appeal to women voters on the peaceable aspects of the League made it inconsistent to talk of balance of power relations and preparedness except in negative terms.

FDR also dropped all mention of his support for UMT as a moral and physical benefit to the nation's manhood. This was partly because he no longer made calls for an increase in armaments, but was also because of a series of awkward scandals involving the moral welfare of sailors serving in the US Navy. The first was a dispute with the navy director of enlisted personnel, Captain Joseph K. Taussig during January 1920 and concerned the return of convicted homosexuals to active service. An article by FDR in the January issue of *Army and Navy Journal* supporting rehabilitation prompted Taussig to charge FDR with condoning the dangers of associating "with these moral perverts, and thereby exposed [other sailors] to contamination" and was responsible for returning something like one hundred of them back to active service. The dispute worsened in the public via the pages of the *Army and Navy Journal* until Taussig called for a court of public inquiry asserting that Roosevelt "questions my veracity, impugns my motives and tends to publicly discredit me." FDR filed the request to avoid further public embarrassment, but it had been a nasty dispute in which FDR had to defend his position as guardian of the morality of sailors in the service.

The second scandal was more serious because FDR was more directly implicated in questionable activities that impacted on the morality of sailors. Vice had long been a concern to local residents around the navy yard at Newport, Rhode Island, and there had been several attempts to "clean up" the "unwholesome" conditions there. FDR showed an interest in these attempts and by June 1919 had established "Section A—Office of Assistant Secretary" charged with gathering evidence to convict both servicemen and civilians involved in criminal activity—largely prostitution and homosexuality. How much FDR actually knew of the methods used by Section A is unclear, but their use of enlisted men to entrap homosexuals came to light after a respected member of the local clergy, Father Samuel Kent, was arrested for "immoral acts." FDR halted the work of Section A in September 1919, which he claimed was as soon as he learned of their activities, but refused to drop charges against Kent despite appeals from the Bishop of Rhode Island. The affair became a public scandal when newspaperman John J. Rathom published the matter in the Providence *Journal* during January 1920.

Father Kent was acquitted the same month, but the court of inquiry appointed by Daniels initially found FDR's actions had been "unfortunate and ill-advised" when he "either directed or permitted the use of enlisted men to investigate perversion." FDR refused to accept these findings or to be made a "scapegoat" for navy officers and managed to expunge the criticisms from the report. The scandal would come back to haunt him when the Republicans took power in 1921, but even in 1920 it had the potential to end his career and FDR sensed the very real danger. It also made any discussion of the moral benefits of naval service impossible—the slightest mention would expose him to attacks of complicity on the moral degradation of enlisted men. What had started as a skilful example of dissimulation to justify preparedness had now reached the end of its useful political life.

The final and most significant development on FDR's position on internationalism was with regard to self-determination. Throughout the 1920 campaign FDR continued to support nationalism along Wilsonian lines— like Wilson he focused on Europe as the major source of disruption and conflict in recent years and argued that the purpose of the war was "to prevent a recurrence of that terrible struggle and give smaller nations of earth a chance to secure their own independence and liberty—the right to self-determination."[49] At one level this was clearly a desire to protect smaller, weaker nations from larger aggressive military states and ultimately prevent the domination of Europe by such powers.[50] FDR had long viewed this eventuality as a threat to US national security and Germany as the major source of insecurity. He had the example of Belgium whose neutrality had been violated by the German armies during the war, but also held a concern for the newly created states such as Poland. Wilson's thirteenth point had called for the creation of "an independent Polish state" and FDR viewed the Polish-Soviet War 1919–1921 as a valiant struggle for Polish independence against Bolshevist aggression. The Polish-Soviet War, ongoing during the summer of 1920, exposed FDR's rather awkward position—in theory the United States, if it joined the League, could be called to contribute troops to defend Polish sovereignty. To further complicate the question, Republican campaigners pounced on the issue and delighted in spreading false rumors that Canada was preparing to send troops to Poland.[51] FDR had always called for compromise on articles of the League Covenant demanding members protect the territorial and political integrity of member nations and was not prepared to advocate the sending of US troops as part of a collective security regime in this instance. The United States would only, presumably, intervene unilaterally if its interests were significantly challenged at any point as they had been during the war.

This rejection of forceful collective security left FDR resorting to Wilsonian arguments for the League as a moral force that he had not previously used. Blaming the Senate for not ratifying the League he argued, "If America had been able to throw into scale the splendid moral force of its hundred million people, the Bolshevist armies would not be where they are now... [and] it would not have been necessary for a single American soldier to cross the sea."[52] Thus for FDR self-determination for nations was a goal, not an enforceable right. As such it merged with the other aspects of his liberal international agenda to be promoted and encouraged by the League. FDR continued to think that liberal, democratic regimes would pursue peaceable and progressive foreign policies and would therefore pose less of a threat to US security, but the League was a route to encourage this rather than enforce it.

Aside from the Wilsonian moral point, nothing in this outlook on self-determination was particularly new or specific to the 1920 election for FDR—he showed the beginnings of a liberal approach to foreign policy in the previous year. What did come out of the campaign was a new appreciation by FDR of how his liberal agenda and, in particular, belief in self-determination should apply to all the nations of the world. Although FDR had long held old-world political colonialism in disdain, he did not initially read Wilson's calls for self-determination for Europe as a critique of global imperialism. The campaign soon brought the issue to the surface, but FDR, unlike Cox, deftly avoided ever discussing thorny issues such as the transfer of the former German concession of Shantung in China to the Japanese as part of the Versailles Treaty and ongoing calls from Irish-Americans for independence from British rule.[53] Global questions of self-determination were clearly intimately linked to anti-imperialism and another issue soon arose that forced FDR to confront difficult questions.

There is little agreement on either the form or origins of FDR's anti-imperialism among historians. To many of the more pragmatic school his anti-imperialism had no theoretical basis and was a flexible stance taken when it suited him—questions of origin and influence are seemingly unimportant. Those taking a more long term ideological view of FDR's attitude have attempted, albeit briefly, to shed light on this apparent contradiction in his position. Willard Range argued that the humanitarian imperialist FDR underwent something of a conversion during the 1920s in reaction to the methods deployed by the Republican administration in South and Central America. When these became increasingly questionable the advantages in leaving sovereign nations alone were more apparent. This account, however, does not explain FDR's denial of imperialism with regard to the Western Hemisphere during the 1920 election campaign before the Republicans had won their crushing victory and begun to direct policy. Later historians, such as Warren Kimball, have focused on the key influence of Wilson in the process and this certainly has some validity. Wilson renounced imperialism in his speech at Mobile, Alabama, in October 1913 though he had gone on to be the most interventionist president up to that point and had seen his fifth point calling for "free, open minded, and absolutely impartial adjustment of all colonial claims" fudged by the mandate system of the Versailles Peace. In addition, Kimball and Pollock argue that FDR's generation had witnessed how European imperialism had exacerbated the conditions for war and greatly complicated the peace.[54] Again, however, there arises a question of how FDR's utterances fit the chronology—his humanitarian imperialism continued through Wilson's administration and at no point did he modify his personal position to fit with that of the president or experience a postwar distaste for colonialism or support for nationalist movements.[55]

FDR had always been an anti-imperialist in the wider world, but his rejection of the paternalistic humanitarian imperialism practiced by the United States in the Caribbean and Latin America stems from a very specific incident during the election campaign. Remarks made by him in Deer Lodge, Butte, and Helena, Montana on the August 18 incurred the wrath, not only of liberals and the left but also exposed him to attacks from the right-wing opponents of the League. In effect, his position became unsustainable in the face of radically changed opinion in society since the war. From this moment, while he could still justify intervention in sovereign states affairs on humanitarian grounds, there was a new awareness of the need to include anti-imperialist rhetoric focusing on the Wilsonian concern for self-determination. Ultimately unimportant in terms of the election, it was crucial to the development of his personal internationalist language.

Montana was the home state of Bruce Kremer, the vice chairman of the DNC, and he sent word to FDR that he would like speeches with a "rough and peppy Americanism" with extemporaneous flourishes.[56] FDR took the opportunity to react to the common charge that Great Britain would outvote the United States in the League because her Dominions also held seats in the Assembly—in effect the sinister hand of imperialist ambition would thwart democracy in the League. This was a favorite argument of the more isolationist irreconcilables in the Senate such as William E. Borah of Idaho, but had increasingly been adopted by the more mainstream opponents of the League.

The record of FDR's campaign speeches in the archives at Hyde Park is missing for August 18, 1920. Whether some hidden hand removed the record or not, it is possible to reconstruct with confidence, from press coverage and a press release from Helena, what he said as he travelled through Montana that day. The first comment that caused concern was:

> Does anyone suppose that the vote of Cuba, Haiti, San Domingo, Panama, Nicaragua and of the other Central American states would be cast differently from the vote of the United States? We are in a very true sense the big brother of these little republics. We are actually acting as trustee at the present time for many of them. Their lot is our lot, and in the final analysis the United States will have far more than six votes which will stick with us through thick and thin.[57]

Criticism of FDR's comments came initially from his Republican opponents—they instinctively sensed a gaffe and moved to exploit it by focusing on the "big brother" image of the United States controlling the rest of the hemisphere. Out on campaign, however, and not in regular contact with his advisers, FDR appears not to have realized initially how explosive his comments were and he sought to make light of the charges beginning to be leveled at him. FDR's casual response to the situation continued as he reached San Francisco where he described the idea that "Haiti, Panama, Nicaragua, Salvador and others" being untrue to the United States as a "joke and a palpable lie."[58]

Sensing some political mileage from the issue the Republicans upped their attacks on FDR in the press. The *New York Telegraph* commented he was "a spoiled child to be spanked." Josephus Daniels' diary for August 24 recorded that the "Tribune roasted FDR for saying he had had Haiti and San Domingo." Importantly, however, more liberal opinion was also beginning to take notice. The retiring director general of the Pan-American Union, John Barnett, declared that FDR had made a grave diplomatic mistake if he had been correctly quoted. The growing furor forced FDR to reevaluate and modify his position with regard to other nations in the Western Hemisphere and crucially imperialism generally. On September 2, as the dispute rumbled on, FDR issued a denial to Associated Press claiming he had been misquoted. He claimed that he merely said that history showed the international interests of the United States and "at least a dozen of these Republics are broadly identical" and they would vote in accordance with "mutual interests." By applying a softened form of the "Unit Rule" to the Western Hemisphere and appealing to the past FDR may have satisfied himself, but more than 20 reporters signed a statement saying he had said what they had reported. Even the sympathetic *New York Times*, relying on local reporters, repeated their version of his comments.[59]

The Republicans aimed to make as much political capital from the controversy as possible. In addition to his comments on voting patterns on the August 18, FDR reportedly joked: "You know I have had something to do with the running of a couple of little republics. The facts are that I wrote Haiti's constitution myself and, if I do say it, I think it's a pretty good constitution." Harding himself entered the fray and took up a new line of attack to exploit the issue by highlighting the conduct of US Marines in Haiti. Focusing on FDR's junior position enabled Harding to attach blame to the former Assistant Secretary of the Navy personally while also blaming the Wilson administration. "I will not" Harding said "empower an Assistant Secretary of the Navy to draft the constitution for helpless neighbors in the West Indies and jam it down their throats at the point of bayonets borne by US Marines." Harding kept the issue rumbling on through September with further comments calling it "the first official admission of the rape of Hayti and San Domingo by the present Administration...To my mind, moreover, it is the most shocking assertion that ever emanated from a responsible member of the government of the United States." In the same speech, while being careful not to lay blame with the troops themselves he said: "many of our gallant men have sacrificed their lives for the benefit of an executive department in order to establish laws drafted by an Assistant Secretary of the Navy to secure a vote in the League, and to continue at the point of the bayonet, a military domination."[60]

Harding was following the lead of the African American, James Weldon Johnson, who the Republicans sent on a two month fact finding trip to Haiti in summer 1920 and who cultivated Harding's interest in Wilson's most glaring foreign policy contradiction. The situation in Haiti had got steadily worse as local resistance to the *corvée* system of forced labor run by the Marines created a fully fledged revolt by 1919 in which an estimated two or three thousand Haitians died.[61] Harding hoped to exploit Haiti as a particularly sensitive issue for African American voters returning from the war and reeling from the bloody race riots of 1918 and 1919. In his charges, Harding was also following the moral lead of Oswald Garrison Villard's liberal *Nation* that had run the article "The Conquest of Haiti" on July 10 by Herbert J. Seligmann. Villard had been attacking the presence of the United States in Haiti from February 1917 and the article provoked outrage among liberals who perhaps recalled Wilson's idealistic reasons for entering the war in Europe. Villard sent a copy of the article to FDR after his comments with a note attached saying that the charges were clear and specific and added up to "one of the blackest records of dishonor in the history of military imperialism the world over."[62]

Harding hoped the exposure of poor Marine conduct in Haiti would reflect badly on their chiefs, Daniels and FDR at the Navy Department, and on a dictatorial executive in the person of Wilson. The Republican presidential candidate's attacks on FDR were incessant and could not be batted away with telegrams denying he had ever said anything of the sort or calling his rival's charges the "merest dribble." In the immediate term Secretary Daniels was forced to take charge of the publicity disaster by ordering Major General George Barnett, Commandant of the Marine Corp, to prepare a detailed report on Marine occupation of Haiti.[63] When this proved insufficient he instituted a full court of inquiry under Rear Admiral Henry T. Mayo to investigate the charges of Marine brutality. FDR, finally realizing the enormity of his miscalculation, wrote a contrite letter to Daniels suggesting that he abandon his campaign and return to Washington to help in the defense of the Navy Department and Marines, but the damage was done and it now remained only to salvage what was possible and learn from the miscalculation.

Although historians agree that the imperialism controversy springing from FDR's comments in Montana ultimately had a negligible effect on votes, it was personally important for his internationalism.[64] He found himself trapped between liberal and conservative opinion on an issue he had previously not needed to consider. The moral orientation of US society had shifted to a more negative opinion of all imperialism because of its connection to European powers, the recent war and their own experiences of the Haiti involvement. It took the 1920 election campaign to teach FDR this and force him to once more refine his internationalism. In the case of Haiti this required a stressing of self-determination where he now argued US intervention had been "to enable them as soon as possible to operate again under their own legislatures." Referring to another US imperial adventure in Cuba, FDR now argued: "We are an unselfish nation, with a mission in the world. We care about the rights of the downtrodden people, we care about the rights of small nations that cannot defend against aggression."[65] In effect, this was an augmentation of humanitarian paternalism with a much more Wilsonian emphasis on rights and republican government. Crucially, though, it came out of the failings of Wilsonianism in the Caribbean rather than any positive inspiration.

From this point as the campaign progressed in the aftermath of his comments in Montana, FDR developed the Wilsonian theme of extending the

Monroe Doctrine to the world first mentioned by the president in his "Peace without Victory" speech in January 1917. To FDR the Monroe Doctrine was the "first expression of self-determination for nations, the first championing of new and relatively weak states against the power of imperialism and despotism." Referring to nations in South and Central America, FDR argued the "US proposes from now on that these nations shall live their natural life in freedom, that they shall maintain their independence, work out their own system of government. Did not James Monroe say in 1821 'We guarantee the territorial integrity of those nations against external aggression.'" Noting the Wilsonian heritage to his thinking FDR suggested the League might even be "called an extension of the theory of the Pan-American Union of American Republics."[66]

The important point to note is that whereas once intervention had been acceptable and Wilson always justified his many interventions in the name of democracy and republican government, FDR was now fully aware of the limitations of such a strategy. It was one thing to talk of protecting the Western Hemisphere, but this was a rhetorical strategy that could no longer, as in Europe, necessarily imply physical intervention. The major threat of Germany that had always guided his thoughts on intervention in the Western Hemisphere was now gone. If US security interests were threatened sufficiently to warrant intervention the terms of FDR's justification had now changed. Instead of humanitarian uplift, any intervention would have to be for a country not conforming to the Wilsonian ideal of the sovereign, self-governing nation state. Security for FDR became less about throwing US weight around and more about encouraging the development of democracy and liberal relations. In a report drawn up for to the National Council for the Reduction of Armaments in April 1922, FDR now argued that Haiti had been occupied because it had "lapsed back into despotism" and "existed practically as a slave state" ruled by "small educated upper class...divided between the 'ins' and the 'outs.'" As such "It was a menace to the health and prosperity of the neighboring islands." With the United States occupying Haiti and FDR so clearly implicated in his country's actions he could do little more than drop humanitarian justifications and attempt to refute nationalist claims to self-determination that "so deceived high-minded altruistic Americans."[67]

Thus the origin of FDR's own "Good Neighbor" policy as president did not lie just in a straightforward conversion to Wilsonian principles of self-determination. Crucial to the process was an awareness of the failures and vulnerabilities brought by the Wilson administration's intervention in Haiti and Santo Domingo that were exposed during the 1920 election campaign. In case he was inclined to forget the lesson, the controversy surrounding his comments in Montana refused to go away completely and always threatened to catch him out. In 1928, *Nation* was still referring to the "Roosevelt Constitution" and during his career as president he occasionally had to defend against the "old stuff and nonsense" of his 1920 comments.[68] After his experiences of 1920, FDR would judge government policy on its ability to conform to liberal Wilsonian ideals in the same way that he had been judged. Intervention in support of nationalist movements was not something he would ever seriously consider, but reaffirming his anti-imperial credentials at every opportunity maintained his flexibility, encouraged an ideal, and made it more difficult for him to be caught out in such a way again.

The 1920 campaign ultimately proved a dismal failure for the Democrats and led to a humiliating defeat. Cox failed to gain a single Electoral College vote in any of the 18 western states and only secured 127 to Harding's 404 in total. In the popular contest Harding's 16,181,750 votes crushed Cox's 8,141,750.[69] While chastening for Cox it was a great educational experience for FDR who commented to an aide "thank the Lord we are both comparatively youthful!"[70] The campaign had clarified and strengthened much of FDR's existing thinking as it had developed to that point. He continued to believe, for instance, that the United States was inextricably linked to the world, that power was not sufficient alone to guarantee national security and that a liberal ideological approach to international relations was a vital part of any attempt to do so. Much of FDR's thinking was Wilsonian in origin, but a great deal of it was not—FDR continued to reject Wilson's pure notions of collective security and his legal internationalism had a distinctly conservative heritage. Yet by the close of 1920, FDR's internationalism had changed dramatically from that of only two years previously. His internationalism was central to his nomination as vice presidential candidate and the campaign exposed many of the inconsistencies and contradictions of his new position. FDR was now much more aware of these issues and could begin to address them.

The political aspects of FDR's internationalism became particularly visible at this time. His position on world affairs was vital to his selection by Cox as running mate in 1920 and he proved a vital player in the campaign strategy. FDR also, for the first time, put together a first-rate political team able to deal with both domestic and international concerns. Most of them would remain associated with his political fortunes into his presidency. In the immediate term the campaign also led not only to a cultivation and development of valuable nationwide political contacts, but increased FDR's awareness of issues and opinions outside of Washington and the eastern United States. Mistakes aside, the campaign demonstrates a clear sensitivity and interest in the western voice evident in FDR that would continue to develop in the years to come.

In addition to a more cohesive articulation of recently acquired ideas, there was also a raft of new aspects to FDR's internationalism. During the campaign he focused on new aspects such as international law and disarmament. His advocacy of multilateralist causes was also transformed by his campaign experiences. He lost his regional, European focus and made the conceptual shift to a global basis for his liberal ideology. Although tentative at this point, it would become a major feature of FDR's internationalism during the 1920s. This was the result of a further Wilsonian lesson for FDR. The failures of the president's policies in the Caribbean, and Haiti in particular, rather than any successful articulation of his ideals, provided a searing lesson for FDR that American society had now changed. It was now more difficult to attract public opinion from across the political spectrum to support actions that conflicted with American ideals. The world had changed and so too had FDR's thinking.

This personal globalization of FDR's liberal ideology had a further implication. During the campaign FDR had conceptually divided the world into liberal and nonliberal nations and crucially saw the survival of reform abroad as vital to US security. Liberal regimes abroad were less likely to attack the United States and could provide a bulwark against alternative ideologies that might eventually surround the United States and either attack it or subvert its democratic way of life. In lessening the chances of conflict, a liberal foreign policy could also buttress progressive reform against the assaults of domestic reactionary forces. At least two recent studies of FDR's foreign policy as president locate his interest in liberal multilateralist solutions of the world's problems in the experience of the Great Depression and World War II.[71] Admittedly these were huge and important events in the development of his outlook, but his interest in legal and social justice programs was already clearly in situ and this pushes the causative explanation back to the pivotal years of 1919 and 1920.

CHAPTER 5

FINDING A VOICE,
1921–1928

IN 1921, A DEVASTATING ATTACK OF POLIO LEFT FDR an invalid and his political career in tatters. The contrast with the later successful president could not be starker—clearly FDR faced a deeply personal ordeal and yet strangely, it is said, this was necessary for his development as a leader.[1] Such personal events, according to some, had a deep impact on FDR's thinking, making him more determined, empathetic, and even intellectual as a person. The reality was more complex—polio was but one of a range of daunting obstacles facing the aspiring politician during the 1920s. Articulating his thoughts on international affairs would require increasing care and attention to negotiate these challenges and ensure his ambitions were not thwarted.

FDR faced many personal changes during the early 1920s that made the articulation of a clear approach to foreign affairs difficult and certainly not his primary concern. No longer a member of the administration, his priority was to find a job to provide for his large family and finance his patrician lifestyle. Despite his mother's generosity, a return to private employment was a necessity. FDR was in such financial straits by 1925 that he was forced to sell some of his prized naval prints at auction.[2] Working his extensive connections soon brought a lucrative post at the Fidelity and Deposit Company of Maryland to "glad-hand" the Wall Street business community for bond business. It also brought some secondary legal work, first with partners Langdon Marvin and Grenville T. Emmet until 1924 and then with Basil D. O'Connor. Already well-connected from his wartime government service, FDR now met businessmen who would play an important role in Republican foreign policy during the 1920s. For instance, at a welcome dinner in his honor given by Fidelity and Deposit on January 7, 1921, he cemented his acquaintance with Owen D. Young, head of General Electric and later key negotiator of the Dawes Plan. FDR had previously dealt with Young in 1919 during the sale of naval radio stations.[3] Such contacts proved useful, but FDR's need to make a living also took up valuable time that was not devoted to his interest in politics and foreign affairs.[4]

No analysis of FDR in the early 1920s would be complete without discussing the implications of his contraction of polio in 1921. While holidaying with his family at Campobello in August he returned from a day of vigorous outdoor activity chilled and unwell. Going to bed early, he rose the next day with numbness in his legs that quickly led to his collapse accompanied by a high fever, excruciating pain, and loss of control of his bladder and bowel. Doctors eventually diagnosed a case of infantile paralysis that was to have a profound impact on FDR's life.[5] Although he recovered the use of his bodily functions, he remained bedridden well into 1922. When he did recover the 39-year-old politician was left wheelchair bound for much of the time. Polio left him able to walk only short distances on his withered legs with cumbersome leg braces and crutches or the supporting arm of a family member or aide. Even the smallest of everyday tasks required meticulous planning or rethinking and could involve countless minor indignities for the once vigorous and active man.

There were, of course, also more long-term physical implications of his illness that first became apparent during the 1920s. There were demands on his time of his own choosing—his unfailing determination to overcome his physical disability led him to spend hours undergoing treatments and exercises in the attempt to regain the use of his legs. The seemingly endless attempts to reach the end of the driveway at Hyde Park on crutches, the exercise programs, the sailing trips to the Florida Keys in 1924, 1925, and 1926, and the discovery and eventual purchase of the Warm Springs resort in Georgia as a treatment center all demanded intense dedication, concentration, and above all, time.

FDR's restricted physical ability had a dramatic impact on the attention he was able to devote to politics and more specifically to international affairs. The immediate period of his illness prevented him from commenting on international events close to his heart such as a separate peace with Germany for the United States on July 21 and the opening of the Washington Naval Conference on November 12, 1921. Then there were family squabbles over his future in the years immediately following the attack. FDR's mother, Sara, with the experience of caring for FDR's father as a virtual invalid following his heart attack, was keen to reassert her commanding position in her son's life when the full extent of his disability became apparent. She wanted her son to forget any political ambitions and return to Hyde Park where he could become, much like his father, an infirm country squire attended to by his doting family.[6] Ranged against this were FDR's political adviser Louis

Howe who, along with Eleanor, worked doggedly to keep FDR in politics covering his correspondence and arranging for Eleanor to speak for him on many occasions. The conflict over FDR's future became intense and, while there was probably little chance of a determined man like FDR retiring completely from public life, the struggle added to the stresses he experienced. Eleanor and Howe's activities on FDR's behalf also made them his "eyes and ears" in situations that were now impossible for him to attend to directly. In the longer term, this experience encouraged his use of personal diplomatic emissaries that he had first picked up from Wilson as a practical solution to a very physical problem.

The physical impact of FDR's illness is apparent, but what of the mental cost? Eleanor's understated comment to FDR's half-brother that "he's getting back his grip and a better mental attitude though he has of course times of great discouragement" speaks volumes about the calamity unfolding at Campobello at the time.[7] Important questions must therefore be asked about whether and exactly how polio affected FDR's personality and thinking, both in the immediate sense and in the longer term. Those who knew him, and historians since, have divided over the impact his illness had on his personality. Some view it as a clear dividing line after which a more determined and empathetic FDR emerges. Others see the illness as having no impact at all or merely heightening existing traits.[8]

There is a real danger of subjectivity in relying on such personal observations, but the context and chronology of any change can help to explain polio's role. The timing and characteristics of the significant change in FDR's approach toward internationalism during the 1920s does not point toward the polio attack as a significant factor. True, by 1921, FDR had gone through an enormously stressful period of his life due to the impact of the war, the discovery by Eleanor of his affair with Lucy Mercer, the 1920 election defeat, and the Congressional report on the Newport scandal, but he did not demonstrate any significant difference in the way he approached international relations. In the immediate term, polio did not provide him with any opportunity to achieve greater intellectual coherence in his world view. Despite time to do more reading and reflection, he still struggled, as before, to develop his thoughts in any extended fashion. FDR wrote a few introductory pages and then abandoned a string of writing projects at this time. These included initial drafts and plans for a history of the United States, a biography of John Paul Jones, and a book on government that appear at this time.[9]

Strangely polio did bring benefits because of the way FDR chose to use his disability. It gave him an excuse not to attend to tiresome chores or political meetings unless he wanted to. He could always claim to be too ill to participate in any meeting, scheme, or effort that failed to fire his enthusiasm. Many historians have made the observation that polio also kept FDR out of the damaging political fights of the 1920s and therefore perhaps saved his later political career.[10] FDR's crippling by polio also gave him the equivalent of a political "log-cabin" upbringing. Long conscious of his class origins and the aspersions this brought against his masculinity, polio and his efforts to master the cruel blow that fate had dealt him was a clear indication that he was no "feather-duster" or effete upper-class patrician. Although he had already largely dispensed with the exaggerated physical masculinity of his younger political self, he would never again feel the need to adopt it. Polio delivered a final blow to his public enthusiasm for a martial spirit and henceforth his advocacy of physical and moral development was limited to support for nothing more adventurous than the Boy Scouts Association.[11]

The impact of polio also brought a much more careful and planned management of FDR's public persona. An undignified sprawling on the floor could kill his political career instantly, while more insidious charges of infirmity and ill health could be equally damaging in a time when physical disability was largely hidden from public view. Indeed, some Republicans attempted to make an issue of FDR's health in every election he fought from 1928. Louis Howe, together with other friends, family, and aides, kept up constant efforts to limit the perceived extent of FDR's disability so that he was seen as "merely lame." This careful management extended into FDR's public spoken and written word. As a physically disabled person, he found getting his message across much more difficult. Speaking engagements and tours became immensely complicated endeavors. It is little surprise, therefore, that FDR became a pioneer in the use of the radio to communicate with the public. Indeed, his nominating speech to the 1928 Democratic Convention was written specifically with the radio audience in mind.[12] The printed word also provided another outlet not cramped by disability and FDR continued his journalistic output during the 1920s, producing his first book, a book review, and two substantial articles on foreign affairs during the decade.[13] Given the restrictions he faced this is a solid indication of the continuing interest of international affairs to him.

Speaking or writing for a national audience required a greater deal of focused attention to avoid embarrassing contradictions—as FDR well knew from his comments on the Haiti constitution during the 1920 election. Here perhaps is the greatest contribution polio made to FDR's public persona and to his internationalist language. His interest in getting his message across on a national scale combined with his disability to compel him to put renewed effort into the projection of his ideas. Clarity and simplicity became essential to obtaining the attention of a national audience. The well-known and loved style of the presidential "Fireside chats" and speeches that did so much to explain complex international problems to a world audience perhaps owed a lot to the techniques FDR developed during the 1920s.[14]

FDR's personal problems were, of course, not the only ones he faced. The Democratic Party was plagued with disunity throughout the 1920s. Prohibition, religion, urban-rural friction, and even splits over conservative and liberal ideology were issues that almost tore the party apart. Internationalism too was a source of division—Wilson lived on in Washington in increasingly poor health until 1924 and continued to act as a focus for supporters and opponents alike. Internationalists such as Hamilton Holt attempted to smooth out some of the arguments of recent years by setting up the League of Nations Non-Partisan Association (LNNPA) in late 1922 from the predominantly Republican American Association for International Cooperation and the Democratic League of Nations Nonpartisan Committee. Its rather vague statement of purpose calling for membership of the League "under whatever terms seemed wise [and] consistent with the Constitution" allowed almost all prominent supporters of some form of League to join the organization and by 1923 it was publishing the *League of Nations Herald* with a biweekly circulation of 35,000. The League remained a divisive issue, however, and Holt also set up a more direct political organization called the Woodrow Wilson Democracy (WWD) in May 1921 to pressure the Democratic Party to adopt "popular, progressive and humanitarian ideals" and a pro-League stance for the 1922 Congressional and 1924 presidential elections.[15]

After their drubbing in the 1920 election, the professional politicians of the Democratic Party wanted to avoid the League as an issue at all costs and both the LNNPA and WWD were roundly ignored by them.[16] There was still a small group of Wilsonian idealists in the Senate who concentrated on domestic issues, but the rest of the party had fragmented into a multitude of positions on international affairs.[17] The two most important positions were Southern conservatives who supported Republican foreign policy, particularly the Washington Treaty, and a centrist bloc of Claude Swanson, Joe Robinson, Key Pittman, and Carter Glass. They claimed to be Wilsonians, but in reality they let the League issue wane into a call for cooperation with existing international agencies.[18] The Democratic Party lacked anyone to push a strong alternative to Republican foreign policy and Robert Johnson has argued that this left the "Peace Progressives" free to articulate a strong alternative of anti-imperialism and antimilitarism that supplanted Wilsonianism during the 1920s. It seems too much, however, to suggest that Wilsonianism did not survive within the Democrats as a link to the 1930s.[19] True, it may not have been in a pure form, but there were plenty of figures who would go on to powerful positions within the party that subscribed to large elements of Wilson's program—FDR and Cordell Hull to name but two.

Frank Freidel painted a picture of FDR in the 1920s as a valiant Wilsonian forlornly battling against an overwhelming "isolationist tide." His portrayal of FDR as a determined internationalist is convincing yet Roosevelt was never the narrow Wilsonian that Freidel described.[20] FDR's experiences in 1919 and 1920 meant that he never supported a Wilsonian League in its pure form. This was still true in 1922 when he wrote in a letter to his 1920 running mate James M. Cox, "I am not wholly convinced that this country is quite ready for a definite stand on our part in favor of immediate entry into the League of Nations."[21] A year later, upon visiting Wilson at his home in April 1923, FDR was careful to issue a statement that he believed "everyone who thinks the United States should join a league believes it must be a revised league. It has been said, and I think correctly, that the Versailles Treaty no longer exists as it was written. Conditions have changed vitally in Europe since those days."[22] FDR still subscribed to the League of Nations as an approach to international relations, but as before, he qualified his acceptance.

The clearest evidence of FDR's position is provided by the internationalist essay prize run by the retired former editor of the *Ladies Home Journal* Edward Bok. In 1923, Bok announced a $100,000 American Peace Award for an essay detailing the most practical plan whereby the United States could cooperate in preserving peace.[23] FDR was caught up in the initial enthusiasm and enormous publicity the prize generated and he decided to enter. His detailed plan, though based on Wilson's Covenant, was essentially the same qualified League he had advocated since early 1919. First he suggested a name change to the "Society of Nations" because the public were apparently so hostile to the League. He then offered what were in effect reservations dealing with the debate of 1919—in response to concerns over the two-years notice period to leave, he proposed members could leave after three months and offered specific protection to "regional understandings" such as the Monroe Doctrine.[24]

More fundamentally, he proposed an "Executive Council" of 11 members with permanent representation for the "five so-called Great Powers" of the United States, the British Empire, France, Italy, and Japan and a rotating further 6 members not including dominions and colonies. The Council only required a two-thirds majority, rather than Wilson's unanimous rule, to make "recommendations" and any enforcement would be purely by "severance of all trade and financial relations" and "prohibition of all intercourse" though he also mentioned a vague "invitation to contribute" armed forces. Linked to this was a clear statement that "we seek not to become involved as a nation in the purely regional affairs of groups of other nations," or to be compelled by "representative of other peoples" to use "armed force." In the plan FDR was very specific that nothing in US membership should in any way "supersede, abrogate or limit the Constitutional or other powers of the governmental system of any member nation." Nations would now "undertake to respect the territorial integrity an existing political independence of all members" and not "guarantee and preserve" in the controversial language of Article X. Freidel notes that in later years FDR liked to refer back to his Executive suggestions with some pride. On January 19, 1944, Roosevelt commented on the plan, "It is interesting to note…that I recommended an Executive Committee instead of a Council of the League." Then during the Quebec Conference on September 15, 1944, he compared his plan with that for the United Nation: "The plan sets up an Assembly as does the plan discussed at Dumbarton Oaks. It sets up an Executive Committee instead of a Council, to be [in] continuing session."[25]

Some historians have viewed the plan as a comprehensive repudiation of Wilsonian idealism—to them FDR by this time was a thoroughly disenchanted idealist and an "expert" in realpolitik.[26] Such an interpretation fails to note both FDR's position on the League since early 1919 and ignores the rest of the contents of FDR's plan for world peace. In essence, it mistakes a rejection of collective security and a deep appreciation of the problems and limitations of power for a comprehensive rejection of the League. FDR's wartime experience had taught him that power alone was insufficient to guarantee US security and he remained committed to his liberal internationalist measures from 1919. He had not changed his belief that "no plan to preserve world peace can be successful without the participation of the United States." He also included plans to reduce armaments, promote judicial settlement, create a Permanent Court of International Justice akin to the existing one, and implement a raft of social justice measures covering labor conditions, just treatment of "natives," antitrafficking measures, freedom of communications, and disease control.[27] This was hardly the program of a firm believer in realpolitik and represented a genuine belief in the necessity of other measures to augment the deployment of power as a function of US security.

It is by no means clear that FDR ever actually entered his plan for the Bok Peace Prize. It is easy to sense that his political alarm bells would begin to ring at such public exposure—even if he was not a finalist, it was yet another referendum on a League and it might not take journalists long to see that FDR was flogging a League plan again. Close association with Wilson's League is exactly what FDR did not want at this time as he tried to maintain a more broad-gauged internationalism. Despite the qualifications of FDR's plan, if made public, it could make him appear a staunch Wilsonian because of the obvious similarities to the League. It is therefore hardly surprising that he would chose either not to enter, or say he had never entered. Indeed, he became critical of the ethos of the competition saying "the world patient cannot be cured overnight, by a simple surgical operation. A systematic course of treatment extending through the years will prove the only means of saving his life."[28]

Although FDR realized that the League should probably be avoided as an issue, he also appreciated that Wilson was still an important figure among liberals and the Democratic Party. Any attempt to appeal to liberal opinion required grappling with Wilson's legacy in a way sufficient to appeal to his supporters without alienating his many opponents. FDR saw a route to achieving this through the Woodrow Wilson Foundation and elbowed his way into the Chair of the National Committee, proceeding to use his considerable influence to guide its direction.[29] His intention was to capitalize on support for Wilson by keeping the Foundation vague in its stated aims and by preventing any specific support for Wilsonian projects such as the League. Despite some lingering animosity from Wilson's wife, who refused to forgive FDR for entertaining Lord Grey, FDR finally got an audience with Wilson in June 1921.[30] He followed up his visit with a letter of June 29 suggesting the purpose of the Foundation be deliberately "vague" because anything "concrete...might restrict the usefulness of the fund later on."[31] This was a pretty direct admission that FDR thought any mention of the League or the form of world assemblies would hamper the usefulness of the fund and, implicitly, Wilson's political legacy. It would also give FDR the maximum amount of flexibility in his involvement.

FDR did magnanimously offer Wilson an opportunity to contribute to the process of setting the "basic principles" of the Foundation.[32] Wilson responded to the request on July 4 with the suggestion that the Foundation be created in recognition of himself, who "was instrumental in pointing out an effective method for the cooperation of the liberal forces of mankind throughout the whole world who love liberty and who intend to promote peace by the means of justice." FDR did not see anything in Wilson's statement that was too "Wilsonian" to risk the usefulness of the project and was, no doubt, pleased to gain Wilson's approval for such a vague remit.[33]

Direct correspondence between Wilson and FDR then ceased with the onset of the latter's polio and did not resume for several months. Wilson does seem to have personally warmed to FDR when he learnt that he had, like him, suffered a debilitating illness. When news of FDR's illness was released to the press in September, Wilson wrote his best wishes to him at the Presbyterian Hospital in New York and inquired of his progress again in November. For the remainder of his life Wilson received and cordially acknowledged birthday greetings from FDR on behalf of the Woodrow

Wilson Foundation. On FDR's birthday in 1923, Wilson even sent him birthday wishes signed off as "Always your Friend Woodrow Wilson."[34]

Wilson, of course, was not the political tool of FDR and, despite being in poor health, played, or his wife played, his own complex game to manage his political legacy. FDR was important on the national Democratic scene and would be worth cultivating as the 1924 election approached. Wilson's support for the Foundation was also not the ex-president's only attempt to manage and secure his legacy—Woodrow Wilson Clubs and WWD formed important alternatives to the actions of the Foundation. Wilson also got his friend Ray Stannard Baker to become involved in the vast project of his biography and papers.

FDR could not control biographers, but he could deploy his influence and connections to kill off rival Wilson legacy projects. The Woodrow Wilson Clubs were college-based organizations begun at Harvard by Robert C. Stuart Jr., which by December 1921 had 54 chapters and a national council. They planned to raise $250,000 that would defray the expenses of a director and enable the supply of important books and materials to smaller college libraries.[35] The obvious similarity in purpose and FDR's championing fundraising for the Foundation on college campuses soon brought the two organizations into conflict. The lack of connections and inexperience of Stuart soon told and, despite initial support from Wilson and considerable encouragement from his secretary Bolling, the outclassed clubs folded.[36]

With FDR's victory over the clubs, Wilson now relied on the Foundation to promote his own personal reputation, philosophy, and legacy in the future. Although he congratulated FDR on his handling of the organization, by early 1922, there was an indication that he was far from happy that his suggestions for the wording of aims were being "overlooked or rejected."[37] Wilson was annoyed because the final statement of the Foundation had replaced "practical contribution to the liberal thought of the world with regard to human rights or international relationships" with "meritorious service to democracy, public welfare, liberal thought or peace through justice." "Liberal thought" was Wilson's phrase and "peace through justice" was a contraction of his words, but democracy and public welfare had not featured in his suggestions. Wilson thought his own wording "more definite and more serviceable" than the formula suggested by the committee and felt "their formula leaves me exceedingly vague."[38]

Exceedingly vague was exactly what FDR wanted for Wilson's legacy. Indeed, he was beginning to show his frustrations with Wilson's attempts to control it and wished he would cease to interfere. A letter from FDR at the end of 1922 gives good indication of this attitude when he wrote, "As you say, his [Wilson's] spirit is stronger than his body and I only wish that the newspapers could stop saying anything about him at all. He would continue to grow with the nation."[39] On May 1, 1923, the 15 permanent trustees were invested at the Biltmore Hotel at which point FDR turned over more than $800,000 in subscriptions—Wilson was unable to attend.[40] The subsequent history of the Foundation and awards quickly descended into farce as it was reduced to essay competitions and financing memorial doors at the League headquarters in Geneva.[41] FDR was replaced as chairman in 1923, but continued as a committee member until 1933. FDR was probably more than glad to end his association when he entered the White House though he, no doubt, gained enormously valuable experience in the management of a presidential legacy that helped when he came to planning his own at Hyde Park in 1940. The direct association with the League was too apparent and he had personally long since moved on from seeing Wilson as an essential central pillar of his internationalism.[42]

In the aftermath of World War I and the League Fight, the American public was less interested in their government actively pursuing international relations. This mood was reinforced by a more assertive Congress willing to attack and defeat any administration plans that appeared internationalist in orientation. Thus, foreign relations remained a highly charged issue; for a politician to express an opinion often courted controversy. In response, the Harding administration acquiesced in a broadly nationalistic policy—one of the first things the president announced in April 1921 was his abandonment of the Versailles Treaty in favor of a Congressional peace resolution eventually passed on July 2 and signed by Germany on August 25 as the Treaty of Berlin.[43] Determined not to divide his party or antagonize the nation, Harding's secretary of state, Charles Evans Hughes, used unofficial observers at the League of Nations, the European Reparation Commission, the Lausanne Conference in 1923, and the later Dawes Conference.[44] Congress too enacted a raft of distinctly nationalist legislation—the Emergency Tariff Act of 1921 and Fordney-McCumber Tariff of September 1922 raised the average tariff to 38.5 percent; the Immigration Restriction Act of 1921 and Immigration Act of 1924 placed a cap on immigration and effectively barred it from many countries. In many ways, it seemed the United States was attempting to put up a wall between itself and the rest of the world. Indeed, when French and Belgium troops occupied the Ruhr in an attempt to secure German payment of reparations beginning January 1923, Harding opted to withdraw the remaining US troops, arguing that America had no vital interest—effectively severing military support for former wartime allies.[45]

The popularity of Republican policy and the complexity of European politics made it difficult for FDR to articulate an approach to foreign affairs in the early 1920s. He was clearly "convinced that we should stand firmly against the isolationist policy of Harding's administration," but the damage that Wilson's policies had caused made him unsure as to how to go about this.[46] FDR was also wary of becoming tangled in political controversy—domestically Harding's administration was a disaster with his untimely death and a succession of scandals culminating in the Teapot Dome affair, but by contrast the administration's foreign policy under Hughes had been hailed a success. Asked to write an article on foreign affairs in September 1922, FDR made excuses about his inability to complete writing projects, but more revealingly wrote "there is another complication—i.e., I am carefully trying to stay out of print on controversial subjects, and by all that is holy if I got started on any kind of article on international matters my remarks would most assuredly be controversial."[47] With the League still a very raw topic, FDR avoided a clear entry to the Bok competition and still could not see a way to articulate principle without becoming mired in the specifics of a past debate.

This meant ignoring the Ruhr crisis of 1923—touching on it only obliquely through the issue of war debts but not reparations. FDR's economic thinking remained unsophisticated and largely constrained by domestic opinion that demanded complete repayment of war debts by the Allies. He sent congratulations to George P. Auld, accountant general of the Reparation Committee, when Auld attacked the position of John Maynard Keynes and other economists who argued that debts should be reduced. FDR wrote: "I particularly love the way you hand things to Mr. Keynes" then went on to condemn England's "silly notions" and "selfish attitude" in her trend toward imperial tariffs. While this is probably the first evidence of FDR considering issues of international economics in any depth, it seems more in tune with Coolidge's nationalistic stance that "they hired the money, didn't they?" Yet in the same letter to Auld, FDR wrote: "we won't guarantee loans or put up a lot of cas[h], but we will soon be ready to discuss"—which was indicative of the more flexible American approach that would soon develop.[48] Although they were not prepared to acknowledge a link between reparations and war debts, the Americans steadily made agreements with individual countries to reduce and reschedule payments. Agreement was reached with the British in June 1923, the Italians in November 1925, and with the French, finally, in April 1926.

The Italian settlement reduced the debt by about four-fifths and left FDR pondering whether the Democrats should make an issue over its ratification in Congress. There was a concern that Mussolini would use attached private loans to finance a small war and raised the ethical issue whether proclaimed liberals should tacitly support a fascist regime.[49] Democratic opposition out of an election year was centered on Congress and at a dinner hosted by Senator Walsh in February 1926 FDR appeared to give the impression he favored a firm stand against the agreement.[50] Louis Howe set about thoroughly researching the problem and consulted with Owen D. Young,

Walter Lippmann, Newton D. Baker, George W. Wickersham, and the acting head of J. P. Morgan, Thomas Cochran. He quickly concluded that the
complexities of the debt question meant it was a potential quagmire for the
Democrats and therefore advocated speedy ratification of the Italian agreement. This advice seemed to be in line with what FDR's political sense had
already told him. He wrote to Walsh: "The ratification of the Italian Debt
Settlement worries me considerably...to oppose, without clear and sound
reasons, would be an act of folly."[51] In a keynote speech to the New York
Democratic State Convention in 1926, he therefore implied, rather than
clearly stated, that he advocated a sympathetic and tactful settlement or
compromise rather than insistence on full and immediate payment of debts.
By not committing or advocating any specific plan while indicating a readi-
ness to talk he could neutralize what was a potentially divisive issue for the
Democrats.[52] As before with his stance toward collective security, FDR held
liberal principles, but did not see forceful economic coercion by the United
States as a viable foreign policy.

European immigration posed a problem because of the diverse demands
of industry, labor, and immigrant communities, but was also avoided by FDR
who focused on Americanization rather than exclusion.[53] Japanese immigration, however, continued to have a more direct impact on US foreign policy.
The 1917 Immigration Act created the so-called Asian barred zone that
virtually cut off any further Asian immigration not already circumscribed
by the series of Chinese Exclusion Acts and the Gentleman's Agreement of
1907 covering the Japanese. Further xenophobic exclusion culminated in
the Immigration Act of 1924 that included the Japanese who had long been
perceived as a problem in the United States, particularly California, where
tensions had almost brought war on several occasions. FDR had originally
viewed the problem purely in terms of the Japanese military threat and a
political attempt to exploit Republican Party divisions. The domestic pressure of the postwar period meant he accepted the implications of 1924 Act
that formalized the notion of a white American race that excluded Asians
as inferior and separate. Acknowledging that Americans believed "that the
mingling of white with oriental blood on an extensive scale is harmful to
our future citizenship" he argued that "[f]rankly [Americans] do not want
non-assimilable [sic] immigrants as citizens, nor do they desire any extensive
proprietorship of land without citizenship."[54] He justified his position by
arguing that the Japanese wanted the same thing themselves—they wanted
nothing that threatened "racial purity." This was not just the opinion of
the Japanese according to FDR but "extends to and affects...other oriental
peoples of acknowledged dignity and integrity."[55] Thus, the internment of
Japanese-American citizens during World War II and the prosecution of the
war in the Pacific with such vehement racial stereotypes had an extended

heritage. It was grounded more in FDR's inability to craft a coherent foreign policy that dealt with American prejudice in the early 1920s than in any earlier more fundamental racism toward the Japanese.

Further frustrating FDR's attempts to differentiate the Democrats from the Republicans in foreign policy was the fact that he actually found himself agreeing with major parts of the Republican approach. Since the 1920 election, he had made it plain that he did not have objections to Elihu Root's efforts to create a Permanent Court of International Justice at The Hague. It was also difficult to disagree with the apparent success of the Washington Conference orchestrated by Hughes. Prompted by mounting public concern over armaments and possible action by other governments and the pressure to do something constructive in world affairs, Hughes had pursued a nationalistic policy and achieved an impressive set of agreements. Convening on November 12, the Conference led to the Four Power Treaty that guaranteed signatories Pacific possessions and resulted in the dissolving of the Anglo-Japanese Alliance; the Five Power Treaty that set the famous 5:5:3 naval ratio and a host of other restrictions and the Nine Power Treaty that served to guarantee the territorial integrity of China and resolved the thorny issue of the Japanese occupation of Shantung province with their promise to withdraw. The United States without the aid of an international political organization had achieved arms control, abrogation of the Anglo-Japanese treaty, limits on imperialism in China, and protections of its rights there. Following on from his wartime experience, FDR certainly agreed with Republican moves toward disarmament in Europe—he had been calling for naval arms reduction since early 1919 and had done so again as recently as May 1921.[56] The policy was popular domestically because it promised to reduce taxation and was favored by pacifists. Internationally, it would not antagonize the French, would help to reduce world tensions and could potentially ease pressure on European budgets.

The relevance of the Washington Treaty to Japan was slightly more difficult to interpret and produced FDR's first foreign policy article of the decade written for the July 1923 issue of *Asia* magazine and entitled "Shall We Trust Japan?" In some ways, it was inevitable that he should want to address a subject so close to his heart and recent career experience, but again the fact that he chose to respond purely to the Pacific aspects of the treaty is indicative of the difficulty in producing a coherent approach to world foreign policy.[57] FDR's article did not neglect more realist based arguments, but did demonstrate the full impact of his wartime experience. There now existed what he called a "naval strategical dead-lock." Military planners, according to FDR, had long acknowledged that, even before the advent of submarines and aircraft, the Philippines were indefensible and similarly the Japanese would be unable to maintain an attack on the Pacific coast of the United

States. Conflict between the two nations was something neither could win and would lead to "Japan and the United States, four or five thousand miles apart, making faces at one another across a no-man's-water as broad as the Pacific...until one or the other, or both had bled to death through the pocketbook." The Washington Conference, he argued, had ended the naval race.[58] FDR also argued that there had been a change of heart in the normally tense Japanese-American relations based on the new conditions existing in the postwar era. Continuing to think of Japan and the Japanese in terms of war was an "apprehensive habit of mind," and "an impediment to progress in world relations." The Washington agreements were evidence of the new basis of trust between nations. "Great Britain," FDR wrote, "has faithfully lived up to her part in the agreement...Japan, contrary to her tactics on certain past occasions, has lived up not only to the letter but to the spirit of the treaty." Hector C. Bywater, the London correspondent to the Baltimore *Sun* and author of *Sea Power in the Pacific* (1921), criticized FDR's view and saw a clash as almost inevitable, particularly in the South Pacific because Japan's population pressure and need for resources. FDR dismissed this with a mixture of bizarre racial logic and internationalism stating the Japanese were not "a tropical race and do not thrive near the equator" and arguing that the "whole tide of the times is against wars for colonial expansion. The thought of the world leans the other way" with "a new spirit of international relations."[59]

According to FDR it was up to the nations that had come out of the war in a strong position, having lost few men or resources, to play the role in stabilizing the world through peaceable cooperation. He stated optimistically: "Today the school of those who believe that the solvent nations, those who are in a position to help restore the world, must play their magnanimous part, is almost daily receiving accessions of strength." This meant that trade could now be an area of agreement. The "idea of the partition of China, which hung like a cloud on the horizon of two generations of Japanese growth" had been dispelled, "if not forever, then for our own times by the Great War." The United States could now "recognize that there is a real necessity to Japan of the markets and raw products of that part of the Chinese mainland contiguous to her island shores."[60] This was almost an admission of Japan's special interest except that FDR argued that there was enough room for both nations in the Pacific and both were very different in trade anyway—Japan did not feature in the great staples of American export oil, cotton, and tobacco and both powers held sway in different areas of manufacturing.

The acceptance of Republican foreign policy in the Pacific left FDR lamely searching for plausible reasons to criticize it—the only one he found was that the Coolidge administration had failed to educate the people on the new relations with Japan.[61] There is, however, a more fundamental point— FDR, by abandoning his previous nationalistic approach to the Japanese and replacing it with bipartisan notions of difference and mutual trust laid the foundation for his later adoption of the Stimson Doctrine in 1933. His wartime appreciation of the limitations of force, the bitter memory of domestic reaction to Wilson's acquiescence to Japanese demands in Shantung, and the nationalistic mood of the country left him few options other than to agree with Republican foreign policy in the Pacific. This surrendered the initiative to the Japanese and their willingness to follow agreements. It also set the parameters, a decade before he became president, for his own response to Japanese aggression.

FDR would likely have found all the obstacles to a coherent approach to foreign affairs in the 1920s insurmountable had it not been for three key developments coinciding in 1924. These, rather than the polio attack of 1921, proved pivotal to the development of FDR's internationalism because they prompted him to examine and formulate mechanisms for its exposition. The first event was the death of Wilson on February 3, 1924. His passing removed one of the greatest obstacles to Democratic unity and party members began to experience more room for maneuver. Suddenly, Wilson was a figure of the past and his image inexorably lost power rather than remaining the center of liberal internationalism within the Democratic Party.

The second development was yet another defeat for the Democrats in the presidential election of 1924. Wilson's death did not have a huge impact on the party's electoral success. Still divided between rural and urban, catholic and protestant, wet and dry, conservative and liberal, the Democrats failed to achieve the unity to win power. It was still difficult to form a position that was different from the Republicans in foreign affairs while avoiding controversy. FDR attributed the problem partly to Harding's taciturn successor, Calvin Coolidge, arguing, "To rise superior to Coolidge will be a hard thing, as Coolidge is inarticulate to the extent of being thought a mystery. To stick the knife into ghosts is always hard, but I trust that the voters as a whole will come to realize that there is nothing behind Coolidge's silence and mystery except a spectr[e]."[62] As a politician FDR had to find a way to "stick the knife" into Coolidge and ensure the Democrats did not go down to another defeat in 1928. He embarked on an extended period of hand-wringing in a determined effort to learn the lessons of defeat. In the years after 1924, FDR paid increased attention to both the presentation and content of the Democratic Party message.

The third, and perhaps most important, development in 1924 was that two fundamental aspects of Republican foreign policy began to be much more pronounced and visible. Traditional interpretations of the 1920s, and indeed that of FDR himself, view this as a period of isolationist foreign policy for the United States. In reality, however, the Republicans developed new ways, acceptable to Congress and the public, to engage with the world and promote US interests. In parallel to their domestic laissez-faire liberalism, Republicans eschewed military and political commitments abroad and instead emphasized informal, private business contacts. In addition to the moral commitments promoted in their legal strategies, they developed a new form of economic diplomacy. Peaceful world relations were to be achieved through commerce benefiting from the promotion of finance and exchange stability. The Republican administration argued that strict adherence to the gold standard, balanced budgets and (in Europe) the funding of war debts was the key to this stability. This developed into "dollar diplomacy" or the use of private bank loans to leverage the use of financial advisers by foreign governments, predominantly in Latin America but also in European nations such as Poland.

As Emily Rosenberg has shown this was nothing new—dollar diplomacy developed during TR's presidency and even Wilson indulged in it, but the scale and scope of such "private" US schemes vastly increased during the 1920s to stretch across the globe. Opposition drew on existing populist and progressive antibanking discourses and, as Republican policies became more widely known in the 1920s, an increasingly powerful anti-imperialist discourse.[63] For FDR, the burgeoning corporatism and dollar diplomacy of the Republicans abroad was the same reactionary laissez-faire liberal approach he described as conservatism in regimes at home and abroad in 1919. The Republicans now seemed to be showing their true colors and this provided an important way to differentiate the Democrats ideologically.

Thomas Jefferson's concept of popular democracy was crucial to FDR's attempts to bring the Democrat's differences from the Republicans into relief and to transcend the difficulties he previously experienced in articulating a position on foreign affairs. FDR, from his education and early career, was familiar with the history and ideas surrounding Jefferson and the Democratic Party. His knowledge of Jefferson, however, was that of rather a one dimensional party hero whose name could be summoned to give gravitas and import to speeches. FDR was actually uncomfortable alluding to great statesmen and preferred military, particularly naval, figures. Even during the 1920 election campaign, he was dismissive of the suggestion that "people should vote Democratic this year on the grounds Thomas Jefferson was the great founder of the principles of the Democratic Party."[64] This continued during the early twenties with FDR turning down several entreaties to become involved in plans to buy Jefferson's former home, Monticello. His stated reason was that he was heavily involved with the Woodrow Wilson Foundation—his hopes for Democratic unity clearly still lay with the more recent former president at this point.[65]

Following the defeat of John W. Davis in 1924, FDR seems to have experienced a change of heart toward the political use of Jefferson. The images of historical figures in politics had long been tools of partisans, but it increased dramatically during the progressive era and particularly during World War I as organizations such as the Committee on Public Information (CPI) sought to justify difficult policy positions. This did not let up after the war with a huge growth in the number of biographies published focusing on figures such as Lincoln and Jefferson. These fed the increasing need of Americans to orientate their lives with reference to the wisdom of historical figures. During the 1920 campaign, Cox had made frequent use of both Jefferson and Lincoln, the former in a very conservative, states' rights guise, and it seems likely that the political utility of such figures began to rub off on FDR.[66] Anniversaries also seemed to favor a revival of Jefferson at this time with the sesquicentennial of the Declaration of Independence and the centennial of Jefferson's death both falling in 1926.[67]

There were also more immediate political causes for FDR's "discovery" of Jefferson. Following the 1924 election, FDR decided to write to every delegate of the National Convention to ask what should be done to make the party more successful.[68] The replies he received reflected many of the divisions still raw within the party, but several respondents called for reform and invoked the name of Jefferson to sanction their suggestions.[69] FDR, with Howe's assistance, produced what purported to be the summary of the replies he received and set it out in an open letter to Senator Thomas J. Walsh, permanent chairman of the Democratic Convention, as part of a maneuver to bring about a national party conference.[70] FDR and Howe thought they saw a way to use Jefferson to contrast the domestic and foreign policy antics of the Republicans with that of the Democrats. In his letter, FDR linked Jefferson to the division he had long seen between liberal and conservative politics:

> [T]he Democracy must be unqualifiedly the Party representative of progress and liberal thought. In other words, the clear line of debarkation [sic] which differentiated the political thought of Jefferson on the one side, and of Hamilton on the other, must be restored. The Democracy must make it clear that it seeks primarily the good of the average citizen through the free rule of the whole electorate, as opposed to the Republican Party which seeks a mere moneyed prosperity of the nation through the control of government by a self-appointed aristocracy of wealth and of social and economic power.[71]

Senator Walsh approved, but most party leaders were not impressed.[72] The press were also scathing of what they saw as FDR's cynical attempts to use Jefferson as a rallying point for the party and a blatant political tool. Herbert

Croly in the *New Republic* called it "The Great Jefferson Joke," whereby challenging issues were met by shouting "hurrah for Jefferson."[73]

FDR still "boil[ed] inwardly" at the attacks by the press months later, but undeterred, and rather characteristically, he attempted to get someone else to develop the idea of reviving Jefferson as a central party pillar. In a letter to Hollins N. Randolph in May, FDR suggested the Atlanta lawyer undertake a comparative study of Jefferson and Hamilton and relate it to contemporary problems faced by the Democratic Party. Randolph agreed that the project would be helpful, but could not undertake the project.[74] Luckily, Claude Bowers published a book that did exactly this. His *Jefferson and Hamilton* (1925) mixed literary style with historical drama and pictured the differences between Jefferson and Hamilton along similar lines to FDR—in his preface, Bowers wrote: "Throughout the struggle we shall find the forces well defined—aristocracy against democracy."[75] Bowers had a distinguished editorial career with Democratic newspapers and asked FDR to review his book for the *New York World*. In it, FDR found a clear articulation of what he had been trying to achieve—a political blue print for uniting the Democratic Party on general principles of opposition to government by the privileged few and support of government by the many. FDR wrote: "I feel like saying 'At Last' as I read Mr. Claude G. Bowers' thrilling 'Jefferson & Hamilton.'"[76] His enthusiasm was palpable, demonstrated more than anything by his writing of the review—his only one. FDR was entranced by Bowers' picture of warring democracy and aristocracy—closing the review he wrote, "I have a breathless feeling as I lay down this book...Hamilton's [*sic*] we have today. Is a Jefferson on the horizon?"[77]

At first glance, this seems compelling evidence for an important intellectual development in FDR, but what, if anything, did he really gain from his encounter with Jeffersonian thought? Central to FDR's interest was Jefferson's emphasis on democracy, but this was nothing new to FDR in 1925—he had talked of democracy rather than special privilege, albeit more vaguely, as something around which the Democratic Party could rally and contrast themselves against the Republicans since 1919. He also learned powerful lessons on the global extent of calls for self-determination during the 1920 election. Neither should FDR's interest be confused with more theoretical and philosophical conceptions of democracy current during the 1920s. FDR was talking very much about the immediate political conception of democracy and there is no evidence to suggest he appreciated the theories of the philosopher John Dewey, who viewed democracy as a much wider community of ideas and interests that generated a deep and rich communication between citizens and intelligent action. This is an important point because Dewey's brand of philosophical "pragmatism" or "experimentalism," that quantified truth and value through experience and thus placed a great deal of emphasis on democratic openness, is often described as a key philosophic underpinning of FDR's administration. While he had little reason to quarrel with much of his adviser's suggestions there is a real danger of mistaking the pragmatic experimental approach of "Brains Trust" advisers Raymond Moley, Rexford Tugwell, and Adolf Berle as FDR's own. Indeed, FDR's famous speech of May 22, 1932, in which he declared the country needed "bold, persistent experimentation" and should "take a method and try it: If it fails, admit it and try another" was actually penned by the journalist Ernest K. Lindley.[78] In truth, FDR's emphasis on democracy lay in his own American nationalism, much of which may well ultimately have been Jeffersonian or Wilsonian in origin.

By founding his outlook on democracy, FDR encountered another problem that seemed exceptionally powerful during the 1920s—how could he be sure that the public would chose to do the right thing? There were plenty of recent examples to indicate they would not do so. Refusal to join the League, isolationist sentiment, and even the Scopes Trial of 1925 highlighted to critics that people could use their power to effect what could be described as nonprogressive actions. Journalists such as H. L. Mencken fired barbed salvos at the idiocy of "Main Street" and even some liberal progressives began to lose faith in the abilities of the general public. The publicist and intellectual Walter Lippmann published two damning critiques of the public's inability to take intelligent action. In *Public Opinion* (1922) and *Phantom Public* (1925), Lippmann painted a picture of a public that was an ignorant, unteachable victim of propaganda and false information, and so preoccupied with life's trials that they did not have the time, or inclination, to acquire the knowledge necessary for informed action.[79]

After World War I, Lippmann became an increasingly disenchanted liberal idealist whereas FDR experienced none of the crisis of conscience that wracked many of his fellow liberals. Indeed, an indication of FDR's apparent contentment was his first book—*Whither Bound?*—published in 1926, which was a statement of continuing simple, unreflective faith in human progress. Unlike Lippmann, FDR also retained his confidence in the democratic majority for two further reasons. The first of these was his agreement with the Republican emphasis on classical legalism, particularly in solutions to world order, as a restraint on democratic power. Classicism stressed the fact that law reflected custom and was, in effect, morally self enforcing. All that was needed was codification of that custom and a court for it to be recognized in to create a substantial force for world peace. FDR's classicist credentials were clearly demonstrated by a 1925 piece titled "Reign of Law Sustained by Public Opinion" in which he wrote: "The history of our country shows that with few exceptions legislative action does represent majority will, and that in most cases where a majority opinion of the electorate is opposed to a law the law itself is repealed or changed by legislative representatives."[80] Thus, FDR stuck rigidly to his faith in the law despite domestic events that questioned that faith during the 1920s. Prohibition generated questions of enforcement throughout the decade while the dubious conviction of immigrants Sacco and Vanzetti proved a scandal to many liberals. FDR also fully supported the ongoing attempts by prominent Republicans to join the World Court. Thwarted in 1926 by stringent reservations set by Congress, FDR would continue to support World Court membership, making his own unsuccessful attempt to get the United States to join in 1935.

FDR clearly saw international legal structures as useful institutions for articulating the customs and moral beliefs of humanity and that this would bring greater stability in the world. Insufficient codification of international law by the Republicans therefore formed one strand of his critique of their policies.[81] Declaring war illegal, however, as the Kellogg-Briand Pact attempted to do, was clearly nonsense to FDR because it contradicted what he knew about humanity and its customs. In a 1928 editorial he wrote, "unfortunately history records that these pious resolutions were duly forgotten or explained away when these…nations got involved in some subsequent quarrel."[82] This did not mean, however, that a world court would have to rely on power to enforce its decisions. FDR believed strongly that the force of public opinion and custom was sufficient to encourage adherence if it reflected reality. This sounds like Wilson, but the origins of FDR's views clearly lay in legal classicism. Wilson was never an enthusiastic supporter of legal solutions while FDR followed Republicans such as Root and even directly quoted an article of his in which he argued that the court was an "indispensable institution" for public opinion against war and should be welcomed by those looking to outlaw and abolish war.[83]

The second reason for FDR's continued faith in mass democracy was that he continued to believe, unlike Lippmann, that the public could be educated. He was keenly aware that foreign policy was increasingly the concern of the people. "Foreign affairs are" he wrote "discussed by the average citizen. Wars and armaments are the concern of more than kings." Thus, any successful foreign policy required broad public support.[84] The problem facing liberals, however, FDR explained in a letter to Thaddeus A. Adams was the tendency to "do nothing" by conservatives while progressives divided over "details" and were "unable to control the government because of their subdivisions and unwillingness to agree a method and machinery."[85]

FDR thought he found the answer to the problem of creating public liberal concern in Jefferson's democratic writings. He wrote to Claude Bowers that "Jefferson organized by disseminating facts." In another letter to Dr. D. C. Martin, FDR advocated bringing "the government back to the hands of the average voter, through insistence on fundamental principle, and the education of the average voter."[86] Yet this emphasis on voter education was not particularly novel. TR had long spoken of the "bully pulpit" and Wilson likewise often talked of "counsel" with the people and advocated direct appeals such as his 1919 tour in support of the League. Jefferson provided a convenient presentational aid and his emphasis on education brought new energy, as it had done with democracy, to FDR's politics, but did not represent a fundamental new direction to FDR's internationalist thinking.

FDR's emphasis on educating the voting public had two practical implications for his internationalism. The first was an increased awareness that he must speak in clear, understandable language and should avoid complex linked discussions that would only serve to confuse the average member of the public. As the 1928 presidential election approached, FDR set about attempting to persuade the domestically focused Democratic candidate Al Smith to become more internationalist in his outlook. His main method was an article for the journal *Foreign Affairs* published in July 1928. From the start he was very clear in the intent of his article, namely that "he [Smith] would be the probable nominee of the Democratic Party, and that the article would be used more or less as guidance in the treatment of foreign affairs in the campaign."[87] Although *Foreign Affairs* was an elite journal, FDR's democratic concern made him quite sure that the piece "must be couched in language which will be understood by the average reader, i.e., a more simple and direct form than many of the average run of articles in Foreign Affairs."[88] All the issues FDR touched upon in the article were clearly explained and were treated as autonomous subjects only linked by the liberal approach he advocated—solutions to one problem were not necessarily linked to others. This tension between the public's need to understand issues individually and the actual interconnected nature of world problems would go on to become one of the major challenges FDR faced as president.

The second important implication of FDR's approach to education is that he clearly did not just have US domestic opinion in mind. In his *Foreign Affairs* article, FDR articulated his appreciation of self-determination and anti-imperialism discourses, partly as a response to Republican foreign policy, but mainly due to his experiences of 1919 and 1920. This produced what, at first sight, seems a fundamental and important shift in FDR's internationalism and critique of Republican foreign policy. Again Jefferson proved a useful tool—this time through FDR's twisting of the Declaration of Independence. FDR argued that the Declaration attempted to influence "the relations of one state with another" by calling for a "decent respect to the opinions of mankind."[89] Thus, he argued that US foreign policy should no longer be unilateral, but should instead pay heed to world opinion. This was not entirely true to the Declaration that described the need for "decent respect" when declaring the reasons for breaking political bonds (in this case with the British) rather than suggesting that it was unwise to hold the opinions of mankind in contempt with regard to US foreign policy.

Nevertheless FDR used this as a stepping off point for a critique Republican foreign policy:

> [W]e must admit also that the outside world almost unanimously views us with less good will today than at any previous period. This is serious unless we take the deliberate position that the people of the United States owe nothing to the rest of mankind and care nothing for the opinions of others.[90]

To support his point, FDR argued that in Europe the huge amount of interest the United States stood to make from war debts made them appear "greedy."[91] In Latin America, he deployed the language of anti-imperialism he had developed since the 1920 election. Glossing over the interventions of the Democratic administration in the Caribbean, he argued:

> The time has come when we must accept not only certain facts but many new principles of a higher law, a newer and better standard in international relations...Single handed intervention by us in the internal affairs of other nations must end; with the cooperation of others we shall have more order in this hemisphere and less dislike.[92]

Freidel suggests the major influence in appreciating the opinion of Latin America was discussions with Norman Davis, Hamilton Fish Armstrong, and Sumner Welles. As early as a Jefferson Day Banquet on March 27, 1928, Roosevelt called for "a definite policy of non interference in the internal affairs of other nations...and a definite effort to end the hate and dislike of America, now shared by every other civilized nation in the world."[93] The ultimate source went a little further back—FDR's critique was nothing actually new and echoed Wilson's 1916 call for a more "wholesome" form of diplomacy. Thus, the Jeffersonian message FDR promoted was, in fact, a cleverly repackaged Wilsonianism that avoided direct linkage to the former president and hopefully offered a clear principle around which the Democratic Party could unite. Jefferson served to both clarify FDR's existing thinking and confirm his beliefs, but when the immediate context is considered one detects a distinctly political flavor to FDR's enthusiasm. Jefferson was merely one of several former presidents that FDR learnt to use to give his own actions power and he was loyal to none of them. Jefferson's image just happened to be particularly useful to FDR in the context of the mid-1920s.

The preoccupation with Jefferson by some historians has also led to the neglect of an equally important figure in the articulation of FDR's internationalism during the 1920s.[94] If anything, Jefferson was out of favor with many leading politicians in the period immediately before that under discussion. Taking the lead from writers such as Herbert Croly and politicians such as TR the emphasis was very much on Jefferson's great rival Alexander Hamilton with his alternative vision of strong, centralized, aristocratic government—even Wilson had proved somewhat Hamiltonian in office.

FDR's experiences of the presidencies of TR and Wilson gave him a passionate belief in the efficacy of strong executive-led government that was distinctly Hamiltonian. Indeed, at the same time he was writing on Jefferson, he wrote an unpublished short biographical sketch of Hamilton of similar length to his Bowers' review that follows the more conventional historic hero image of Hamilton rather than following any Jeffersonian democratic critique.[95] Hitherto, this has gone unnoticed by historians focusing on Jefferson and seems all the more important because of the comparative rarity of FDR putting his thoughts down on paper. In 1924, he also wrote a 23-page article on the nature of federal government that was positive toward a strong executive and clearly critical of both the legislative arm and the small government corporatism of the 1920s. In a speech to the New York State Democratic Convention in September 1926, FDR was more direct stating that "a nation or a state which is unwilling to take governmental action to tackle the new problems, caused by immense increase of population and by the astounding strides of modern science, is headed for decline and ultimate death from inaction."[96] It was clear from this that FDR's "discovery" of Jeffersonian democracy did not eliminate his preference for Hamiltonian means.[97]

This Hamiltonian streak had a very direct implication for FDR's internationalism because it helped shape his assessment of Republican foreign policy. The London Reparations Conference of August 1924 and the Dawes plan that followed (and arguably the Washington Treaties) indicated a return by Anglo-American powers to European affairs. As Patrick Cohrs has argued, these treaties, and that at Locarno the following October, represented a bold new attempt at pacific settlement of disputes rather than looking back to the solutions proposed by Wilson. Thus, they represented a serious, if truncated, attempt at postwar territorial settlement in Europe outside Wilsonian political structures.[98] This argument does have much merit, but many internationalists such as FDR maintained a Hamiltonian interest in political structures. They may not have subscribed fully to Wilson's schemes, but they were aghast at the lack of supporting executive structures created by these arrangements and this formed a growing aspect of their critique of Republican foreign policy.

In foreign affairs, FDR, therefore, developed a twofold critique of the "nine gray years" of Republican foreign policy.[99] First, although he was a supporter of disarmament proposals, the sacrifices made at the Washington Conference were not productive, according to FDR, because "we assumed that a mere signature was enough; no machinery was set up to finish the work."[100] This threatened disaster if the machinery for discussion and cooperation were not in place for the next conference due to take place in 1931 and when the naval treaty expired in 1936. FDR made a similar charge about the discussions of Secretary Kellogg that would eventually lead to the Kellogg-Briand Pact. FDR felt they could "do no direct harm," but viewed them as "words without deeds" and a cynical preelection attempt to make the nation feel self-righteous by making it think war could be outlawed by "resolution alone." For FDR, the "primary cause for failure in the past has been lack of machinery for the elimination of the causes of disputes before they reach grave proportions. Practical machinery must be erected and be kept in good working order."[101] This was a direct rejection of the nonpolitical nature of Republican foreign policy and its adherence to private corporate solutions.

Second, although FDR acknowledged that membership of the League was impossible, he saw that even without US participation it had become "the principal agency for the settlement of international controversy, for constructive administration of many duties which are primarily international in scope, and for the correction of abuses that have been all too common in our civilization." And that "best of all, it offers a common round table where threats against the peace of the world can be discussed and divergent views compromised." Thus, he argued: "We should cooperate with the League as the first great agency for the maintenance of peace and for the solution of common problems ever known to civilization, and, without entering into European politics, we should take an active, hearty and official part in all those proceedings which bear on the general good of mankind."[102] FDR still firmly believed in political structures as an essential to US security, just as he had in 1919 and 1920. He had long abandoned advocacy of membership of the League in any form, but continued to support political solutions to the world's problems as vital to US security and as an alternative to Republican corporatism and dollar diplomacy.

FDR placed his faith in executive-led government solutions founded on broad democratic principles as his answer to overcoming the problems liberal reformers in the Democratic Party faced with regard to internationalism during the 1920s. He clearly advocated some forms of "entanglements" in world affairs, even if they were not direct political commitments. Shaping this was FDR's long-standing conviction that "Democrats...do not believe in the possibility or the desirability of an isolated national existence or national development heedless of the welfare, prosperity and peace of the other peoples of the world." His definition of progress also still demanded an interest in social justice around the world—recognition that "all the rest of the world is one big family." The United States may not have joined the League, but he still enthused over its "great effectiveness... in many matters which do concern us—international health work, improvement of labor conditions, aid to backward peoples, the improving of education, the clarification of international law, assistance to world trade."[103] This was his liberal creed and a foundation stone of his conception of US security.

Although FDR experienced no fundamental change in his thinking on foreign affairs, the 1920s are still an important decade for the consolidation of his internationalism and development of its presentation. The challenges of polio, Democratic divisions, public opinion, and Republican foreign policy were more important for the way he articulated rather than formed his ideas. The years following Wilson's death and the Democratic defeat in the presidential election of 1924 were particularly important in this respect. In the face of a dominating Republican foreign policy, FDR developed a new clarity, coherence, and energy in his positions on internationalism.

Jefferson was pivotal to the form, but not the substance of FDR's thinking at this time. FDR's Americanism had long contained a Jeffersonian streak and he "rediscovered" it during the 1920s because it worked so well to disguise the Wilsonian origins of much of his internationalism. The intellectual origins of FDR's more idealistic internationalism clearly lay with the twenty-eighth rather than the third president of the United States. Neither was Jefferson the sole rhetorical inspiration for FDR's outlook during the 1920s. Equally important was the neglected figure of Alexander Hamilton who provided FDR with a further critique of Republican foreign policy by enhancing his existing preference for working through executive structures. Both figures represented thinking that had long coexisted in FDR's internationalism—Jefferson just proved the more immediately useful in the political context of the mid-1920s.

FDR still believed that the United States should be involved in the world and that power was not enough to permanently reshape the world and guarantee security. He also still divided the world conceptually into the liberal and nonliberal spheres. Adherence to international law, implementation of disarmament schemes and social justice plans, and belief in self-determination and republican government were indicators of like-minded nations. This was his stated approach and yet the public clearly did not always choose what FDR saw as the right course—mass democracy in the United States had failed in its exclusion of Japanese immigration, its refusal to cancel war debts and in its support for Republican "dollar diplomacy" and corporatism. This was where FDR's faith in the public, his belief in education, the law, "decent respect to the opinions of mankind," and a firm executive-led action came to the fore. The position he refined during the 1920s was more coherent, but was nothing new with its long heritage in the influences and experiences of his earlier life and career.

The significant period when FDR formed important aspects of his prepresidential approach to foreign affairs is clearly located in the period up to 1919–1920. The liberal ideological position he had developed then, which included aspects of Wilsonianism, survived to the late 1920s along with aspects of his earlier outlook and remained with him when he returned to elected office. Throughout the period though FDR had steered clear of difficult economic issues such as the tariff—Wilson's third point of 1918 "the removal, so far as possible, of all economic barriers and the establishment of equality of trade conditions among all nations" had not formed a central pillar of his internationalism thus far. FDR did, however, maintain a political friendship with his future secretary of state and prominent free trader, Cordell Hull, through regular meetings in Washington during the 1920s.[104] Now the United States was moving, along with the rest of the world, into a time of great economic hardship that required a deep understanding of economic issues and a flexible response to the crisis of the Great Depression. Whether FDR's internationalism would survive these challenges as he assumed power, first as the governor of New York and then as president, is the subject of the next chapter.

CHAPTER 6

INTERNATIONALISM, 1928–1933

FDR's SUCCESS IN NEW YORK'S GUBERNATORIAL ELECTION OF 1928 marked his triumphant return to political office. His occupancy of the Governor's mansion in Albany led to a successful reelection campaign in 1930 and opened the way for his equally successful presidential bid in 1932. In place of idle speculation, the media now paid serious attention to this rising star and asked probing questions about his ambitions for higher office. Coming less than a year after FDR's inauguration as governor, however, was a sharp downturn in the worldwide economy that became the Great Depression. This brought untold economic hardship for millions of Americans and people around the world. Inextricably linked to the collapse in the world economy was a heightening of tensions in some areas of the globe. International relations suddenly became increasingly complex, less predictable, and more volatile. The pressures originating from increased public scrutiny of FDR, the appalling economic conditions around the world and the rising potential for armed conflict would provide some of the biggest challenges yet to his position.

The Democratic presidential nomination of 1928 was a poisoned chalice. While the years of Republican economic prosperity continued any Democratic candidate had scant chance of being elected. The Grand Old Party (GOP) had also settled on a strong candidate in Herbert Hoover—a well known and popular man of public affairs. His most recent assignment was secretary of commerce to the Harding and Coolidge administrations, but he had also served in the Wilson administration during World War I. At the Democratic Convention in June, party leaders awarded Al Smith an empty honor by nominating him on the first ballot. Predictably, the election held on November 6 was a landslide for Hoover who had wisely promised little more than policies to continue the economic boom. Smith's candidacy suffered not only under the prevailing positive economic conditions, but many Americans were not prepared to vote for him because he was a catholic and of Irish immigrant stock. Although Smith had a progressive record as a governor, his abrasive New York manner and links to business and Tammany Hall tainted him in the eyes of many—particularly in the Midwest and West. The prejudice displayed also gave the campaign an unpleasant flavor, particularly in the South.

The Republican landslide, however, was not complete—the Democrats managed to win the New York gubernatorial contest with FDR as their candidate. He had been reluctant to take the nomination, preferring to concentrate on his continuing recovery from polio and developing his foundation at Warm Springs. Smith, however, saw Roosevelt as crucial to his attempt to win the contest because of FDR's upstate protestant appeal and persuaded him to stand. Once in the race, FDR embarked on a characteristically active campaign.[1] He praised Smith's progressive program as governor and concentrated on the state issues of social welfare legislation, development of water power, aid to agriculture, and government and law reform. In addition, he attacked the religious bigotry that was damaging Smith's campaign. His personal campaign style proved effective and he managed to narrowly beat his conservative Republican opponent, Albert Ottinger, by 25,000 votes— FDR in his first term jokingly referred to himself as the "one half of one percent Governor."[2]

It was a triumphant return to elective office for FDR who now became a leading Democrat with a clear shot at his presidential nomination. The job of governor of New York was tough in itself. During his first term, FDR would be extremely busy learning his role in addition to dealing with the many challenges and issues of running one of the most populous states with close to 13 million people. With election promises to deliver on and Republican opponents in the state congress determined to undermine him, he more than had his work cut out. Issues such as public ownership of water power, budgets, and Tammany corruption were to stretch him during his time as governor. Increasingly, he also became concerned with issues of public welfare as the Great Depression began to bite. His main focus had to be doing a good enough job to be reelected in 1930, which he achieved with an enormous majority of 725,000, to keep alive any presidential hopes he might have.

The amount of work as governor and his desire to avoid difficult issues that might embarrass a later presidential bid meant that FDR kept his comments on foreign affairs to a minimum. As he said himself in March 1931: "I am just sitting tight, sawing wood, and keeping my mouth shut."[3] FDR largely maintained his existing positions and opposition to Republican foreign policy though he rarely articulated his position. Disarmament was still a concern to him—in 1929, Hoover and his secretary of state, Henry Stimson, wished to reinforce the idealism of the Kellogg-Briand Pact with concrete action and planned another attempt at naval reductions with a conference for 1930. This resulted in the Rapidan Conference between Hoover and British prime minister Ramsay MacDonald in October 1929 and a subsequent conference in London from January to April 1930, but there was little visible progress. FDR, who had previously been critical of Republican lack of planning and machinery to implement agreements in his *Foreign Affairs* article, was probably keenly interested in all these developments. The only comment from him, however, was in a private letter that indicated a frustration at Stimson's failure to curtail the expensive naval building projects to any degree.[4] Any public comment by FDR at this time would have been seen as a virtual announcement of candidacy for president.

Also linked to disarmament was the Nine Power Treaty signed as part of the Washington Naval Conference that aimed to achieve stability in the Far East by respecting Chinese sovereignty, independence, integrity, and the American "open door" policy. FDR had argued in his *Asia* article of 1923 for acceptance of this and for placing trust in Japanese intentions. Indeed, by 1929, no country had yet violated the treaty, though the United States had said nothing on Chinese rights since 1923. The more recent Kellogg-Briand Pact of 1928 in which 56 states solemnly renounced war aimed to reinforce the earlier efforts at Washington. The Pact was enormously popular and had been somewhat forced on Secretary of State Kellogg by popular opinion—proof if it were needed that the public was now an important factor in foreign policy formation. FDR saw nothing wrong with this approach, but took a more realistic view that human nature made it impossible to outlaw war and that therefore the Pact should not constitute the only approach to foreign relations—the important thing for FDR was "not to resolve against war, but to eliminate the causes of war."[5] If FDR had commented he would, no doubt, have taken a similar position on Kellogg's revival of treaties of arbitration and reconciliation in 1927. Hoover continued the policy and drew up 25 treaties of arbitration and 17 treaties of conciliation, not one of which were ever used.

The Republicans continued to advocate membership of the World Court that was promoted in particular by elder statesman Elihu Root. Entrance into the Court had failed in 1926 when the Senate had attached unacceptable reservations to the treaty. Stimson was an admirer of Root and began a new effort to enter the Court in 1929, but was hampered by the complex problems of the underdeveloped state of international law and the question of enforcement. Ultimately, however, it was the fact of the Court's close connection to the League of Nations (a problem that similarly hampered FDR as president) that frustrated US attempts to join. FDR, however, felt on safer ground with a larger degree of bipartisan support for the Court. Writing to Viscount Robert Cecil, a British League delegate, in August 1930, FDR stated: "I hope you realize how important some of us think it is that the general spirit which underlies the League and the World Court should be kept alive."[6] In August 1931, he was even comfortable making a firm declaration when he wrote to the head of the National World Court Committee confirming, "I approve of American membership in the World Court."[7]

Congress and the American people still demanded repayment of European war debts. Stimson, in line with respectable intellectual and elite opinion, would rather solve a thorny problem by writing off the debts, but Hoover refused this suggestion as politically unacceptable. In addition, he steadfastly refused to admit any link between reparations and war debts as this was liable to drag the United States into European politics.[8] The Dawes Plan had tried to avoid this linkage by giving private loans and credits to Germany that enabled them to pay reparations and the Allies then completed the bizarre circular monetary exchange by making war-debt payments back to the United States. By 1929, the Germans were struggling to maintain the scheduled payments and a new plan was drawn up under the name of Owen D. Young, the American industrialist and lawyer, who had coauthored the Dawes Plan. FDR thought the administration was disingenuous for claiming responsibility for what was a private arrangement, but what really bothered him was the ill-feeling the handling of war debts bred toward the United States.[9] In a sensitive position, FDR stuck to his decision and to the advice Howe had given in 1926, namely that the issue was too controversial to focus on.

Following the Federal Reserve's tightening of discount rate in 1927 to halt leveraged stock speculation, loans to Germany began to dry up and this cut off the circular movement of reparations and payment of war debts. In May 1931, the important Credit Anstalt bank in Austria closed its doors but, despite US banks being heavily exposed on private loans to Germany and Austria, Hoover did nothing for virtually a month. On June 20, he finally proposed a one-year moratorium on debt and reparation payments. This failed to achieve financial stability and, after a run on the Bank of England, Great Britain was forced off the Gold Standard that fixed the price of its currency. Not until Hoover extended the moratorium until March 1, 1933, did he finally restore confidence in the European banking system.[10]

Many saw Hoover's intervention as an act of statesmanship. In public FDR said nothing while in private he was critical because it neglected to take account of a large body of nationalist public opinion. In a letter to Senator Joe Robinson in June, he noted that it was the first effort of the present administration to improve world conditions but doubted "whether it will do much to put people back to work all through this country."[11] For a governor of one of the nation's largest states this was a legitimate concern, but it was not his main point of difference. Privately, FDR maintained his criticism of Republican corporatism and lack of direct involvement in the problem. Writing to Josephus Daniels, he stated: "They [the Hoover administration] jumped into this German moratorium business on twenty four hours notice and without previous study just because they were told by the New York bankers that if Germany went into bankruptcy... most of our biggest banks would be seriously embarrassed."[12] It seems, therefore, not so much the involvement that FDR objected to, but the lack of government planning and the reliance on private banks.

The tariff was closely connected to the problem of war debts and reparations because American policies directly affected the world's ability to trade with America and earn the money to pay back loans. Despite previous tariff increases Hoover actually requested a tariff reduction but, against his wishes, the Smoot-Hawley Tariff Act of June 1930 raised the average duty to 59 percent. At the same time that the loans to Germany dried up, the United States erected a high tariff wall that prevented nations earning currency to pay debts. The tariff matched FDR's long-standing critique of "the interests" that ran the Republican Party and he certainly kept his eye on the issue. He wrote to Cordell Hull in May 1929 that he was "more inclined to believe that in 1932 the tariff issue will be more to the front than at any other time since 1892. Our objective should be to get the facts and the Democratic position so clearly before the nation that Republican misstatements and propaganda will come too late to hurt us." Although publicly he remained silent, FDR saw it as an issue with which to hit the Republicans and was happy to let others such as Hull and Jouett Shouse, chairman of the executive committee of the Democratic National Committee (DNC), to "give it the right kind of publicity."[13]

Despite FDR's plans, by 1932, a host of other issues in international affairs were attracting public attention. A growing crisis between Japan and China in the Far East exposed the dangers of "international complications" once more and the ineffectiveness of the League and the treaties signed by world powers during the 1920s. In Europe, the Disarmament Conference that opened in Geneva on February 2, 1932, appeared lame duck because of the Japanese aggression in China and an immediate impasse over French security. The majority of delegates were also the national League representatives that gave the appearance that the United States had actually been brought into a League meeting.[14] This is an important context for a speech made by FDR to the New York Grange in Albany on the same day. These issues combined with the ongoing problem of war-debt payments—Congress had only approved Hoover's moratorium in December on the condition that there was no renegotiation of debts. Isolationists could see real dangers in the darkening international situation, while internationalists felt the only hope was through increased international cooperation. In the fluid political debate, there were dangers for an aspiring presidential candidate.

FDR's silence on many issues was beginning to be noticed by the press. The *New York Times* columnist Arthur Krock had publicly criticized FDR's silence on the moratorium in the summer of 1931. Now Walter Lippmann attacked him at the end of December for failing to state clearly his economic views and noting that "Governor Roosevelt belongs to the new post-war school of politicians who do not believe in stating their views unless and until there is no avoiding it."[15] On New Year's Day 1932, the press magnate William Randolph Hearst made a firmly nationalist speech over the radio in which he denounced the potential candidates FDR, Baker, Young, and Smith as internationalist followers of Wilson and called for a president with a motto of "America First." He then openly declared his support for John Nance Garner as a candidate who was anti-League and strong on the payment of war debts.[16]

As Lippmann had rightly observed, FDR still aimed to keep silent on the issue as long as he could to avoid unnecessarily upsetting potential supporters. He had the example of Newton D. Baker, long seen as heir apparent to Wilson's internationalism, who bungled his candidacy over a botched statement on the League.[17] To head off Hearst's attacks, FDR made his notorious speech to the New York Grange in February 1932 in which he is supposed to have dumped his internationalism for a more pragmatic nationalist approach. The section of his speech that drew most attention was an apparent rejection of the League in which he stated:

> The League has not developed through these years along the course contemplated by its founder…American participation in the League would not serve the highest purpose of the prevention of war and a settlement of international difficulties in accordance with fundamental American ideals. Because of these facts, therefore, I do not favor American participation.[18]

This infuriated Wilsonian internationalists who roundly condemned FDR's comments. Eleanor refused to speak to him for four days and even his old chief, Josephus Daniels, felt the speech had gone entirely too far.[19] Historians have largely agreed with this picture of FDR disowning his internationalism in an act of "political cynicism," of "eating his words," of "selling out his Wilsonian heritage" all to placate Hearst and gain the nomination.[20]

Was FDR's speech really such an act of political cynicism? The rest of the speech is actually remarkable for the clear internationalism it expressed while further nationalist sounding rhetoric is notably absent. FDR opened by noting that the nation's problems were "world-wide in their scope" and "vitally affected…[by] the relationship between this Nation and other nations." He then discussed how the people of New York State were deeply involved in the search for foreign markets and then launched an attack on the Smoot-Hawley Tariff that "stifled" demand for the products of industry and farms. He also called for "reciprocal methods to start the interchange of goods," a statement clearly designed to appeal to internationalist supporters like Cordell Hull and a precursor to FDR's support for the Reciprocal Trade Act of 1934. In addition, FDR made a firm statement of his existing critique of Republican foreign policy. The corporatism underwritten by private bank loans during the 1920s had now "stopped" for "good and obvious reasons." In its place, he proposed a political solution—an unspecified international conference where nations could "put all cards on the table" to break the deadlock that had paralyzed world trade. "By economic cooperation" FDR argued, "this Nation can revive the trade of the world as well as trade within our border."[21] All of this was consistent with the internationalist position FDR had articulated during the 1920s. Neither did it preclude cooperation with the League in its many and varied operations. In FDR's first term, the United States would join the International Labor Organization, attempt to join the World Court, and even propose appointing an ambassador to the League. He also continued to publicly praise its work in health, education, commerce, and dispute resolution demonstrating that there was much he viewed as workable in the League.[22]

The problem facing FDR in early 1932 was that the worsening world situation, particularly in the Far East, was increasing the calls from some Wilsonian internationalists to cooperate with the League in a more direct fashion. FDR, however, had clearly rejected Wilson's notion of collective security many times in 1919 and throughout the decade that followed—most recently in his 1928 *Foreign Affairs* article. Yet up to that point FDR's sometimes opaque language failed to distinguish clearly enough, for many hopeful Wilsonian internationalists, the distinction he saw between his rejection of collective security and support for Wilson's wider liberal internationalist agenda.

The Grange speech provided clarity, but what FDR said was entirely predictable and should not have been such a great surprise. In this light, it is perhaps easier to understand the frustration FDR exhibited at the shocked response of many Wilsonian supporters of the League. In a letter to one, he wrote: "I am looking for the best modern vehicle to reach the goal of an ideal while they insist on a vehicle which was brand new and in good running order twelve years ago. Think it over! And for heaven's sake have a little faith."[23] FDR saw that US relations with the League were once more becoming too closely associated with notions of collective security and this was therefore not a viable route to wider international liberal goals. The speech actually represents an important restatement of his internationalist beliefs prior to the presidential election. The place given to it in FDR mythology by historians has more to do with the disappointed reaction of some Wilsonian internationalists than with FDR's actual oft-stated position.

FDR's speech had its desired effect in the neutralizing of a potentially damaging foreign policy issue. By the opening of the Democratic Convention in Chicago on June 27, 1932, FDR was certainly a favorite. His nomination was by no means a foregone conclusion, however, and was only achieved after four nerve-racking ballots. In the event, foreign policy would not play a huge role in the campaign as both candidates (Hoover was renominated by the Republicans) focused more on domestic issues. In fact, FDR received an assurance from Hoover via Anne O'Hare McCormick that international issues would not be mentioned.[24] FDR, as usual, planned an active campaign focusing on the South, Midwest and West—he had not yet fully realized the growing power of urban immigrant support for the Democrats. Accepting the nomination on July 2 FDR pledged himself and the American people "to a New Deal" based on a "liberal thought, of planned action, of enlightened international outlook, and of the greatest good to the greatest number of our citizens."[25] Throughout the campaign, FDR concentrated on the issues of social welfare and relief contrasted with the "destruction, delay, deceit, despair" of the Republican leadership in desperate conditions.[26] His strategy worked and on November 8, the nation repudiated Hoover's leadership in an electoral landslide of 472 to 56 in the Electoral College and a popular vote of 22,821,277 to 15,761,254.[27]

The question now became one of how FDR's thinking would reflect his position of power. In the Western Hemisphere, Herbert Hoover had made great strides toward improving relations with Latin America. After his election in 1928, he conducted a goodwill tour of Central and South America that lasted until January 1929. The tour was notable because it was Hoover who first used the phrase "Good Neighbor" in a speech on November 26 and made frequent reference to it after that. Linked to this was Hoover's publication in March 1930 of a memorandum produced by undersecretary of state J. Reuben Clark in 1928, who found that the Roosevelt Corollary to the Monroe Doctrine of 1905 (under which the United States claimed the right of intervention to stabilize the affairs of Central American and Caribbean nations) was only applicable in the event of threatened European intervention. While the Clark memo indicated that Coolidge had already considered improving relations with the region, Hoover moved things along by initiating steps to remove the controversial Marine presence from Nicaragua by January 1933 and from Haiti by October 1934. Though FDR made no comment, there is nothing in his previous actions to suggest that he would have disagreed with any of Hoover's moves. Indeed, Hoover's new Latin American policy sounded very much like the "many new principles of a higher law [and] a newer and better standard in international relations" that FDR had called for in his *Foreign Affairs* article.[28]

There was one problem FDR saw with the new policy—on September 30, 1930, Hoover's administration announced a new recognition policy to reflect his noninterference stance. Recognition criteria were now set solely as de facto control of the country, the intention to fulfill international obligations, and the intention to hold elections in due course. With so many revolutions and upheavals in the area, there was a pragmatic element to this approach, but it was also in stark contrast to Wilson's more moralistic approach. On February 6, 1931, Stimson addressed the Council of Foreign Relations defending Hoover's policy and attacking the Wilsonian position of de jure recognition. This was a direct challenge to the views FDR had developed since the 1920 election and, avoiding public comment himself, he suggested that Norman Davis write an article for the July 1931 issue of *Foreign Affairs* critical of Stimson's move. FDR saw de facto recognition as a crucial aspect of Republican "dollar diplomacy" of which he had been so critical in his own *Foreign Affairs* article. It was not so much that FDR advocated enforcing de jure conditions on recognition in Latin America, but rather that de facto recognition was associated with private banking missions that often relied on pliable autocratic regimes and represented some of the worst corporatist excesses of the decade. The policy also unnecessarily restricted US latitude for action in a key strategic area. In a time when intervention was becoming impossible, it remained one of the few ways to influence an unwelcome regime as FDR's controversial 1933 nonrecognition of the Grau administration in Cuba would demonstrate. FDR also evidenced a concern that debate was being closed off by Hoover and Stimson and retained an appreciation of the need for public education. In a letter to Sumner Welles, he noted: "[I]t is a subject that the average citizen knows very little about." These reservations aside, FDR would have been more than happy with the policy. Indeed, it was even incorporated in his inaugural speech as president on March 4, 1933, and was reaffirmed a month later.[29]

As world economic conditions worsened during the Great Depression, pressure also mounted on some governments to seek solutions outside their borders—as with the case of Japan's actions in China. In the months before FDR's announcement of his candidacy for the presidency on January 23, 1932, the situation in the Far East had become increasingly unstable. On the night of September 18, 1931, the Japanese military claimed several stretches of the South Manchurian railway had been destroyed and used this as a pretext for launching a campaign of conquest. In the following months, they swept through Southern Manchuria setting up the "independent" state of Manchukuo in September 1932. In January 1932, the Japanese also launched a fierce separate attack on Shanghai in response to a Chinese economic boycott.

Japanese aggression appeared a clear test case for the Kellogg-Briand Pact and the League of Nations. Secretary Stimson's initial inclination was to cooperate with the League but its resolutions were ignored by the Japanese. This left Stimson wanting to respond more firmly and he hit upon the idea of nonrecognition as a way to make US opinion clear while keeping his options open for further action. Stimson sent his now famous letter to both the Japanese and Chinese on January 7, 1932, detailing what was to become known as the "Stimson Doctrine." This reaffirmed that the United States regarded treaties as sacrosanct and listed them, highlighting particularly the Nine Power Treaty's protection of the open door and China's territorial and administrative integrity and the Kellogg-Briand Pact. Stimson made no mention of implementation of the doctrine, whether by embargo or direct conflict, and at this stage it was essentially a moral position. Stimson sent a further open letter to Senator Borah on February 23, 1932, that strongly affirmed American rights and contained an implicit threat that further aggression might compromise the naval and fortification agreements of the Washington Treaty. Hoover, a Quaker, undermined Stimson's efforts by insisting that the United States would only rely on peaceful means which meant the Japanese simply ignored them.

As with other major international controversies at the time, FDR ignored this one and his position would not become clear until after he won the 1932 election. As he prepared to assume power, FDR had a key meeting with Stimson at Hyde Park on January 9, 1933, and during five hours of discussions appeared to agree with the Hoover administration's policies on the Far East.[30] There were still clearly at least two administration interpretations of the policy though. Hoover viewed it as a moral position and was at pains to prevent any chance of escalation to armed confrontation. Stimson, however, viewed it as the first step to economic sanctions and possible conflict.[31] The distinction is important because some revisionist historians attributed a fateful tone to the meeting at which Stimson convinced FDR to adopt the policies that were to lead directly to the attack on Pearl Harbor nearly a decade later.[32] The implication is that FDR already thought it was too late to appeal to liberal opinion in Japan and head off the inevitable war. Stimson, clearly thinking he had FDR's agreement to maintain his doctrine, told the League that the US policy of nonrecognition would stand and thus set in motion a chain of events that led to Japan leaving the League of Nations on February 24.[33]

Stimson, and historians since, was perhaps unwise in taking FDR's agreement at face value without questioning the basis on which he gave it. The

Stimson Doctrine had proven an acceptable method of communicating displeasure to the Japanese, but would FDR really consider embargo and war as possible consequences at this stage? This seems unlikely given his appreciation of the limitations of power coming out of World War I and his conciliatory stance toward the Japanese during the 1920s. Instead, he probably leaned more toward Hoover's interpretation of the Stimson Doctrine. This offered a rhetorical strategy of nonrecognition based on moral principle without committing to either unilateral or collective intervention. In the absence of concerted international action, the United States was clearly not at the stage where war was a realistic proposition. This approach gave FDR the utmost flexibility while continuing to educate the public on what view they should take toward the Japanese aggression.

Economic problems continued to loom large in world affairs after FDR assumed power and only added to the problems he faced. The New York stock market crash in October 1929 heralded, even if it did not necessarily cause, the start of the Great Depression. The collapsing economy brought a growing army of unemployed in the United States who by 1932 numbered some 11.5 million people out of work with twice that number as dependants. President Hoover had certainly felt he was well informed about economic problems—he viewed the Depression as international in origin and advocated currency stabilization, balanced budgets, and a return to the Gold Standard as the only sensible cure. Realizing that European powers wanted reductions in war debts he hoped to trade this for his proposed cures for the Depression at the forthcoming World Economic Conference scheduled to convene in London. He viewed the interregnum between the election and FDR assuming power on March 4 as a vital time to take the necessary action and begin the long climb out of Depression. To achieve this, he would need the cooperation of FDR—because Hoover was leaving office no government would take his initiatives seriously if proposed alone. With this in mind, on November 12, the president invited FDR to visit him at the White House to discuss war debts and preparations for the London Conference.

Hoover's invitation did two things—first, it surprised FDR and his advisers because such an appeal for cooperation was unheard of between incumbent and president-elect. Second, it forced the FDR team to spend time on the consideration of foreign affairs. While this may not have concerned FDR, it certainly would bother some of his key advisers such as Raymond Moley and Rexford Tugwell who saw the solution to the Depression as the most pressing problem and clearly located its cure in the domestic sphere.[34] FDR, aware of the political implications of discussing such topics with Hoover, agreed to the meeting and opted to take his adviser Raymond Moley with him. The meeting took place at the White House on November 22. A dour Hoover proposed joint appeal to Congress for the reviving of a debt commission that would take coordinated steps on debt, disarmament, and the London Conference. FDR, however, was evasive and the meeting proved inconclusive.

The debt situation continued to deteriorate and on December 15, the French and Polish defaulted on their payments. US banks were beginning to close their doors at an alarming rate as the "Banking Crisis" began to take hold. This prompted Hoover to try again with his idea of a debt commission and on December 17, he sent FDR a lengthy telegram inviting him to select its membership. He also continued to try and link debts to other questions such as disarmament and the London Conference. FDR replied on December 20 again disagreeing that a "permanent economic program for the world" should be linked to questions of disarmament or debts.[35] In addition, FDR requested that any delegate selection be held in abeyance until after March 4 and pointed out disingenuously that he held no authority until that date. Hoover then sent a second conciliatory reply to FDR on the same day asking if FDR would like to send someone like Owen D. Young or Colonel House to sit down with the administration to see what steps could be taken to avoid unnecessary delays, but this was again rejected by FDR.[36] Hoover then released the correspondence to the press in disgust and initiated an undignified series of press releases from the rival camps. Hoover made one last attempt at linkage in a second meeting with FDR on January 20, but the president-elect still managed to evade being tied to Hoover's policy. Exasperated, at this point, Hoover effectively turned debt policy over to the incoming FDR administration.[37]

FDR opposed the president's moves for several reasons. It was tantamount to accepting Hoover's position on war debts that linked them to the international recovery. Linking debts to other complicated European issues would strain the electorate's understanding and frustrate any attempt to elucidate the issues. On Hoover's election in 1928, FDR had observed that the new president lacked a "versatility of mind that can take up one subject after another during the day and find itself equally at home in all of them." [38] Any Republican solution was also sure to centre on the banks rather than government and that went against FDR's belief in political solutions. Visiting FDR in New York on January 10, the French ambassador Paul Claudel reported the president-elect, commenting, "Mr. Hoover has a confidence in commissions and conferences which I do not share...It is much better to speak frankly through friendly conversations on all subjects and with all parties." Stimson also recorded in his diary for January 15 that FDR "was tired" of commissions. Hoover was asking FDR to take responsibility for his policy and at the same time lose any control of it. Unsurprisingly, FDR opted to deal with the debt problem through existing diplomatic channels and refused to accept a commission.[39]

FDR's decision not to link discussion of debts to other policies left his disarmament policy floundering. He remained convinced in the efficacy of political solutions to the world's worsening security problems, but was unable to find a workable solution for disarmament separate from wider issues. When Prime Minister MacDonald proposed consultation among European powers and a reduction in armed forces shortly after FDR's inaugural, the new president leapt at the suggestion offering to relinquish traditional neutral rights and refrain from doing anything that would defeat collective effort.[40] He also renewed his proposal that MacDonald visit the United States to discuss the issue. This was accepted and FDR immediately invited ten other countries, including France, Italy, Germany, and Japan, to similar conferences in Washington. FDR had no specific proposals to make, but the visits during April and May did generate a great deal of publicity and discussion on disarmament that may have been FDR's intention. In this light, FDR made one last appeal calling for the elimination of weapons along the lines of MacDonald's March proposals, augmented by an arms moratorium and a "solemn and definite pact of non-aggression." This fell flat and FDR had to be content with a Four Power Pact of June 7 in which Britain, France, Germany, and Italy would consult on disarmament and peace.[41] FDR's only hope again lay in a future process of discussion that was effectively doomed on October 14 when Germany withdrew from the Conference and the League.

The forthcoming World Economic Conference in London also entertained hopes of a return to international financial stability. FDR's handling of the issue appears, in its display of both nationalist and internationalist elements, erratic and contradictory. The Hoover administration took an internationalist view feeling that the recovery depended on currency stabilization to create the right conditions for private business to lead the recovery. FDR himself said he hoped to get the world back on some form of Gold Standard on April 19 even as the United States left it. With the French and British prime ministers in Washington at that time, FDR's comments led them to believe that he wanted stabilization of the dollar's international exchange rate. Indeed, FDR actually offered the French a Dollar/Pound/Franc stabilization agreement provided the ratio was satisfactory, which they turned down because of inflationary fears.[42] In his second "Fireside chat" to the American public on May 7, FDR emphasized an internationalist line that the "domestic situation is inevitably and deeply tied in with the conditions in all other nations of the world." He then clearly stated that "we seek the setting up of a stabilization of currencies."[43] In his message to the heads of the Nations at Geneva, he argued that the World Economic Conference "must establish order in place of the present chaos by a stabilization of currencies." He later sent the American delegates a memorandum of policy calling for stability as quickly as possible. There was also substantial pressure from abroad for stabilization, of the 66 countries attending all but 2 supported stabilization measures.[44]

This pressure, however, was contrasted with the domestic need to raise prices to halt a speculative drain of gold and inflate the dollar to aid indebted farmers and the depressed domestic economy. At the same time that FDR was articulating an internationalist policy, he was also detailing nationalist concerns. In his inaugural address, he declared that "our international trade relations, though vastly important, are in point of time and necessity secondary to the establishment of a sound national economy." In his "Fireside chat" of May 7, he added that "the administration has the definite objective of raising commodity prices to such an extent that those who have borrowed money will, on the average, be able to repay that money in the same kind of dollar which they borrowed." If FDR's internationalist Secretary of State Cordell Hull needed any indication of the turn of policy, the president gave it with his dropping of the reciprocal trade bill in Congress. When FDR informed Hull on June 7, he only just managed to keep his secretary of state from resigning. As the months passed, FDR began to appreciate the strength of domestic pressure for the raising of prices.[45]

FDR realized he needed to rein in expectations for the London Conference and in May allowed Moley to publish a newspaper column warning against these hopes for the conference. He also tried to limit the conference to eight weeks duration and crucially the general principles of tariff truce, coordination of monetary and fiscal policies for stimulating national economies and improving prices, removal of foreign exchange restrictions, establishment of an adequate and enduring international money standard, gradual abolition of artificial barriers to trade, control of production and distribution of basic commodities. The selection of diverse and nondescript delegates underlined the fact that FDR wanted to keep control of policy at the conference himself.[46] If he could demonstrate the extremes to the electorate they may well be prepared to accept general compromise agreements at the Conference.

The situation became acute when the tripartite stabilization discussions began. Feeling that his advisers were not following his directions sufficiently, FDR decided to send Moley to the conference. Moley's dramatic manner of travel made it appear that he had something new to offer but when he plunged into discussion of foreign exchanges upon his arrival on June 28, it became clear he had nothing in particular to add. At home, the stock market fell dramatically in fear of a disadvantageous stabilization of the dollar and FDR was forced to end discussion of stabilization with his famous "bombshell" message of July 3, which almost put an end to the conference completely. Only the interventions of Cordell Hull kept it limping on for several more weeks after the president's intervention. Moley was not the source of FDR's apparent turn—he was a sound money man who advocated government planning rather than monetary manipulation to raise the general domestic price level. The major influence pushing for a policy of price rising and who was with FDR when he composed his "bombshell" message was Henry Morgenthau.[47]

Morgenthau's influence is not as clear cut as it may first appear. The domestic conditions of the Depression clearly influenced FDR's responses, but the way he couched his rejection of stabilization agreements is also interesting. He attacked the "old fetishes of so called international bankers" and the "specious fallacy of achieving a probably artificial stability in foreign exchange." FDR went on to describe it as a "temporary experiment affecting the monetary exchange of a few nations only" and indicated he preferred measures to "mitigate" the restrictions on world trade and cure "fundamental economic ills."[48] This was a classic example of his antibanking and propolitical critique of Republican foreign policy. FDR probably realized that the direction the Conference was taking was unlikely to conform to his own Democratic principles developed over the last 20 years and so he had little qualms about killing it even though this also appeared a politically nationalist move.

In truth, the tools FDR had at his disposal for alternatives were also extremely limited and using government money as part of a currency stabilization scheme to benefit only a few European countries and, of course, bankers and speculators lacked appeal to his internationalist ideals. The innovative Export-Import Bank did begin to replace private loans in Latin America, but this was on a small experimental scale and it was not until FDR's own recession of 1937–1938 that he would begin to appreciate the power of government finance to prime the national and international economy. This in time led to the World Bank and International Monetary Fund (IMF) set up by the Bretton Woods agreements in 1944 to ensure world financial stability, but this was a long way from FDR's dominant economic experience in 1932 and 1933. Approaches to economic recovery remained overwhelmingly conservative in fiscal terms and offered few alternatives to policy makers. Although FDR's economic moves appeared nationalist, they were as much driven by a rejection of Republican corporatism and in this sense he actually remained true to the internationalist position he had articulated throughout the 1920s.[49]

The pressures of the governorship and the presidential campaign placed enormous demands on FDR's time and constraints on his ability to discuss foreign affairs publicly. The worsening Depression and growing global nationalism also made international affairs much more complicated and interconnected. Despite this, FDR did not dispense with his internationalist position to get elected. Indeed, there is a great deal of continuity between his position during the 1920s and that in 1932 and 1933. Neither did FDR neglect, as it is often suggested, international problems for more important domestic concerns once in the White House. He may well have said on many occasions that the situation at home was more urgent, but this did not translate into the neglect of international sphere. The interregnum and first "Hundred days" were a time when FDR was fully involved and concerned with world problems and consistently pursuing his existing internationalist agenda.

In the background was FDR's deep conviction that the United States could not avoid involvement in the world. He often stated his belief in many speeches throughout 1932 and 1933 that international trade and connections were vital to the United States. Crucially FDR's conception of links with the rest of the world were based on an appreciation of power that realized its limits and he never countenanced collective security or enforcement where the United States did not have clear strategic security interests. FDR believed force alone could not provide a permanent solution to the world's problems and he made this patently clear in both his New York Grange speech of February 1932 and in his agreement with Hoover's pacific interpretation of the Stimson Doctrine. He also made it clear in his support for the International Labor Organization, US representation to the League, and attempts to join the World Court.

In his approach to internationalism, FDR exhibited both similarities and differences with Hoover. FDR's focus on international law and belief in democracy and self-determination against imperialism and militarism was something both men could agree upon. This was a largely educative field with no ultimate commitment to either unilateral or collective enforcement through sanctions or military action. Hoover and FDR differed in their conception of government's role in foreign affairs where FDR maintained his critique of Republican corporatist foreign policy. This was clearly evident in FDR's rejection of aspects of the "Good Neighbor" policy implied by Hoover's de facto recognition policy and in his rejection of currency stabilization attempts at the London Economic Conference. FDR called for political executive-led solutions to world problems. Hoover, in contrast, offered solutions that relegated the government to an advisory capacity in favor of private fronted "corporatist" solutions.

The price FDR paid for this difference was twofold. First, by placing government in a central role he was forced to avoid linking issues as Hoover did because it risked confusing the public. Thus, FDR's educative conception of the democratic process, as demonstrated in his handling of war debts and disarmament, dictated a separate treatment of issues that placed restraint on the policy options available to him. Second, after a decade of private focus by the Republicans, the tools available to government for a lead in international cooperation were quite limited. Political structures existed, but before theories of international economics developed there was little more than rhetoric and Hoover's orthodox approach to promoting world stability. FDR was himself a confirmed fiscal conservative who had criticized Hoover for government deficits he ran and implemented his own retrenchment measures that resulted in the "Roosevelt recession" as late as 1938. FDR's experience to date gave him little, except calls for free trade, to alleviate the increasing economic nationalism around the world that would contribute to so much war by the end of the decade.

FDR's rejection of collective security, his critique of Republican corporatist foreign policy, and his continuing desire for political solutions to the world's problems were fundamental aspects of his approach to international affairs at this time. Viewed through this lens, cynical or nationalist actions by FDR appear instead to be part of a more broadly defined and principled internationalism. His actions were not clear cut, but he was searching for an effective way to remain true to his ideals. His position was deeply rooted in the experiences of his prepresidential life and career that are vital to understanding his foreign policy as president.

CONCLUSION

FDR SO DEFINED THE YEARS OF THE GREAT DEPRESSION and World War II in the United States that when he died on April 12, 1945, the nation experienced a deep sense of shock. Such was his skill at leading the American people through the many challenges and traumas of those years that it was difficult for many Americans to imagine their country without him. A comprehensive interpretation of these pivotal years on the further development of FDR's internationalism is beyond the scope of this study. Yet FDR's position as it stood in 1933 can provide important hints to the directions this development would take. He entered the White House with a clear approach that would help guide his actions as president. His thinking was complex and would continue to develop, but as FDR assumed power it was clear and consistent rather than confused, contradictory, and impossible to fathom.

FDR's precocious awareness of strategic thinking, particularly in relation to the operation of national power (predominantly naval) in a world of rivals, is vital to understanding his early international outlook. National power would continue to form an important base to his thinking throughout his life. In this respect, he was shaped and molded by the influence of Theodore Roosevelt and Alfred Thayer Mahan. Following them, FDR's dominant view prior to World War I was that the United States needed to be able to project military power unilaterally. This theorized a global defense that could meet potential enemies long before they reached the coasts of the United States or brought instability to areas of strategic importance. In a time of increasing global trade it also meant that material interests around the world could be protected by force if necessary. Like TR and Mahan, FDR saw sufficient national power articulated primarily through the battleship as the only sure route to international respect and security. As war erupted in Europe and a series of disturbances occurred in the Western Hemisphere, FDR adhered to this doctrine ever more closely.

Later theorists would categorize FDR's outlook at this time as that of a realist who pictured national forces competing to protect interests. There are, however, important qualifiers to this description. FDR's immersion in traditional Americanism made his international outlook more resistant to the more ideological aspects of TR and Mahan's thinking. There is no evidence, for instance, to suggest that FDR shared Mahan's belief in aggressive economic expansion; his economic thinking at this stage was likely limited to free trade, a low tariff, and the open door. Neither did FDR demonstrate a broader ideological preference for a particular type of civilization as both TR and Mahan did. In his youth there was no demonstrable preference for the British or any other powers and this fact frustrates attempts to explain his presidential actions as driven by an inherent distrust of particular nations originating in his childhood. His position did change, however, when German naval power began to threaten US security in the years before World War I. FDR then quickly began to appreciate the value of British naval power in the Atlantic and see the common ground between the United States and Allies.

FDR's upbringing, education, and religion also meant he rejected the deterministic implications of such a power-based view of the world. He steadfastly maintained an optimistic belief in the ability of humans to influence world affairs. As he entered the political arena for the first time this view became more and more difficult to maintain in the face of seemingly vast impersonal forces driving the world to war. Public opinion and direct involvement in the complex problems of the world as a member of the Wilson administration further challenged his views. In the immediate term, FDR's advocacy of an assertive US foreign policy on the world stage only became exaggerated and more visible. In a series of crisis from Japan, Mexico, and the war in Europe FDR advocated an aggressive response that lacked any degree of sophisticated intellectual justification. His simple strategic calculus perceived only a direct threat to US security from other powers. This was in stark contrast to TR and Wilson at this time. Both were prepared, as evidenced in the case of Japanese tensions in California, to sacrifice domestic political capital for wider global diplomatic trade-offs in the balance of power to protect US interests.

FDR's aggressive calls for military intervention also contrasted with the moral ideological views of TR and Wilson. TR saw the threat to US security from Mexico and Europe, but justified his calls for intervention on the basis of a duty to protect civilization—something FDR never did at this stage. Wilson too pursued a more ideological line in Mexico where he was insistent on the type of regime that should be in power and offered de jure recognition as an alternative to traditional US policy. Wilson also remained steadfastly aloof from the conflict in Europe and refused to take sides, much to FDR's annoyance. Similarly, FDR did not at this point see global or even regional reform as a key to US security. Instead, he supported intervention because of the direct threat posed to the United States by aggressive military powers and the indirect threat of rival power intervention in unstable countries in which the United States held a strategic interest. This remained his private view, however, as public opinion and service in the Wilson administration restricted his ability to articulate it openly. Instead, he chose to promote his concerns indirectly via a concern for preparedness and universal military training.

FDR's impressive early grasp of world geography is also crucial to understanding his early international outlook. The cosmopolitan aspects of his upbringing, particularly his education and extensive European travel, made him aware of the growing interconnectedness of nations. His practical experience of the late nineteenth and early twentieth century revolution in communication and transportation technology made the world seem smaller and less parochial. Important individuals he encountered during his early life augmented this view. At Groton an interest in world affairs was encouraged while TR and Mahan were particularly verbose on US global interests during the period and even Wilson displayed an impressive grasp of geography before and during World War I. This all contributed to FDR's conception of an interconnected world that was only reinforced by the experience of war and his participation in the planning of transatlantic flights by US Navy aircraft in the early postwar years.

Historians have rightly focused on the extraordinarily integrated concept and understanding of the worldwide arena FDR continued to demonstrate as president. His airman's view of an interconnected world, it is said, made him unusual among Americans until at least the end of World War II. Crucially, it is argued, FDR was able to share and communicate his geographically based global understanding to humanity in a way that helped change global perceptions.[1] This world view certainly enabled FDR to picture the interconnections of the strategic conflict during World War II and communicate this to the American public. In the years preceding that conflict it also enabled him to perceive a threat to the US security via land forces from Latin America, from airpower in West Africa, and even from sea should the British Atlantic fleet fall into enemy hands. Indeed, FDR's calls for increased aircraft construction following the Munich Crisis of 1938 was a good indication of his priorities at that time, but would also appear to be part of a much longer term awakening to both the diplomatic and offensive potential of airpower stretching back at least to his experiences during World War I.

Less attention has been given to FDR's understanding of more traditional US geographic nationalism. From the start there were many tensions in his expansive worldview. FDR appreciated that most Americans saw the United States and Western Hemisphere as geographically secure in relation to the rest of the world and he understood their confidence in the limited ability of hostile foreign powers to pursue their ambitions in the region. He also shared their faith in the Monroe Doctrine barring foreign powers from interference in the Western Hemisphere—though in its early years this was arguably a colossal bluff by the United States that relied on the Royal Navy, rather than any ability of the Americans to enforce their will. This did not change by the time he became president as, in the years immediately prior to World War II, the majority of Americans continued to view the Western Hemisphere as immune from attack by an enemy power. Thus, FDR was able to manage the complex interplay of domestic opinion with his own expanded geography of US security. Indeed, it has been suggested that FDR argued for intervention on the basis of a more nationalist defensive realism that saw a threat of continental attack rather than the danger to wider global US interests and values he actually perceived.[2]

FDR's knowledge of the more common American hemispheric perception was highly useful to him as a political leader in overcoming the curious mixture of insecurities and overconfidence existing in the United States during his presidency. This was, of course, nothing new—FDR had been similarly opaque in his public pronouncements during the preparedness debates of 1915–1916. The important point is that it seems problematic to try to understand FDR's hemispheric awareness as purely a product of the significant isolationist opposition he faced prior to US entry into World War II. His prepresidential career clearly demonstrates he had an early and deep appreciation of more parochial geographic concerns and of the complex interplay with his broader global viewpoint.

World War I brought a profound and fundamental change to FDR's international outlook by making the limitations of US power on the world stage fully apparent to him. FDR's early unilateralism broke down in the face of his experience of war. His firm belief in the sole efficacy of national power reeled under a succession of challenges. The development of new weapons such as the submarine and aircraft along with tactical necessities of destroyer warfare undermined his conception of the ultimate projection of US power via the battleship. Much of his existing strategic doctrine effectively became redundant in the face of modern war. As well as robbing him of strategic certainties the conflict also underlined the need to work with other powers, such as the British and French, to achieve security goals—even if they were not always a perfect ideological match. Wilson's perceived failure to achieve a peace based on his Fourteen Points only further underlined the limitations of power and the necessity of dealing with other powers to achieve security goals. Even the United States, in a preponderantly powerful position in Europe, was unable to impose its will at the end of a calamitous war.

Despite this, FDR still maintained a belief in the need for the United States to effectively deploy its military, economic, and diplomatic power when needed to support national security goals. This is clearly demonstrated by his appreciation of Wilson's naval diplomacy with the British during the Versailles negotiations and his similar appreciation of aviation rivalry with Britain later in 1919. Ultimately FDR did not, like Wilson, subscribe to schemes of collective security through moral, economic, diplomatic, political, or even military coercion as the heart of a new peaceful world order. In this respect he was never a true Wilsonian—the reality of powerful nations being able to frustrate US policy with their own ambition was all too apparent to FDR. Throughout the 1920s, although he supported aspects of the League of Nations and its liberal measures, he remained firm in this conviction and restated it on many occasions.

FDR's appreciation of power would certainly have continued to influence his perception of national importance as president. Although he was confident in the strength of the United States to protect its interests, his unusual grasp of the limitations of his nation's capabilities and the effect this had on policy needs further investigation. In his early presidency he maintained that power could be challenged and subverted in many ways. This was clearly evident in his interest in disarmament measures, his acceptance of Hoover's passive interpretation of the Stimson Doctrine and continued rejection of collective security via the League. This is not to say that FDR rejected power entirely—when the United States was strategically threatened he placed a central importance on forming a Grand Alliance during World War II to defeat Germany, Italy, and Japan. Yet a host of issues from the response to German, Italian, and Japanese aggression during the 1930s, to relations with the Soviet Union and plans for Great Power cooperation and order in the postwar world clearly need to be understood in the context of his firm views on the limitations of power.

In his youth, FDR's worldview was also strongly influenced by traditional conceptions of US ideological isolation from the rest of the world. This outlook was cultivated by his family upbringing, education, and interaction with wider American society. For FDR, like many Americans, the United States was set apart from the world, particularly Europe, by its adherence to ideals such as mass democracy, equality, and republican government. This sense of difference directed that the United States should remain aloof from political, diplomatic, and military commitments to the rest of the world. Dangerous entanglements and possible contamination by erroneous ideologies were to be carefully avoided. Though restricted and increasingly suppressed in the years prior to US entry into World War I, there was clearly always a vestigial remnant of this Americanism contained within FDR's international outlook.

The difference FDR's Americanism created in his early international outlook is most evident in his attitude toward imperialism. Witnessing the great debates at the turn of the century FDR rejected, in stark contrast to TR and Mahan, empire in the wider world as a viable policy for his country. Imperial expansion in the Western Hemisphere where the United States had very clear strategic interests, however, appeared unavoidable. This led FDR to justify intervention and imperialism in a way that he saw as consistent with his Americanism. Almost unconsciously, FDR's personal religious notions of "doing the right thing" and of progress under God's plan combined with his ideals of noblesse oblige and appreciation of the secular Enlightenment. He advocated what was, in effect, an imperialism couched in a humanitarian and racial language that emphasized development and progress. Again this was very different to TR and Mahan who eschewed humanitarianism and called for straightforward intervention of the "big-stick" or "dollar diplomacy" variety in areas of perceived strategic importance.

Whereas Wilson, in the years prior and during World War I, moved to a more idealistic stance as a route to world peace, FDR initially demonstrated no interest in this line of thought. He clearly favored a more belligerent stance where he perceived direct threats to US strategic interests, as with Germany in Europe and Japan in California. The war, however, brought a fundamental shift in his international outlook. In an unusually reflective mood resulting from his experiences of war, the discovery by Eleanor of his affair and, perhaps, with his advancing age, FDR saw that something in addition to power was needed to achieve US security. He now became open to a more ideological approach to international relations. Wilson and his approach to the peace through his scheme for the League of Nations played an important part in this awakening. In the absence of much guidance or contact with the president, however, FDR was also influenced by other organizations promoting reform such as the League of Free Nations Association (LFNA) and the more conservative legally orientated League to Enforce Peace (LEP). Over the following months and years FDR became increasingly vocal in calls for schemes of world reform that promoted democracy, self-determination, disarmament, international law, and social justice measures as a vital part of US security.

There are two important qualifiers to this statement. First, FDR, like Wilson, was focused largely on Europe at this point. FDR still applied humanitarianism to other areas of the world where the United States had strategic interests. Second, as discussed above, his appreciation of the limitation of power meant that these were all nonenforceable goals. Thus, he supported liberal reform abroad by example and exhortation and through the practical measures of the League as a vital part of US security, but never ventured into the more defined realms of coercion and collective security. The unilateral or multilateral exercise of power alone was not a route to world stability for FDR. Instead, nations adhering to these "American" standards would, in FDR's mind, be less likely to attack the United States directly or cause external pressures that could subvert both domestic Americanism and schemes for liberal reform. Ultimately FDR did not agree with the forceful coercion of nations in anything other than a direct threat to US security.

This, perhaps, indicates that FDR's experience of World War I was fairly unusual—though he denounced war in general, he remained convinced of the righteousness of the most recent example. He experienced none of the liberal angst or rejection of the war common during the 1920s and 1930s. FDR was therefore able to pay careful attention to the liberal mood during 1919 and instead of being drawn into the destructive League Fight he concentrated on retaining liberal support by reminding them of the wider agenda at stake. In a key speech to the Democratic Party in May 1919, he clearly linked Republican reactionary conservatism at home with similar policies abroad. This served to separate the wider liberal agenda from the League while remaining entirely consistent with his internationalist position.

The practical liberal agenda advocated by FDR got him noticed by the Democratic Party and formed the basis of his 1920 vice presidential election campaign. FDR's position on internationalism was a key reason for his selection by Cox as running mate because he was able to appear close to Wilson and yet talk a language of compromise on the League. The 1920 campaign also exposed FDR's position to intense public and partisan scrutiny. This highlighted some of the problems and contradictions in his new outlook and prompted the globalization of FDR's new liberal approach to world affairs to countries outside Europe. During the campaign, FDR rhetorically extended his 1919 description of the United States as divided between "sane liberal" and "conservative" forces to the wider world. Liberal regimes, for FDR, were now a bulwark against the reactionary, revolutionary, and anarchic alternatives that chose to stay out of the world organization. Not joining the League, he argued, would place the United States with these nations and pose a threat to US security by not encouraging the development of other liberal regimes. It was not, however, until FDR's gaffe regarding Latin American League votes and the Haitian constitution during the campaign that he began to use a specific Wilsoninan-sounding democratic rhetoric with regard to the rest of the world. Thus, it was the failures of Wilson's policies in the Western Hemisphere rather than his successes that provided a final lesson for FDR and prompted a broadening of his liberal agenda on a global basis. In this lay the origins both of his global liberal internationalism and comprehensive anti-imperialism.

As president FDR divided the world rhetorically into liberal and nonliberal spheres. This was evident in his stressing of Jeffersonian mass democracy, his strong animus against imperialism, and his increasing discomfort with totalitarianism. The common explanation for the latter stance was that it was essentially reactive to the Germans and Japanese creating diplomatic links between themselves and threatening to surround the United States with an alternative ideological system. Through his moral interpretation of the Stimson Doctrine, attempts at a moral embargo during the Spanish Civil War, the later Quarantine Address, Four Freedoms, and Atlantic Charter, FDR rhetorically divided the world into the forces of "light and dark" and applied his liberal ideology "everywhere in the world." When war broke out in Europe FDR did not equivocate, as Wilson had done, and did not ask for neutrality in thought or deed—he clearly sided with the Allies even if he did not immediately involve the United States in the conflict. This strong ideological imagery of division continued throughout the war and, it has been suggested, set much of the tone for the Cold War. The global points of division may have been outlined clearly by FDR in the months and years before Pearl Harbor, but much of his language clearly predated any interaction with Japanese and German ambition during the late 1930s. At least some of the origins of FDR's view of a bipolar world can instead be found in the years 1919–1920.

The Great Depression and World War II are seen by historians as a prime driver of change to American liberalism. Americans, it is said, increasingly dropped reform liberalism that focused on broader national and economic interests and replaced it with a concern for rights and freedoms or "rights based" liberalism.[3] This idea has been picked up and developed by a historiography that sees a similar transition due to the Depression and war in US foreign relations.[4] Sunstein identifies an ideological shift shaping public aspirations for freedom from "want," as expressed by FDR in his famous Four Freedoms address of 1941 and developed further in his December 1944 State of the Union Address calling for rights of employment, adequate food, clothing, shelter, education, recreation, and medical care on a world basis. Borgwardt has developed the rights issue and stresses the essential newness of this because of its focus on individual accountability to international law.[5] As Donohue has noted, however, although the war and Depression played a big role, this focus on the individual in liberalism has a much longer heritage dating back to the Civil War representing an accommodation between public and business interests.[6] This accommodation is visible in FDR's early life and career, particularly in his distinction between "sane liberalism" and "reactionary" conservatism in May 1919, his animus toward "dollar diplomacy." While the Depression and war brought these issues into sharp focus for liberals, in FDR's case the developmental chronology has to be pushed back.

Borgwardt also argues for the development of an emphasis on large-scale institutional solutions during the period. These institutions highlighted traditional political and civil rights, economic justice applicable within and across national boundaries through the policy architecture of the UN, IMF, World Bank, and the Nuremburg Trial regime.[7] These international civil and economic rights, it is argued, were an innovative aspect contained within FDR's "Four Freedoms" speech and the Atlantic Charter. FDR's early life again shows precedents—he made repeated pleas throughout the 1920s for an increase in government machinery and executive-led solutions. True these were not envisaged on the scale of the World Bank and IMF, but the propensity was certainly evident. Likewise, his support for legalism and the World Court during the 1920s and 1930s laid some of the foundations for the proposed postwar Nuremburg regime. Finally, self-determination, republican government, and social justice were ideals he began to rhetorically apply on a worldwide basis from 1920—the ability to project an integrated vision of social and economic rights as a function of US domestic and international security was clearly not just a product of the Depression and the New Deal Response or his encounter with polio for that matter. This is not to argue that FDR was entirely responsible for these innovative measures, but his presidency did create an accepting environment for them to flourish.

The approach to politics FDR developed during his early life and career is immensely important to understanding his position on international relations. His upbringing and education firmly cemented American ideals of democracy, equality, and republican government into his outlook. This belief in the virtue of mass democracy became particularly evident when he embarked on a public career. Time and again he demonstrated that he was prepared to compromise firm beliefs on international affairs to protect his own career or build public support for issues he considered important. His dissimulation during the preparedness debate and refusal to articulate the real threat he saw emanating from Germany, his avoidance of war debts as an issue during the 1920s, and his failure to make virtually any public comment on international relations from the late 1920s until he was elected are but a few prominent examples. He was also prepared to push particular issues to legitimate his public position. In his early public career, his patrician background was clearly a handicap and his support for universal military training and preparedness certainly aided his democratic credentials and were quickly discarded by him when no longer useful.

As a natural politician FDR was highly sensitive and responsive to public opinion, but he also learnt from key politicians around him. TR provided a model and route map to power for FDR to follow. He was also immensely popular on a personal level and was an attractive personality to emulate. TR's career, however, had gone off the rails when he left the Republican Party in 1912 and ended in disappointment and his early death in 1919. Wilson in his earlier presidency, of course, provided an important positive example of practical politics for FDR. The president's cooperation with Congress to push through progressive legislation during his first term, his handling of the preparedness issue and his effective strategy to attract votes in the West during the 1916 presidential election deeply impressed FDR. Wilson, however, had ultimately failed at politics in FDR's eyes. The president had built up liberal expectations during the war to a degree that could not be satisfied by the conditions of the eventual peace and badly divided his support. At the same time his rigid position on the League precluded any workable compromise with his opponents. Although FDR did not need a lesson in practical politics, Wilson's tragic demise during the League Fight still underlined the importance of compromise and it remained a powerful image for him throughout his life.

Nevertheless, TR and Wilson were a good source of political imagery for FDR to use in justifying his positions. Throughout FDR's early career there are dangers in taking his Rooseveltian or Wilsonian language as evidence of his true position. On numerous occasions during his early life he appropriated their language to support positions they did not or no longer supported—the same was true during FDR's presidency.[8] FDR may well have sounded like his two illustrious predecessors on many occasions, but he was enormously skilled in draping himself in their rhetorical mantels to garner support for his policies. FDR's 1932 speech to the New York Grange had plenty of Wilsonian rhetoric, but actually revealed FDR's distinct differences with the former president's internationalism over collective security. Similarly, TR was fond of proposing the distinctly unilateral "exercise of international police power" most famously in his 1904 corollary to the Monroe Doctrine to justify unilateral action by the United States in areas where he chose to forcefully secure national interests.[9] FDR found the "police" imagery appealing and the language was filed away in his mind and popped up again from 1942 onward when he began to talk of the "four policeman" as the key to world stability and security.[10] Yet again this was something very different from TR's position—FDR was using the imagery to suggest cooperation with a power whose ideology he knew to be antithetical to that of the United States—TR always saw the world in terms of balance created by the cooperation of like-minded powers. Not only that, FDR was also attempting to integrate the concept with a set of liberal structures that TR would have rejected as a worthless new version of Wilson's League. Clearly, great care is required when suggesting a direct heritage to FDR's positions.

Still, FDR was no egregious politician defined by shallowness and complete lack of principle—he placed clear limits on his reliance on public opinion developed during his early career. Though much of his activity was dissimulation and posturing, it is possible to cut through this to see his true consistent positions and the important points of development. There was an overall progressive-liberal direction to FDR's politics after 1919–1920. During the 1920s FDR devoted considerable time and effort to articulating his thoughts on the failure of Americans to support progressive issues such as the League and their continuing isolationist sentiment. Thus, he recognized there were instances whereby the public could get it wrong and fail in his mind to do the right thing. Yet this did not diminish his confidence in their judgment as it did with important commentators such as Walter Lippmann or H. L. Mencken. FDR saw important restraints on democracy provided by what he called a "decent respect for the opinion of mankind" and the rule of law firmly based in custom. This led to an interpretation of US foreign policy that could respond to world opinion underpinned by international law.

As a further restraint on public opinion FDR also believed firmly in the ongoing education of the public. As president he had an almost instinctive understanding of people that led to an impressive capacity to educate the public and develop support for his policies. His familiar "Fireside chats" and confident use of the press conference were distinctive features of his presidency that had their roots in his painful experiences of polio and the political wilderness during the 1920s. In the international sphere, FDR's attempts at educating public opinion have been explored comprehensively in the period from 1938 when he attempted to pursue more directly internationalist policies. Apart from the educative aim of the "Good Neighbor" policy for rest of world, however, this is a neglected area of investigation for the period 1933–1938.

Public education was clearly important to FDR during the 1920s and the way this approach acted as an inhibitor to his actions as president needs to be understood more clearly. His rejection of linkage between debts and disarmament to wider discussions on economic recovery measures and his keeping open of the Far Eastern question in 1933 suggest that his approach to power itself could sometimes restrain his effective internationalism. His conception of democracy therefore may have some important ramifications for his internationalism during the 1930s. It also raises the interesting question as to whether there were essential differences in his educational approach as president or whether it was purely world conditions that had drastically altered by the late 1930s. By that stage, for instance, he was clearly more experienced in the techniques of public education and was able to plan and mount diplomatic missions for their educative value, in the full knowledge that they would likely fail.[11]

FDR's advocacy of a decent respect for the opinions of mankind and an emphasis on public education had a distinct Jeffersonian ring to them. Using the political image of Thomas Jefferson, FDR argued in the period

after 1925 for a foreign policy directed by mass democracy rather than in
the hands of a privileged few. Yet none of this was intrinsically new and
represented instead a clever Jeffersonian repackaging of his experience and
thought to date. In a review of Claude Bowers' *Jefferson and Hamilton* and
an important article for *Foreign Affairs*, FDR advanced the cause for a
Jeffersonian approach to internationalism, but was really restating many of
the positions he had held from 1919 or even before. Both TR and Wilson
had stressed the education of the public and Wilson had emphasized foreign
policy responsive to world opinion. Thus, the period 1921–1928 brought no
fundamentally new thinking to FDR's internationalism and did not, as has
been suggested, take a Europhobic and nationalist turn at this juncture.

There was a further equally important, though neglected, aspect of
FDR's restraint on democracy that impacted on his internationalism at this
time. From his early experiences FDR was equally drawn to the thought of
Alexander Hamilton on executive government. TR's emphasis and example
of a Hamiltonian executive-led foreign policy was important in this respect.
FDR's outlook owed much to his fifth cousin's vivid demonstration of bold
presidential leadership and personal diplomacy. Wilson too, though slower
in advocating strong executive-led government went on to provide a vivid
example of presidential control of foreign policy. It is also important to
remember just how experienced FDR was in administrative terms. By the
time he became president, FDR had acquired an extraordinarily broad experience—his education, contacts, and extensive career service in the Wilson
administration and as Governor of New York made him one of the most able
executive leaders ever to occupy the White House. He was also president
for an unprecedented 12 years, winning four elections, and he continued to
accumulate useful experience after he assumed power in 1933.

The 1920s were still an important period both personally and in the
way FDR presented his thinking on international relations. The problems
he faced from his attack of polio, the divisions in the Democratic Party,
Wilson's legacy and an astute Republican foreign policy made it difficult for
him to articulate his worldview effectively during this time. This changed
after 1924 with the death of Wilson, another Democratic presidential defeat
and increasing definition in Republican foreign policy that focused FDR's
mind and brought increasing clarity to his ideas. FDR styled his thinking
in terms of Hamiltonian means to achieve Jeffersonian ends. This would
not only act as a further restraint on mass democracy, but was also central to FDR's critique of Republican foreign policy. FDR argued that the
Republican emphasis on a private corporatist approach to international
relations and their neglect of government machinery was anathema to US
security goals because of their reactionary nature. As he returned to elective office this twin Jeffersonian and Hamiltonian critique of Republican

foreign policy remained central to his internationalism and disguised much of its true origins.

FDR's conception of the presidential office could clearly cause problems for US international relations and much of this had its origins in his early career experience. Many historians trace the growth of the imperial presidency, with its extending of executive power way beyond the perceived constitutional limits, to FDR's administration and his foreign policy in particular. His undeclared naval war in the Atlantic prior to American entry into World War II and his authorization of wire taps on isolationist opponents are but a few examples of charges that he overstepped the boundaries of executive power. In much of this, however, he was following the example of TR and Wilson. He ran his own foreign policy, much as they had done, and consequently often neglected the State Department and Cordell Hull. His use of personal envoys in a similar way to Wilson created bitter and destructive rivalries while FDR retained his power to make final decisions. Like his predecessors, FDR's leadership vision was also very much dependent on his personal capabilities—he did not consider his own failings and certainly did not appear to think about the failings of other men. Subsequent presidents in very different times have exposed just how dangerous this level of power can be in office.

FDR's emphasis upon executive government in international relations could also act to restrict his policy options as president in ways that need to be more fully understood. FDR fundamentally opposed Republican foreign policy that was centered on corporatist private banking solutions during the 1920s. Yet FDR's knowledge of alternative government solutions was limited. It was not so much that he rejected internationalist approaches, but that suitable vehicles were not yet available to him. The obvious example is the League of Nations that clearly lacked appeal to the American public. There was, however, for much of his presidency, a large gap between his desire for political solutions to the world's problems and the solutions on the table for a "consumer of ideas" to pick up and use.

This gap seems most evident in the field of economics. It seems somewhat unfair to criticize FDR for failing to embark on currency stabilization measures in 1933, when the only options available to him would have been regional and the very private banking solutions he had railed against throughout the 1920s and during the 1932 election campaign. The Export-Import Bank set up in 1934 to provide finance to foreign governments purchasing US goods was an early attempt at government involvement in wider economic structures, but the really big interventionist schemes did not come about until FDR's own experience of government stimulus during the 1937/38 recession and increased defense spending prior to World War II.[12] The Export-Import Bank is simply not a convincingly large example of government economic involvement on a world scale during the 1930s. The IMF, World Bank and indeed the entire Bretton Woods system were answers provided by others that were not even imagined in the fiscally conservative days of 1933. The evidence of FDR's early life demonstrates an economically unsophisticated man hardly venturing beyond the open door and low tariffs—neither of which were aggressive positions for him. The relationship between FDR's presidential moral stance and the restricted economic solutions available to him is therefore another promising area of investigation.

FDR's position as governor of New York placed great pressures on him as did the worsening Depression and an infinitely more volatile world situation. Although he maintained his position on a string of foreign policy issues in the years to 1931 he rarely commented on them publicly for fear of damaging his presidential ambitions. This did not mean he ditched his international views to get elected. His New York Grange speech of February 1932 was an honest restatement of his position as it had existed for the previous 12 years. FDR was, of course, a politician reluctant to alienate support, but it is disappointed Wilsonian internationalists at the time and since that have given the speech an air of controversy and betrayal rather than FDR's actions. His famous disavowal of the League was necessary because of the threat of Hearst's charges against FDR's candidacy and the risks of being drawn into collective action in the Far East. The speech brought clarity— FDR had long rejected US League membership as a viable means of enforcing a world liberal agenda and was never a supporter of collective security in a pure form.

FDR came to the White House with a well developed and maintained international view. At heart was a duality that valued power and idealism equally. FDR saw the need to forcefully protect US interests across the military, economic, diplomatic, and political spectrum around the globe, but he crucially understood the limitations of US power to do this. In a pluralistic world, security goals could potentially require the cooperation of Allies and the recognition that other nations and peoples had their own ambitions that could frustrate US policy. In FDR's eyes, collective combinations of power did nothing to resolve the underlying problems with power. FDR's liberal idealism was therefore an equally important aspect of his internationalism. His advocacy and emphasis of self-determination and mass democracy restrained by executive-led republican government, education, equality under international law, social justice, disarmament, and a decent respect for the opinions of mankind was, for him, just as vital to US security. This provided the basis for a conceptual division of the world that sought to encourage friendly regimes, but never to enforce adherence unless FDR perceived the threat as direct and immediate.

The internationalist vision that FDR brought to the White House proved a practical and resilient approach to international relations when combined with his superior political understanding and conception of democracy. FDR ultimately believed deeply in his old schoolmaster Peabody's "upward curve of history." Devising a way to keep liberal internationalism on the table, while allowing for the power of alternatives, was to him a large step toward guaranteeing the ultimate triumph of his outlook. Wilson failed to answer the question of how exactly to reconcile Americanism and power as a sound base for stability within a pluralistic world. The question has continued to vex policymakers ever since. Perhaps FDR found at least some of the answers in his appreciation of the limitations of both physical and ideological power stemming from the experiences of his prepresidential life and career.

NOTES

INTRODUCTION

1. Robert Murray and Tim H. Blessing, "The Presidential Performance Study: A Progress Report," *Journal of American History* 70, No. 3 (1983), 542 place him second behind Lincoln. A more recent poll of presidential historians and "professional observers of the presidency" by the C-SPAN organization in 2009 placed FDR third behind Lincoln and Washington. See http://www.c-span. org/presidentialsurvey/overall-ranking.aspx, accessed on April 2, 2010.
2. Charles Beard, *American Foreign Policy in the Making, 1932–1940: A Study in Responsibilities* (New Haven, CT, 1946), 43–46; and Charles Tansill, *Back Door to War: The Roosevelt Foreign Policy, 1933–1941* (Chicago, 1952), 558–583 and 616–652.
3. An early defense of FDR's internationalism was William L. Langer and S. Everett Gleason, *The Challenge to Isolation, 1937–1940* (New York, 1952) and *The Undeclared War, 1940–1941* (New York, 1953); Frederick W. Marks III, *Wind Over Sand: The Diplomacy of Franklin Roosevelt* (Athens, GA, 1988) is a damning critique of a president guided by domestic considerations.
4. Robert A. Divine, *The Reluctant Belligerent: American Entry Into World War II* (2nd edn., New York, 1972). Sympathetic to the prevailing conditions FDR faced is Robert Dallek's comprehensive volume *Franklin D. Roosevelt and American Foreign Policy, 1932–1945* (Oxford, 1979). For the nationalist interpretation, see John Lamberton Harper, *American Visions of Europe: Franklin D. Roosevelt, George F. Kennan, and Dean G. Acheson* (Cambridge, 1994), 7–131; and Fraser J. Harbutt, *Yalta 1945: Europe at the Crossroads* (Cambridge, 2010), 225–279.
5. Michael H. Hunt, *Ideology and U.S. Foreign Policy* (New Haven, CT, 1987), xi and 17–18.
6. Frances Perkins, *The Roosevelt I Knew* (London, 1948), 17–19; and Robert Sherwood, *Roosevelt and Hopkins—An Intimate History* (New York, 1950), 179. The three key early attempts to search for FDR's overarching philosophy were Thomas H. Greer, *What Roosevelt Thought: The Social and Political Ideas of Franklin D. Roosevelt* (reprint edn., East Lansing, MI, 2000); Daniel R. Fusfeld, *The Economic Thought of Franklin D. Roosevelt and the Origins of the New Deal*

(New York, 1956); and Willard Range, *Franklin D. Roosevelt's World Order* (Athens, GA, 1956).

7. The clearest interpretation of FDR as an eventual Wilsonian internationalist is Robert A. Divine, *Second Chance: The Triumph of Internationalism during World War II* (New York, 1967).

8. John Milton Cooper, Jr., *The Warrior and the Priest—Woodrow Wilson and Theodore Roosevelt* (Cambridge, MA, 1983), 359. On FDR's conception of geo-politics as an expanded geography of US security, see David Reynolds, *From Munich to Pearl Harbor: Roosevelt's America and the Origins of the Second World War* (Chicago, 2001), 4.

9. Warren F. Kimball, "This Persistent Evangel of Americanism," in Warren F. Kimball, *The Juggler--Franklin Roosevelt as Wartime Statesman* (Princeton, NJ, 1991), 186; Harper, *American Visions*, 32; Arthur M. Schlesinger, Jr., "Franklin D. Roosevelt's Internationalism," in Cornelis A. Van Minnen and John F. Sears (eds.), *FDR and his Contemporaries—Foreign Perceptions of an American President* (New York, 1992), 7.

10. Kimball, "Persistent Evangel," 271–272.

11. The fascinating linguistic approaches suggested by Hayden White in *Metahistory: The Historical Imagination in Nineteenth-Century Europe* (Baltimore, MD, 1973) and by Quentin Skinner in *Visions of Politics Volume One—Regarding Method* (Cambridge, 2002) are beyond the scope of this present study.

12. Frances Perkins, *Roosevelt*, 9. At least one biographer has felt compelled to dis-cuss the complexity of FDR. See Kenneth S. Davis, "FDR as a Biographer's Problem," *American Scholar* 52 (Winter, 1983/84), 100–108.

1   A Patrician Internationalist, 1882–1910

1. FDR, "Resolved, that Hawaii be promptly annexed" in Elliott Roosevelt (ed.), *The Roosevelt Letters I* (London, 1949), 150 and 152 (hereafter *PL*).

2. Alan K. Henrikson, "FDR and the World-Wide Arena," in David B. Woolner, Warren F. Kimball, and David Reynolds (eds.), *FDR's World: War, Peace, and Legacies* (New York, 2008), 35.

3. FDR participated in six known debates at Groton covering the Nicaraguan Canal Bill, the annexation of Hawaii, Naval expansion, the integrity of China, the Philippine question and the Transvaal. See FDR to Sara and James Roosevelt February 28, 1897; March 11, 1897; January 19, 1898; February 28, 1899; and January 23, 1900, in *PL I*, 74, 77, 240, and 328–329.

4. Christopher Endy, "Travel and World Power: Americans in Europe, 1890–1917," *Diplomatic History*, 22, No. 4 (1998), 565–594.

5. Isabel Leighton and Gabrielle Forbrush, *My Boy Franklin as Told by Mrs James Roosevelt* (New York, 1933), 33.

6. *PL II*, 156.

7. William McKinley, "Last Public Speech," September 5, 1901, (Buffalo, NY). available on: http://www. presidency.ucsb.edu, accessed on February 25, 2012.

8. FDR to Sara Roosevelt March 4, 1897; March 11, 1897; and March 24, 1897, in *PL I*, 75, 77, and 82.

9. James McLachlan, *American Boarding Schools—A Historical Study* (New York, 1970), 259 and 293.

10. Leighton and Forbrush, *My Boy*, 15.

11. FDR to Sara Roosevelt October 26, 1902, in *PL I*, 414–415.

12. As detailed by fellow clerk Grenville Clark in Kenneth S. Davis, *FDR: The Beckoning of Destiny 1882–1928* (New York, 1971), 214.

13. FDR and ER to Sara Roosevelt September 7, 1905, in *PL II*, 78 and 82.

14. For a direct quotation of Carlyle, see FDR "Campaign speech for State Senate, Oct 1910," in *PL II*, 139.

15. FDR to Sara and James Roosevelt May 16, 1899, in *PL I*, 271.

16. FDR to Sara Roosevelt June 11, 1905, and Eleanor Roosevelt to Sara Roosevelt June 13, 1905, in *PL II*, 22–24.

17. Masuda Hajimu, "Rumors of War: Immigration Disputes and the Social Construction of American-Japanese Relations 1905–1913," *Diplomatic History* 33, No. 1 (2009), 22.

18. Kristin L. Hoganson, *Fighting for American Manhood: How Gender Politics Provoked the Spanish American and Philippine Wars* (New Haven, CT, 1998), 10–12 and 22–24.

19. Frank Freidel, *Franklin D. Roosevelt—The Apprenticeship* (Boston, MA, 1952), 158.

20. For FDR's meetings with TR, see FDR to Sara and James Roosevelt June 4, 1897; June 11, 1897; and Apr. 30, 1901, in *PL I*, 108, 111–112 and 394–395. For his mildly critical attitude to TR, see FDR to Sara and James Roosevelt October 26, 1898, in *PL I*, 202 and FDR to Sara Roosevelt October 26, 1902, in *PL I*, 414.

21. FDR quoted in Freidel, *Apprenticeship*, 35.

22. Michael Adams, *The Great Adventure: Male Desire and the Coming of World War I* (Bloomington, IN, 1990), 10, 65, 69, and 82.

23. FDR to Sara and James Roosevelt October 23, 1900, in *PL I*, 371. On the embarrassment Taddy caused FDR at Groton, see Geoffrey C. Ward, *Before the Trumpet—Young Franklin Roosevelt 1882–1905* (New York, 1985), 195.

24. Ward, *Trumpet*, 251.

25. On FDR's difficulties with acceptance at Groton, see Ward, *Trumpet*, 91 and Davis, *Beckoning of Destiny*, 103. For his desire for school spirit, see FDR to Sara and James Roosevelt May 14, 1897, in *PL I*, 97.

26. Ward, *Trumpet*, 236.

27. Endy, "Travel and World Power," 571.

28. Frank Ninkovich, "Theodore Roosevelt: Civilization as Ideology," *Diplomatic History* 10, No. 3 (1986), 221–245.

29. As David Haglund argues in "Roosevelt as Friend of France—But Which One?" *Diplomatic History* 31, No. 5 (2007), 890.

30. This was Sara Roosevelt's sister Deborah Forbes and FDR's "Aunt Doe." See note in *PL II*, 30 and extended discussion of FDR and Eleanor's honeymoon in Paris 29–33 and 65–76.

31. FDR to Sara Roosevelt June 26, 1905, and FDR to Sara Roosevelt August 1, 1905, in *PL II*, 32 and 59, See also ER to Sara Roosevelt July 25, 1905, in *PL II*, 52.

32. For English aristocratic contacts, see John Lamberton Harper, *American Visions of Europe: Franklin D. Roosevelt, George F. Kennan, and Dean G Acheson* (Cambridge, 1994), 19. On the *Illustrated London News,* see FDR to Sara and James Roosevelt September 21, 1896, in *PL I*, 50. For *Punch,* see FDR to Sara and James Roosevelt May 21, 1897, and for the *Spectator,* see FDR to Sara and James Roosevelt February 9, 1899, and May 24, 1899, in *PL I*, 100, 230, and 275.

33. FDR to Sara and James Roosevelt May 26, 1899; February 9, 1899; and May 24, 1899, in *PL I*, 277, 230, and 275.

34. FDR to Sara and James Roosevelt September 21, 1896, and December 5, 1897, in *PL I*, 50 and 138.

35. McLachlan, *American Schools,* 261–265 and 267.

36. FDR "Memorandum for Steve" October 19, 1939, in *PL III*, 282.

37. Harper, *American Visions,* 20–23.

38. Ward, *Trumpet,* 17 and 67.

39. Geoffrey C. Ward, *A First Class Temperament—The Emergence of Franklin Roosevelt* (New York, 1989), 173–174.

40. Thomas G. Dyer, *Theodore Roosevelt and the Idea of Race* (Baton Rouge, LA, 1980), 6–7 and 67 for TR's gradual dropping of the Anglo-Saxon ideal.

41. FDR "Address to People's Forum" Troy, New York, March 3, 1912. Master Speech File (hereafter MSF) Box 1 Fl 1, Franklin Delano Roosevelt Library, Hyde Park, New York (hereafter FDRL).

42. Harper, *American Visions,* 27 and Casey "Franklin D. Roosevelt," in Steven Casey and Jonathan Wright (eds.), *Mental Maps in the Era of the Two World Wars* (Basingstoke, 2008), 222. For the English Speaking Union, see http://www.esuus.org, accessed on March 5, 2010.

43. FDR to Sara and James Roosevelt November 10, 1899, in *PL I*, 311.

44. Sara Roosevelt quoted in Harper, *American Visions,* 26. For FDR response, see FDR to Sara and James Roosevelt January 21, 1900, in *PL I*, 328 and FDR to Sara and James Roosevelt January 11, 1900, in *PL I*, 324.

45. On the fund, see Ward, *Trumpet,* 231–232; Freidel, *Apprenticeship,* 60; Harper, *American Visions,* 26–27. On FDR's sending the money to TR, see Howard K. Beale, *Theodore Roosevelt and the Rise of America to World Power* (Baltimore, MD, 1953), 95.

46. Beale, *Rise of America,* 22–37.

47. FDR "Resolved, that Hawaii be promptly annexed," January 19, 1898, in *PL I*, 150–153.

48. FDR to Sara and James Roosevelt January 23, 1900, in *PL I*, 328–329.

49. FDR to Sara and James Roosevelt February 1, 1900, in *PL I*, 331.

50. Leighton and Forbrush, *My Boy,* 4.

51. FDR "The Roosevelt Family in New Amsterdam" Dec 1901 in Papers Pertaining to Family, Business and Personal File (hereafter PFBP) Box 18, FDRL.

52. FDR to Sara and James Roosevelt June 4, 1897, in *PL I*, 108. For the visit of Jacob Riis to Groton, see FDR to Sara and James Roosevelt January 23, 1900, in *PL I*, 328–329.

53. Quoted in William Leuchtenburg, *The FDR Years: On FDR and his Legacy* (New York, 1995), 2.
54. Raymond Moley, *After Seven Years* (New York, 1939), 376.
55. *PL I*, 46.
56. McLachlan, *American Schools*, 288 and Axel Bundgaard, *Muscle and Manliness: The Rise of Sport in American Boarding Schools* (Syracuse, NY, 2005), 119. Freidel describes Kingsley as the "lodestar" of Groton. See Freidel, *Apprenticeship*, 38.
57. Conrad Black, *Franklin Delano Roosevelt: Champion of Freedom* (London, 2003), 16.
58. FDR to Sara and James Roosevelt December 4, 1898, in *PL I*, 213–214; FDR to Sara and James Roosevelt January 29, 1899, in *PL I*, 224–226.
59. Leighton and Forbrush, *My Boy*, 15.
60. Ernest K. Lindley, Franklin D. Roosevelt—A Career In Progressive Democracy (New York, 1931), 323; See also Thomas H Greer, *What Roosevelt Thought— The Social and Political Ideas of Franklin D. Roosevelt* (East Lansing, MI, 2000), 101–102.
61. Davis, *The Beckoning of Destiny*, (New York, 1971), 87–88
62. Franklin D. Roosevelt, *Whither Bound?* (New York, 1926), 6–7. Elliott Roosevelt's comments are in *PL II*, 429–434; FDR "Montcalm's Victory and Its Lessons," Speech at Osewego, New York September 30, 1913. MSF Box 1, Fl 24, FDRL.
63. FR to Sara Roosevelt January 3, 1919, in *PL II*, 355.
64. James T. Kloppenberg, *Uncertain Victory—Social Democracy and Progressivism in European and American Thought, 1870–1920* (Oxford, 1986), 107–114.
65. Daniel R. Fusfeld, *The Economic Thought of Franklin D. Roosevelt and the Origins of the New Deal* (New York, 1956), 17–18, 23, and 32–37.
66. Arthur M. Schlesinger Jr. *The Age of Roosevelt: The Coming of the New Deal, 1933–1935* (New York, 1958), 14; Conrad Black, *Franklin Delano Roosevelt: Champion of Freedom* (London, 2003), 275–276, notes that it is unclear whether Holmes was referring to FDR or TR, but is overly defensive of his subject. FDR had met Holmes many times from as early as 1913 and visited the latter's house for his famous Sunday afternoon gatherings during World War I.
67. Fusfeld, *Economic Thought*, 17–18.
68. FDR "Resolved, that Hawaii be promptly annexed," January 19, 1898, in *PL I*, 151.
69. Emily S. Rosenberg, *Spreading the American Dream—American Economic and Cultural Expansion 1890–1945* (New York, 1982), 7. On the "glut" thesis, see also 39–40.
70. FDR to Sara and James Roosevelt February 17, 1898, in *PL I*, 163.
71. FDR to Sara and James Roosevelt April 8, 1898, in *PL I*, 175.
72. Hoganson, *Fighting for American Manhood*, Chapter 4 "McKinley's Backbone," 88–105.
73. FDR to Sara and James Roosevelt April 20, 1898, in *PL I*, 182.
74. FDR to Sara and James Roosevelt April 22, 1898, and April 24, 1898, in *PL I*, 183–184. For the perhaps apocryphal enlistment tale, see note on 186.

75. FDR to Sara and James Roosevelt January 29, 1899, in *PL I*, 225; FDR to Sara and James Roosevelt February 28, 1897, in *PL I*, 74.

76. Theodore Roosevelt Annual Address December 6, 1904, available on: http://www.presidency.ucsb.edu, accessed on February 25, 2012.

77. "Gov. Roosevelt in Chicago," *New York Times*, April 11, 1899, 3.

78. Rita Halle Kleeman, *Gracious Lady: The Life of Sara Delano Roosevelt* (New York, 1935), 190; Jonathan Daniels "Franklin Roosevelt and Books," in Daniels et al., *Three Presidents and Their Books—Jefferson, Lincoln and F.D. Roosevelt* (Urbana, IL, 1955), 93; McLachlan, *American Schools*, 276.

2 The Challenges of Public Office, 1910–1917

1. John M. Blum, *The Republican Roosevelt* (Cambridge, MA, 1954), 6. See also Geoffrey C. Ward, *Before the Trumpet—Young Franklin Roosevelt* (New York, 1985), 19.

2. Rita Halle Kleeman, *Gracious Lady: The Life of Sara Delano Roosevelt* (New York, 1935), 253.

3. Geoffrey C. Ward, *A First Class Temperament—The Emergence of Franklin Roosevelt* (New York, 1989), 88–89.

4. *PL II*, 138.

5. Julie M. Fenster, *FDR's Shadow—Louis Howe, The Force That Shaped Franklin and Eleanor Roosevelt* (New York, 2009), 184. Frances Perkins also described graduation from Harvard as "a political handicap." Frances Perkins, *The Roosevelt I Knew* (New York, 1946), 14.

6. FDR to Josephus Daniels February 16, 1916, in Carroll Kilpatrick (ed.), *Roosevelt and Daniels—A Friendship in Politics* (Chapel Hill, NC, 1952), 25.

7. Ronald H. Spector "Josephus Daniels, Franklin Roosevelt, and the Reinvention of the Naval Enlisted Man," in Edward J. Marolda (ed.), *FDR and the United States Navy* (New York, 1998), 19–33.

8. FDR to Sara and James Roosevelt October 31, 1900, in *PL I*, 372. On the Delano side of FDR's family Warren Delano II (his grandfather) was an implacable Republican as was FDR's mother and his wife Eleanor initially; Ward, *Trumpet*, 63 and 338.

9. Ward, *Trumpet*, 256; See FDR to Sara Roosevelt November 6, 1903, in *PL I*, 440.

10. Frank Freidel, *Franklin D. Roosevelt—The Apprenticeship* (Boston, MA, 1952), 94. FDR had both Federalist and Whigs in his ancestry on the Roosevelt side. See Ward. *Before the Trumpet*, 17–19.

11. James MacGregor Burns, *Roosevelt: The Lion and the Fox* (New York, 1956), 25.

12. David Sarasohn, *The Party of Reform: Democrats in the Progressive Era* (Jackson, MS, 1989).

13. John Milton Cooper Jr., *The Warrior and the Priest: Woodrow Wilson and Theodore Roosevelt* (Cambridge, MA, 1983), 161; and Daniel D. Stid, *The President as Statesman—Woodrow Wilson and the Constitution* (Lawrence, KS, 1998), 52.

14. For Daniels' account see his diary entry for March 6, 1913, E. David Cronin (ed.), *The Cabinet Diaries of Josephus Daniels 1913–1921* (Lincoln, 1963), 4.

15. Perkins, *Roosevelt*, 13.

16. Fenster, *FDR's Shadow*, 185.

17. John Lamberton Harper, *American Visions of Europe: Franklin D. Roosevelt, George F. Kennan, and Dean G. Acheson* (Cambridge, 1994), 33–34 quoting Jonathan Daniels.

18. Fenster, *FDR's Shadow*, 184.

19. FDR Speech "The Future of Our Navy," January 30, 1915, MSF, Box 1, Fl 42, FDRL. See also his 1914 article quoted in Ernest K. Lindley, *Franklin D. Roosevelt—A Career in Progressive Democracy* (New York, 1931), 120; and FDR's "Proposed article on the United States Navy/Possible speech before Order of Washington," February 22, 1917, Publications File (hereafter PF) Box 40, Fl 135, FDRL.

20. Wilson "An Address in Mobile, Alabama," in Arthur S. Link (ed.), *The Papers of Woodrow Wilson* (hereafter *PWW*) 28, 449.

21. FDR Speech "The Future of Our Navy," January 30, 1915, MSF, Box 1, Fl 42, FDRL; and FDR "The Cost of the United States Navy," *Economic World* 10 (September 4, 1915), 299–303. On the fleet, see FDR "Proposed article on the United States Navy/Possible speech before Order of Washington," February 22, 1917, PF Box 40, Fl 135, FDRL.

22. FDR Speech "The Future of Our Navy," January 30, 1915, MSF, Box 1, Fl 42, FDRL.

23. FDR, "On Your Own Heads," *Scribner's Magazine* 61 (April 1917), 414; FDR, "Our Navy Blind," *Boston Daily Advertiser* September 29, 1915, in Assistant Secretary of the Navy Papers (hereafter ASNP), Box 86 Scrapbook, FDRL. The Chinese wall theme was TR's—see his "Strenuous Life" speech "Gov. Roosevelt in Chicago," *New York Times* April 11, 1899, 3.

24. Theodore Roosevelt, *America and the World War* (London, 1915), 159.

25. FDR had visited the canal construction in April 1912, see FDR to SR April 22, 1912, in *PL II*, 162. On the exposition, see FDR to ER July 19, 1914, in *PL II*, 192–193.

26. Lindley, *Progressive Democracy*, 120.

27. *Flushing Times* December 22, 1915, quoted in Freidel, *Apprenticeship*, 260.

28. FDR "Proposed article on the United States Navy/Possible speech before Order of Washington" February 22, 1917, PF Box 40, Fl 135, FDRL.

29. Masuda Hajima, "Rumors of War: Immigration Disputes and the Social Construction of American-Japanese Relations, 1905–1913," *Diplomatic History* 33, No. 1 (2009), 23.

30. TR to FDR May 10, 1913, in Elting E. Morrison, John M. Blum, and John J. Buckley (eds.), *Letters of Theodore Roosevelt Vol VII* (Cambridge, MA, 1954), 729. See also the FDR correspondence with Mahan in ASNP Box 53 and with TR in ASNP Box 58, FDRL.

31. See FDR's account in FDR to Mahan June 16, 1914, ASNP Box 53, FDRL.

32. *Los Angeles Examiner* May 26, 1913, quoted in Freidel, *Apprenticeship*, 226.

33. See Woodrow Wilson Annual Address December 2, 1913, available on http://www.presidency.ucsb.edu, accessed on February 25, 2012.

34. FDR to SR July 29, 1913, in *PL II*, 176.

35. "The Sound of Laughter and of Playing Children has been Stilled in Mexico," in Theodore Roosevelt, *Fear Good and Take Your Own Part* (New York, 1916), 231–283.

36. *Milwaukee Sentinel* April 27, 1914, quoted in Freidel, *Apprenticeship*, 232. See also Ward, *Temperament*, 242.

37. FDR to ER July 7, 1916, in *PL II*, 248.

38. Woodrow Wilson "First Annual Message," December 2, 1913, available on http://www.presidency.ucsb.edu, accessed on February 25, 2012.

39. FDR to ER July 14, 1914, in *PL II*, 188; FDR to SR July 18, 1914 in *PL II*, 191; and FDR to ER July 19, 1914 in *PL II*, 192.

40. FDR Speech "The Future of Our Navy," January 30, 1915, MSF, Box 1, Fl 42, FDRL for the first public appearance of the tale. See also note in *PL II*, 189–190; and Ward, *Temperament*, 244.

41. FDR to Daniels August 7, 1915, in Kilpatrick, *Roosevelt and Daniels*, 23.

42. David Healy, *Gunboat Diplomacy in the Wilson Era—The U.S. Navy in Haiti, 1915–1916* (Madison, WI, 1976), 134–135 and 117 on Daniels as "King."

43. FDR to ER August 28, 1915, in *PL II*, 236. See also FDR to SR August 29, 1915, in *PL II*, 236–237.

44. FDR "Trip to Haiti and Santo Domingo 1917" (undated) and Livingston Davis "Log of the Trip to Haiti and Santo Domingo," February 15, 1917, ASNP Box 41, FDRL.

45. Woodrow Wilson "An Address in Mobile, Alabama," *PWW* 28, 451, and 448.

46. FDR to ER August 25, 1915, *PL II*, 235.

47. FDR "Trip to Haiti and Santo Domingo 1917" (undated) ASNP Box 41, FDRL.

48. FDR "Proposed Article on Haiti" (circa 1916) PF Box 40, FDRL.

49. FDR "Trip to Haiti and Santo Domingo 1917" (undated) ASNP Box 41, FDRL.

50. *PWW* 36, 7–122.

51. FDR "Proposed Speech on Navy in Foreign Policy" May 19, 1916, MSF Box 40, FDRL.

52. Wilson "Address in Washington to the League to Enforce Peace," in *PWW* 37, 113–116; Wilson's campaign addresses are in *PWW* 38, 127–615; Wilson "An Address to the Senate," January 22, 1917, *PWW* 40, 533–539.

53. Link, *Wilson*, 177 on Gardner's involvement; and Ward, *Temperament*, 301–302 for FDR's part.

54. FDR to Daniels August 3, 1915, in Kilpatrick *Roosevelt and Daniels*, 21–22.

55. TR to FDR May 26, 1916, and FDR to TR June 7, 1916, ASNP Box 58, FDRL.

56. FDR to ER August 1, 1914, in *PL II*, 195; FDR to ER August 2, 1914, in *PL II*, 198; FDR to ER August 5, 1914, in *PL II*, 202; and FDR to ER November 9, 1916, in *PL II*, 274.

57. FDR to ER May 20, 1915, in *PL II*, 221.

58. FDR to A. P. Gardner November 25, 1914, ASNP Box 14, FDRL; and FDR to SR December 17, 1914, *PL II*, 215.

59. FDR "Dutchess County Society Dinner," January 17, 1914, MSF Box 1, Fl 26, FDRL.

60. FDR "The Navy Program and What It Means," *The Nations Business* III, No. 12 (1915), 8–9.

61. FDR Speech "The Privilege of National Service," December 3, 1916, MSF Box 1, FDRL.

62. *Poughkeepsie Evening Enterprise* April 8, 1913, PF Box 39, FDRL.

63. FDR "Relation of Navy to Farmer," September 7, 1916, PF Box 40, FDRL. On universal training, see FDR Speech "The Privilege of National Service," December 3, 1916, MSF Box 1, FDRL.

64. FDR "Safeguarding the Sailors Ashore," *Association Men* 41 (Jan, 1916), 7.

65. FDR to ER July 7, 1916, in *PL II*, 248; and FDR to ER July 19, 1916, in *PL II*, 251.

66. Woodrow Wilson "An Address to the League to Enforce Peace," May 27, 1916, in *PWW* 37, 113–116.

67. FDR to ER August 2, 1914, in *PL II*, 200.

68. FDR to ER August 7, 19 14, in *PL II*, 204.

69. FDR, "The Cost of the United States Navy," *Economic World* 10 (September 2, 1915), 299–303. Also his discussion of the "Kretschmer Formula" for naval comparison in his testimony before the Committee on Naval Affairs of the House of Representatives December 16, 1914. *Congressional Record*, FDRL.

70. FDR to ER August 7, 1914, in *PL II*, 204. See also FDR to ER August 10, 1914, in *PL II*, 207

71. Ward, *Temperament*, 299.

72. TR, *Outlook* 107 (August 22, 1914) quoted in Cooper, *Warrior and the Priest*, 277.

73. Roosevelt, *America and the Great War*, 15–43.

74. FDR, "Our Navy Blind," *Boston Daily Advertiser* September 29, 1915, ASNP, Box 86 Scrapbook, FDRL.

75. FDR to ER August 2, 1914, in *PL II*, 199.

76. FDR Speech "The Future of Our Navy," January 30, 1915, MSF, Box 1, Fl 42, FDRL. See also FDR Speech at Vassar Institute January 4, 1916 (clipping Poughkeepsie *Evening Enterprise* January 5, 1916), MSF Box 1, Fl 150, FDRL; and FDR "Address in Washington" November 15, 1915, MSF Box 1, Fl 45, FDRL.

77. *San Francisco Chronicle*, April 16, 1914, quoted in Freidel, *Apprenticeship*, 220.

78. FDR undated letter to O. J. Merkel quoted in Freidel, *Apprenticeship*, 236.

79. FDR undated letter to O. J. Merkel quoted in Freidel, *Apprenticeship*, 236.

80. *New York Times*, July 18, 1914 quoted in Freidel, *Apprenticeship*, 236.

81. FDR to ER early 1915 (undated) in *PL II*, 220.

82. FDR to ER August 2, 1914, in *PL II*, 199–200.

83. FDR Memo June 22, 1915, quoted in Freidel, *Apprenticeship*, 252.

84. FDR to ER June 10, 1915, in *PL II*, 222.

85. FDR to ER August 21, 1915, in *PL II*, 231.

86. FDR to ER August 28, 1915, in *PL II*, 235–236. See also FDR to SR August 29, 1915, in *PL II*, 236–237; Also Ward, *Temperament*, 308.
87. Cooper, *Warrior and Priest*, 245.

3 WAR AND PEACE, 1917–1919

1. FDR to ER August 10, 1914, in *PL II*, 207.
2. FDR "Address to Harvard Union," April 1918, MSF, Box 1, FDRL.
3. FDR "The Future of the Submarine," *North American Review* 202, No. 4 (1915), 508.
4. For FDR's dire warnings, see FDR "Speech on the Submarine Menace," Jamestown, New York, July 7, 1917, MSF, Box 1, FDRL.
5. FDR to Woodrow Wilson October 29, 1917, in *PL II*, 295; Frank Freidel, *Franklin D. Roosevelt— The Apprenticeship* (Boston, MA, 1952), 301.
6. FDR "Speech at Chautauqua," August 30, 1919, MSF, Box 1, FDRL.
7. Freidel, *Apprenticeship*, 307–310; Geoffrey C. Ward, *A First Class Temperament— The Emergence of Franklin Roosevelt* (New York, 1989), 342 and 355–357. The correspondence between FDR and Winston Churchill including "A General Statement to the President Concerning the Situation I Have Found in the Navy Department," given to the president by Churchill on August 1, 1917, is located in ASNP, Box 44, FDRL.
8. On opposition to the sending of destroyers, see Freidel, *Apprenticeship*, 305; William J. Williams, "Josephus Daniels and the United States Navy's Shipbuilding Program During World War I," *The Journal of Military History* 60, No. 1 (1996), 15.
9. Williams, "Daniels," 9 and 37; Robert H. Ferrell, *Woodrow Wilson and World War I 1917–1921* (New York, 1985), 38–39.
10. Freidel, *Apprenticeship*, 351. For FDR's positive view of unity of Allied command, see London *Times* June 17 and July 4, 1919, both in ASNP, Box 40, FL61, FDRL.
11. Alfred F. Hurley, *Billy Mitchell: Crusader for Air Power* (Bloomington, IN, 1975), 58.
12. Hurley, *Mitchell*, 47, 57–58.
13. FDR "Personal Diary" in *PL II*, 347–348.
14. "Memoir of Livingston Davis," 10, ASNP, Box 41, FDRL. Neither FDR's account of the trip, nor that of his chief of staff for the trip, Capt Edward McCauley, Jr., mentions the attack. FDR's "Personal Diary" of the Trip is in ASNP, Box 33 and McCauley's in ASNP, Box 41, FDRL.
15. Freidel, *Apprenticeship*, 369; McCauley, "Diary," 25, ASNP, Box 41, FDRL.
16. FDR "Attitude of the Navy toward a United Air Service," June 14, 1919, ASNP, Box 40, Fl 160, FDRL.
17. FDR "Speech 31 January 1920" in *Brooklyn Chamber of Commerce Bulletin*, (February, 1920), ASNP, Navy Scrapbooks, Box 88, FDRL.
18. FDR "Fireside Chat 26 May 1940," available on www.presidency.uscb.edu, accessed on Febraury 25, 2012.

19. Hurley, *Mitchell*, 47–48; FDR "Attitude of the Navy toward a United Air Service," June 14, 1919, PF Box 40, Fl 60, FDRL; and FDR "Appearance at Subcommittee on Reorganization," Senate Committee of Military Affairs September 12, 1919, *Congressional Record*, FDRL.

20. FDR "Personal Diary" in *PL II*, 317.

21. FDR "Personal Diary" in *PL II*, 319. FDR also toured British night bombing stations, see *PL II*, 321.

22. Michael S. Sherry, *The Rise of American Airpower: The Creation of Armageddon* (New Haven, CT, 1987), 29.

23. For the navy dirigible see, FDR to ER May 15, 1919, in *PL II*, 376. For the NC flight, see FDR to ER May 18, 1919, in *PL II*, 377; Josephus Daniels, *The Wilson Era: Years of War and After, 1917–1923* (Chapel Hill, NC, 1946), 567–568; Frank Freidel, *Franklin D. Roosevelt—The Ordeal* (Boston, MA, 1954), 26. FDR later went on an extended hunting trip in late 1919 with Byrd. See *PL II*, 383.

24. David Reynolds, *From Munich to Pearl Harbor: Roosevelt's America and the Origins of the Second World War* (Chicago, 2001), 45; FDR "Fireside Chat" December 29, 1940, available on www.presidency.uscb.edu, accessed on February 25, 2012.

25. FDR wrote a syndicated article on "Scouts and Aircraft" in September 1915 and two calls for increased aviation spending and research to catch up with the Europeans in the September 1915 issue of *Flying* and March 1916 issue of *Aerial Age Weekly* and was a member of the National Advisory Committee of Aeronautics. See ASNP, Box 40, FDRL.

26. Ferrell, *Wilson*, 111–112; and Seward W. Livermore, *Politics is Adjourned: Woodrow Wilson and the War Congress, 1916–1918* (Middleton, CT, 1966), 123–136.

27. Freidel, *Ordeal*, 26; FDR "England's Airforce and Ours," *New York Times* June 29, 1919, in ASNP, Navy Scrapbooks, Box 87, FDRL; FDR "Attitude of the Navy toward a United Air Service, June 14, 1919, PF Box 40 Fl 60, FDRL.

28. FDR "America Should Lead in Aviation" Uncredited newspaper clipping March 19, 1919, ASNP, Navy Scrapbooks, Box 87, FDRL. FDR made a similar appeal that summer; See FDR "Must Develop Aero," Poughkeepsie *Evening Star and Enterprise*, June 26, 1919, in ASNP, Box 40, Fl 160, FDRL.

29. Alan P. Dobson, "FDR and the Struggle for a Postwar Civil Aviation Regime: Legacy or Loss?" in David B. Woolner, Warren Kimball, and David Reynolds (eds.), *FDR's World: War, Peace, and Legacies* (New York, 2008), 193–226.

30. Ernest May, *Lessons' of the Past: The Use and Misuse of History in American Foreign Policy*, (Oxford, 1975). See FDR "Speech at Sioux Falls, South Dakota," August 14, 1920, MSF Box 2, Fl 138, FDRL.

31. Lloyd E. Ambrosius, *Woodrow Wilson and the American Diplomatic Tradition— The Treaty Fight in Perspective* (Cambridge, 1987), 52–54 and 115–117 and Josephus Daniels, *The Wilson Era: Years of War and After, 1917–1923* (Chapel Hill, NC, 1946), 369–384.

32. Freidel, *Ordeal*, 25–26.

33. Daniels, *Years of War*, 370 and 382. On Sims, see Ward, *Temperament*, 353, 382, 390, and 426.

34. FDR to Daniels July 29, 1918, in Carroll Kilpatrick (ed.), *Roosevelt and Daniels—A Friendship in Politics* (Chapel Hill, NC, 1952), 46–47. For FDR's visit to Rhineland, see Freidel, *Ordeal*, 13.

35. Ross A. Kennedy, *The Will to Believe: Woodrow Wilson, World War I, and America's Strategy for Peace and Security* (Kent, OH, 2009), 186.

36. Freidel, *Apprenticeship*, 301–302 and 366–367; Ward, *Temperament*, 405 and 409–410; and *PL II*, 300. FDR's note to Daniels September 4, 1918, is in Kilpatrick, *Roosevelt and Daniels*, 50.

37. FDR "What the Navy Can Do for Your Boy," June 1917, ASNP Box 40, Fl 136, FDRL. TR lost his son Quentin who was a pilot on the Western Front in July 1918, Ward, *Temperament*, 387–389.

38. FDR "What the Navy Can Do For Your Boy," June 1917, ASNP Box 40, Fl 136, FDRL. For Walter Camp's activities, see *Letters PL II*, 281–282.

39. FDR "What the Navy Can Do For Your Boy," June 1917, ASN Papers, Box 40, Fl 136, FDRL.

40. Freidel, *Apprenticeship*, 338–343.

41. "Personal Diary" in *PL II*, 308 and 311; ER to SR February 8, 1919, in *PL II*, 371.

42. Freidel, *Ordeal*, 4; and ER to SR January 3, 1919 (Diary Letter) in *PL II*, 355.

43. FDR "Speech at Syracuse, New York" July 4, 1919, MSF, Box 1 FDR; Freidel, *Apprenticeship*, 337.

44. FDR "Personal Diary," in *PL II*, 342; FDR to Daniels August 2, 1918, in Kilpatrick, *Roosevelt and Daniels*, 47.

45. "F. D. Roosevelt Says Nation May Not Need 'Bigger Navy,'" Unattributed Newspaper clipping March 2, 1919, ASNP Box 87, Navy Scrapbook, FDRL.

46. Freidel, *Ordeal*, 14. Elliott Roosevelt also attributed his father's acceptance of the League idea to the crossing with Wilson. See *PL II*, 379.

47. Diary of Dr. Grayson February 22, 1919, in *PWW* 55, 224.

48. For FDR reading of the Covenant, see Freidel, *Ordeal*, 14; and Ward, *Temperament*, 430.

49. *PL II*, 353–375; and Freidel, *Ordeal*, 7.

50. Kennedy, *Will To Believe*, 203 and 216.

51. William C. Widenor, *Henry Cabot Lodge and the Search for American Foreign Policy* (Berkeley, CA, 1980), 304.

52. John Milton Cooper Jr., *Breaking the Heart of the World—Woodrow Wilson and the Fight for the League of Nations* (Cambridge, 2001), 40.

53. Cooper, *Breaking the Heart*, 61.

54. FDR "Would Give League Law Making Power," in *New York Times* March 2, 1919, 25; and "Believes League Will Win," *New York Times* March 30, 1919, 8.

55. FDR "The National Emergency of Peace Times," June 25, 1919, MSF, Box 2, Fl 98, FDRL.

56. FDR "What the Navy Can Do for Your Boy," June 1917, ASNP Box 40, Fl 136, FDRL.

57. FDR "Speech at Poughkeepsie, New York," July 18, 1919, MSF, Box, 2, Fl 95, FDRL.

58. Francis A. Boyle, *Foundations of World Order: The Legalist Approach to International Relations, 1898–1922* (Durham, NC, 1999), 39 and 53.

59. Stuart I. Rochester, American *Liberal Disillusionment in the Wake of World War I* (University Park, PA, 1977), 64; and Thomas, J. Knock, *To End All Wars: Woodrow Wilson and the Quest for a New World Order* (Princeton, NJ, 1992), 161.

60. Ruhl J. Bartlett, *The League to Enforce Peace*, (Chapel Hill, NC, 1944), 221.

61. "F. D. Roosevelt Says Nation May Not Need 'Bigger Navy,'" Unattributed newspaper clipping March 2, 1919, ASNP Box 87, Navy Scrapbook, FDRL.

62. *Baltimore American* March 7, 1919, MSF, Box 2, Fl 186, FDRL.

63. Theodore Roosevelt, *America and the World War* (London, 1915), 104.

64. Cooper, *Breaking the Heart*, 11. On TR's reversal of his internationalism, see Cooper, *Warrior and the Priest: Woodrow Wilson and Theodore Roosevelt* (Cambridge, MA, 1983), 285.

65. Cooper, *Breaking the Heart*, 64–65 and 55; Ambrosius, *Diplomatic Tradition*, 96.

66. Cooper, *Breaking the Heart*, 69; Ambrosius, *Diplomatic Tradition*, 97.

67. Ambrosius, *Diplomatic Tradition*, 96; Cooper, *Breaking the Heart*, 69.

68. http://avalon.law.yale.edu/20th_century/leagcov.asp, accessed on February 25, 2012.

69. *Baltimore American* March 7, 1919, MSF, Box 2, Fl 186, FDRL.

70. FDR "Speech to the Baltimore City Club" March 29, 1919, in "Believes League Will Win," *New York Times* March 30, 1919, 1.

71. FDR "Speech to the Baltimore City Club" 29 March 1919 in "Believes League Will Win" *New York Times* 30 March 1919, 1.

72. FDR "Believes League Will Win," *New York Times* March 30, 1919, 1. LEP member Lowell had offered the argument in his debate with Lodge on March 19, 1919; Ambrosius, *Diplomatic Tradition*, 99–100.

73. Cooper, *Breaking the Heart*, 94.

74. The others on June 6, 9, and 21 were barely reported. FDR also gave short talks in August on the steps of the subtreasury in Washington. See "Will Talk for League," *New York Times* August 3, 1919, 4.

75. FDR "Speech at Poughkeepsie New York," *The Evening Star and Enterprise* July 19, 1919, in MSF Box 2, Fl 98, FDRL.

76. Cooper, *Breaking the Heart*, 85–86.

77. Cooper, *Breaking the Heart*, 96.

78. Wolfgang J. Helbich, "American Liberals in the League of Nations Controversy," *The Public Opinion Quarterly* 31, No. 4 (1967–68), 588.

79. FDR "Speech to Democratic National Committee," Chicago May 29, 1919, MSF, Box 2, Fl 92. FDRL. For TR's speech, see John Milton Cooper, *The Warrior and the Priest*, 259.

80. FDR "The National Emergency of Peace Times," June 25, 1919, in MSF, Box 2, Fl 95. FDRL.

81. FDR "Would Give League Law Making Power," *New York Times* March 2, 1919, 25.

82. FDR "Speech to Democratic National Committee," Chicago May 29, 1919, MSF, Box 2, Fl 92. FDRL. For later expressions, see FDR "The National Emergency of Peace Times," June 25, 1919, in MSF, Box 2, Fl 95. FDRL.

83. Ward, *Temperament*, 455–456.

84. FDR to ER July 23, 1919, in *PL II*, 381–382.

85. FDR "Speech at Poughkeepsie, New York," July 18, 1919, MSF, Box 2, Fl 95, FDRL.

86. FDR "Speech at Syracuse," New York in MSF, Box 2, Fl 96, FDRL.

87. FDR "Speech at Poughkeepsie" New York, July 18, 1919, MSF, Box 2, Fl 95, FDRL; FDR "Speech at Homecoming Celebration," Utica, New York September 15, 1919, in MSF, Box 2, Fl 102. FDRL.

88. FDR "Speech to the Baltimore City Club," March 29, 1919, in "Believes League Will Win" *New York Times* March 30, 1919, 1. See also FDR "Address at Tacoma Park," Washington D.C. March 28, 1920, in MSF, Box 2, Fl 115, FDRL.

89. FDR "Speech at Poughkeepsie, New York," July 18, 1919, MSF, Box, 2, Fl 95, FDRL.

90. FDR "Speech at Poughkeepsie, New York," July 18, 1919, MSF, Box, 2, Fl 95, FDRL. On ILO membership, see Gary B. Ostrower, *Collective Insecurity—The United States and the League of Nations during the Early Thirties*, (London, 1979), 183.

91. FDR "Speech to the Baltimore City Club," March 29, 1919, in "Believes League Will Win" *New York Times* March 30, 1919, 1.

92. FDR "Speech at the Chautauqua Institute," Chautauqua, New York, August 30, 1919, MSF Box 2, Fl 101, FDRL.

93. FDR "The National Emergency of Peace Times," June 25, 1919, in MSF, Box 2, Fl 95, FDRL; and FDR "Speech at Hyde Park," July 7, 1919, in MSF, Box 2, Fl 97, FDRL.

94. FDR "Speech to the Harvard Union," February 26, 1920, MSF, Box 2, Fl 114, FDRL. For FDR's arguments for a strong executive, see "Article for Empire State Democrat," January 1920; FDR "The National Emergency of Peace Times," June 25, 1919, in MSF, Box 2, Fl 95. FDRL.

95. Ambrosius, *Diplomatic Tradition*, 233–239; and Ward, *Temperament*, 481–482.

96. "Broke Law For Navy," in *New York Times* February 2, 1920, 7; E. David Cronin, ed. *The Cabinet Diaries of Josephus Daniels, 1913–1921* (Lincoln, NE, 1963), February 21, 1919, 497.

97. Samuel I. Rosenman, *Working with Roosevelt* (New York, 1952), 167.

4 THE PRESIDENTIAL ELECTION OF 1920

1. Wesley M. Bagby, *The Road to Normalcy—The Presidential Campaign and Election of 1920* (Baltimore, MD, 1962), 134; Warren F. Kuehl and Lynne K. Dunne, *Keeping the Covenant—American Internationalists and the League of*

Nations, 1920–1939 (Kent, OH, 1997), 8; and Douglas B. Craig, *After Wilson: the Struggle for the Democratic Party, 1920–1934* (Chapel Hill, NC, 1992), 22; James MacGregor Burns, *Roosevelt: The Lion and The* Fox, (New York, 1956), 74.

2. The major analysis of the 1920 election remains Bagby, *Road*. See also Donald R. McCoy "Election of 1920" in Arthur M. Schlesinger Jr. and Fred L. Israel (eds.), *History of American Presidential Elections 1900–1936 Volume III* (New York, 1971), 2349–2456; David Burner, *The Politics of Provincialism—The Democratic Party in Transition 1918–1932* (Cambridge, MA, 1986).

3. McCoy, *Presidential Elections*, 2350; Bagby, *Road*, 22; and Burner, *Provincialism*, 43.

4. Frank Freidel, *Franklin D. Roosevelt—The Ordeal* (Boston, MA, 1954), 55.

5. McCoy, *Presidential Elections*, 2365; Josephus Daniels, *The Wilson Era: Years of War and After, 1917–1923* (Chapel Hill, NC, 1946), 555–557; Bagby, *Road*, 118; McCoy, *Presidential Elections*, 2363.

6. "Campaign Issues as Seen by Governor James M. Cox," *New York Times* May 23, 1920, xxi. Craig, *After Wilson*, 3–4.

7. James M. Cox, *Journey Through My Years* (Macon, GA, 2004), 244; Bagby, *Road*, 73–76; McCoy, *Presidential Elections*, 2354.

8. "Campaign Issues," *New York Times* May 23, 1920, 2.

9. "Democratic Party Platform of 1920," available on http://www.presidency.ucsb.edu, accessed on February 25, 2012

10. Cox, *Journey*, 232.

11. Cox, *Journey*, 232.

12. Frederick Boyd Stevenson unaccredited article "Prepare for War," July 14, 1920, PVPC, Box 20 Scrapbook, FDRL.

13. *Brooklyn Eagle* July 7, 1920, PVPC, Box 20 Scrapbook, FDRL. See also "Roosevelt Career Like That of Cousin," *New York Times* July 7, 1920, 4; "Republicans Star Colonel Roosevelt," *New York Times* August 5, 1920, 3. Cox was not averse to using TR style rhetoric.

14. "New Yorkers in Fist Fight," *New York Times* June 29, 1920, 1.

15. "Gov. Cox Accepts," *New York Times* July 7, 1920, 1.

16. Craig, *After Wilson*, 281–283.

17. *PL II*, 398. See also FDR Speech Milwaukee, Wisconsin August 12, 1920, MSF Box 2, Fl 134, FDRL.

18. Bagby, *Road*, 121; See also Freidel, *Ordeal*, 53.

19. The other known meetings are July 18, Washington; July 20, Dayton Ohio; August 31, Columbus, Ohio; October 3, meeting on board Cox's campaign train from Terre Haute to Indianapolis.

20. "Cox Will Make Ratification His Issue," *New York Times* July 10, 1920, 1.

21. "Democracy's Candidate and His Platform," *New York Times* July 11, 1920, xx2.

22. "Not a 'Courtesy Call,'" *New York Times* July 14, 1920, 1.

23. "Nominees Confer on Fight," *New York Times* July 13, 1920, 1. FDR did not resign from the Navy Dept until August 6, 1920. His resignation letter and Daniels' reply is in Carroll Kilpatrick (ed.), *Roosevelt and Daniels—A Friendship in Politics* (Chapel Hill, NC, 1952), 67–69.

24. Frederick Boyd Stevenson unaccredited article "Prepare for War," July 14, 1920, PVCP, Box 20 Scrapbook, FDRL.

25. Cox, *Journey*, 243–244. On Cox's response to Harding's charges at the time, see "Aim of Gov. Cox's Campaign," *New York Times* July 15, 1920, 1. Louis Howe also urged FDR to stress government reform. See Freidel, *Ordeal*, 72–73.

26. "Cheering Crowd Welcomes Cox in Washington," *New York Times* July 18, 1920, 1; "Text of Statements," *New York Times* July 19, 1920, 1; Cox, *Journey*, 241–242 reports on an undated letter from Claude Bowers to James M. Cox.

27. Steve Early to Louis Howe August 16 and 18, 1920, PVPC, Box 5, FDRL.

28. "Cox Warns of 'Staggering Funds,'" *New York Times* July 21, 1920, 1. The other committee men were: Secretary Edward G Hoffman, Ft. Wayne Ind, Vice Chair J. Bruce Kremer, Butte, Montana, Vice Chair S. B. Arnidon of Wichita, Kansas, Treasurer Wilbur W. Marsh, Waterloo, Iowa, Sergeant at Arms John J. Hughes, Oklahoma.

29. McCoy, *Presidential Elections*, 2372; "Cox Warns of 'Staggering Funds,'" *New York Times* July 21, 1920, 1; Cox, *Journey*, 238–240.

30. "Cox and President Agreed on Principles," *New York Times* July 22, 1920, 5. FDR "Can the Vice President be Useful?" for *The Saturday Evening Post* October 16, 1920, PF, Box 3, FDRL.

31. "Cox Mail Shows Backing On League," *New York Times* August 3, 1920, 3; "Cox Sees Pomerene," *New York Times* July 28, 1920, 6; and "Walsh Sees Cox," *New York Times* July 30, 1920, 2.

32. Bagby, *Road*, 130; McCoy, *Presidential Elections*, 2373.

33. Bagby, *Road*, 155–156; Steve Early to Louis Howe August 18, 1920, PVPC, Box 5, FDRL; FDR speech Chicago, Illinois, August 11, 1920, MSF Box 2, Fl 132, FDRL; and "Roosevelt Opens Western Campaign," *New York Times* August 12, 1920, 3.

34. See "Gov. Cox Accepts," *New York Times* July 7, 1920, 1.

35. "Roosevelt Opens Western Campaign," *New York Times* August 12, 1920, 3; See also "Roosevelt Talks on Tour," *New York Times* July 16, 1920, 6.

36. Linda Lotridge Levin, *The Making of FDR*, (New York, 2008), 47 and 50.

37. Craig, *After Wilson*, 22.

38. "Cheering Crowd Welcomes Cox," *New York Times* August 17, 1920, 1; McCoy, *Presidential Elections*, 2376.

39. "Cox Will Make Ratification His Issue," *New York Times* July 10, 1920, 1; "Nominees Confer on Fight," *New York Times* July 13, 1920, 1.

40. "Nominees Confer on Fight," *New York Times* July 13, 1920, 1; and "Roosevelt Opens Western Campaign," *New York Times* August 17, 1920, 3.

41. "Greatest Tour of Any Campaign," *New York Times* July 25, 1920, 1.

42. FDR Acceptance Speech, August 9, 1920, in *PL II*, 395–401.

43. FDR Speech at Wheeling, West Virginia September 29, 1920, in MSF Box 3, Fl 182, FDRL. See also speeches at Des Moines, Iowa and Cincinatti, Ohio, October 8 and 16, 1920, in MSF Box 3, Fl 203 and 212, FDRL.

44. FDR only mentioned Article X directly in his speeches four times during whole campaign. This was on October 1, 16, 20, and 22, 1920.

45. FDR Speech Cincinnati, Ohio, October 16, 1920, MSF Box 3, Fl 212, FDRL; See also *Brooklyn Daily Eagle* October 27, 1920, MSF, Box 4, Fl 238, FDRL.

46. FDR Speech Milwaukee, Wisconsin, August 12, 1920, in MSF Box 2, Fl 134, FDRL. For TR, see Roosevelt, *America and the World War*, 104. For FDR, see Speech Sioux Falls, South Dakota, August 14, 1920, in MSF Box 2, Fl 138, FDRL; FDR Speech Milwaukee, Wisconsin, August 12, 1920, MSF Box 3, Fl 134, FDRL; FDR Speech San Francisco, August 23, 1920, in MSF Box 2, Fl 149, FDRL.

47. FDR Speeches at Seattle, Washington, August 21, and Cincinnatti, Ohio, October 16, 1920, in PVPC Box 21 and MSF Box 3, Fl 212, FDRL.

48. FDR "Press Statement on Maine and the Women Vote," September 4, 1920, Box 41, Fl 17, FDRL; and "Press Release," October 4, 1920, MSF Box 3, Fl 195, FDRL. On mothers and the League, see FDR Acceptance Speech August 9, 1920, in *PL II*, 395–401; Speech at Bangor, Maine, September 11, 1920, in Box 41, Fl 21, FDRL; and Hudson, New York, November 1, 1920, in MSF Box 4, Fl 234, FDRL.

49. FDR Speech at Bridgeport, Connecticut, September 18, 1920, MSF Box 3, Fl 172, FDRL.

50. See for instance FDR Speeches August 9, 1920, in *PL II*, 395–401, San Francisco August 23, 1920, in MSF Box 2, Fl 149, FDRL; Bangor, Maine, September 11, 1920, in Box 41, Fl 21, FDRL; Bridgeport, CN, September 18, 1920, in MSF Box 3 Fl 172, FDRL.

51. FDR Speech at Milwaukee, Wisconsin, August 12, 1920, in MSF Box 2, Fl 34, FDRL; FDR "Press Statement on Maine and the Women Vote," September 4, 1920, in Box 41, Fl 17, FDRL; and Speech at Cincinnatti, Ohio, October 16, 1920, in MSF Box 3, Fl 212, FDRL.

52. FDR Speech at Milwaukee, Wisconsin, August 12, 1920, MSF Box 2, Fl 34, FDRL.

53. On Cox's difficulties, see "Harding Now Cries Kamerad," *New York Times* October 17, 1920, 3; "Calls Harding Idea Bunk," *New York Times* October 19, 1920, 2; "Democracy's Candidate," *New York Times* July 11, 1920, xx2; "Cox Says Congress Balked," *New York Times* September 19, 1920, 1; and "Cox Flays Lodge," *New York Times* October 20, 1920, 1.

54. Willard Range, *Franklin D. Roosevelt's World Order* (Athens, GA, 1959), 102–104; and Warren F. Kimball and Fred E. Pollock, "'In Search of Monsters to Destroy': Roosevelt and Colonialism," in Warren F. Kimball, *The Juggler—Franklin Roosevelt as Wartime Statesman* (Princeton, NJ, 1991) 127–128.

55. Freidel notes that he had already made the "Butte" comments in a speech at Newburgh, New Jersey in January 1920, which would suggest he had not at that point had an anti-imperialist "epiphany." See *Ordeal*, 81.

56. Freidel, *Ordeal*, 81.

57. FDR "Press Release from Helena, Montana," August 18, 1920, MSF Box 2, Fl 142, FDRL.

58. FDR Speech at San Francisco August 23, 1920, MSF Box 2 Fl 149, FDRL.

59. McCoy, *Presidential Elections*, 2376; E. David Cronin (ed.), *The Cabinet Diaries of Josephus Daniels, 1913–1921* (Lincoln, NE, 1963), 552; Freidel,

Ordeal, 82–83; FDR "Press Statement," September 2, 1920, in Box 41, Fl 16, FDRL; FDR "Says America Has 12 League Votes," *New York Times* August 19, 1920, 11.

60. "Says America Has 12 League Votes," *New York Times* August 19, 1920, 11. FDR had nothing to do with the drafting of the new Haitian Constitution according to Frank Freidel, *Franklin D. Roosevelt—The Apprenticeship* (Boston, MA, 1952); Freidel, , 283–84; Freidel, *Ordeal*, 81 and 83; See also "Constitution or League," *New York Times* September 18, 1920, 11; "Constitution or League," *New York Times* September 18, 1920, 11.

61. Mary A. Renda, *Taking Haiti: Military Occupation and the Culture of U.S. Imperialism, 1915–1940* (Chapel Hill, NC, 2001), 187, 151, and 191; David Healy, *Gunboat Diplomacy in the Wilson Era—The U.S. Navy in Haiti, 1915–1916* (Madison, WI, 1976), 211.

62. Freidel, *Ordeal*, 83.

63. "Merest Dribble," *New York Times* September 18, 1920, 11; Daniels, *Diary* September 17, 1920, in David E. Cronin, ed. *The Cabinet Diaries of Josephus Daniels, 1913–1921* (Lincoln, NE, 1963), 558. The report was released in October and confirmed the wanton killings. See Freidel , *Ordeal*, 83.

64. McCoy, *Presidential Elections*, 2376; and Freidel, *Ordeal*, 83.

65. Johnson argues for a powerful non-Wilsonian anti-imperialist bloc in Congress between 1919 and 1930. See Robert D. Johnson, *The Peace Progressives and American Foreign Relations* (Cambridge, MA, 1995), 3–4; FDR Speech at Hartford, Connecticut, September 17, 1920, MSF Box 3, Fl 171, FDRL; and "Merest Dribble," *New York Times* September 18, 1920, 1; FDR "Speech at Cincinnati," Ohio, October 16, 1920, MSF Box 3, Fl 212, FDRL.

66. FDR "Speech at Bangor," Maine, September 11, 1920, MSF Box 3, Fl 162, FDRL; FDR "Speech at Cincinnati," Ohio, October 16, 1920, MSF Box 3, Fl 212, FDRL; "Interview with FDR," October 17, 1920, MSF Box 3, Fl 216, FDRL.

67. FDR "Memorandum in Regard to Hayti," April 8, 1922, ASNP Box 40, FDRL.

68. Freidel, *Ordeal*, 82.

69. Bagby, *Road*, 159.

70. FDR to Steve Early, December 21, 1920, in *PL II*, 406.

71. Cass R. Sunstein, *The Second Bill of Rights: FDR'S Unfinished Revolution and Why We Need It More Than Ever* (New York, 2004); and Elizabeth Borgwardt, *A New Deal for the World: America's Vision For Human Rights* (Cambridge, MA, 2005).

5 FINDING A VOICE, 1921–1928

1. Freidel appropriately titled the second volume of his FDR biography "The Ordeal." See Frank Freidel, *Franklin D. Roosevelt: The Ordeal*, (Boston, 1954).

2. Freidel, *Ordeal*, 138.

3. Freidel, *Ordeal*, 93; and Geoffrey C. Ward, *A First Class Temperament—The Emergence of Franklin Roosevelt* (New York, 1989), 561–562. On the sale of navy

radio stations, see Carroll Kilpatrick (ed.), *Roosevelt and Daniels—A Friendship in Politics* (Chapel Hill, NC, 1952), 101.

4. Freidel, *Ordeal*, 138–143; and Ward, *Temperament*, 656–657.

5. There is a plausible medical case for incorrect diagnosis that posits the hereditary autoimmune illness Guillain-Barré syndrome. See Armond S. Goldman et al. "What was the cause of Franklin Delano Roosevelt's Paralytic Illness?" *Journal of Medical Biography* 11 (2003), 232–240.

6. See note in *PL II*, 419.

7. ER to James Roosevelt Roosevelt August 18, 1921, in *PL II*, 413–414.

8. Frances Perkins developed the polio transformation thesis in her *The Roosevelt I knew* (London, 1948). Eleanor Roosevelt concurs in *This I Remember*, (London, 1950). FDR's son Elliott downplays the impact of polio, see *PL II*, 500 and 430.

9. *PL II*, 122 and 429–435.

10. Donald A. Ritchie, *Electing FDR: The New Deal Campaign of 1932* (Lawrence, KS, 2007), 72.

11. Freidel, *Ordeal*, 108–109; See also FDR "How Boy Scout Work Aids Youth," *New York Times* August 12, 1928, x18.

12. Freidel, *Ordeal*, 242–243.

13. FDR, "Shall We Trust Japan?" *Asia* (July, 1923), 475–528; FDR, "Our Foreign Policy: A Democratic View," *Foreign Affairs* 6, No. 4 (1928), 573–586; and FDR, *Whither Bound?* (New York, 1926).

14. Sadly the major study of FDR's rhetoric fails to cover the prepresidential period. See Halford R. Ryan, *Franklin D. Roosevelt's Rhetorical Presidency* (Westport, CT, 1988).

15. Warren F. Kuehl and Lynne K. Dunn, *Keeping the Covenant: American Internationalists and the League of Nations, 1920–1939* (Kent, OH, 1997), 39–41; and Robert David Johnson, *The Peace Progressives and American Foreign Relations* (Cambridge, MA, 1995), 202.

16. Kuehl and Dunn, *Keeping the Covenant*, 35 and 41–42.

17. Johnson, *Peace Progressives*, 245 places Senators Thomas Walsh, Pat Harrison, and Hugo Black in this group.

18. Johnson, *Peace Progressives*, 237–238 and 250 describes Senators Oscar Underwood, Millard Tydings, and Thomas Byrd as Southern conservatives.

19. Johnson, *Peace Progressives*, 236 and 267.

20. Freidel, *Ordeal*, 122 and 129–130.

21. FDR to James M. Cox December 8, 1922, quoted in Freidel, *Ordeal*, 122.

22. "F. D. Roosevelt Sees Foreign Policy Issue," *New York Times* April 8, 1923, 2.

23. Kuehl and Dunn, *Keeping the Covenant*, 90.

24. Eleanor Roosevelt, "Appendix I: A Plan to Preserve Peace," *This I Remember* (New York, 1949), 275–276 and 282.

25. See Freidel, *Ordeal*, 275–283 and 128.

26. See Townsend Hoopes and Douglas Brinkley, *FDR and the Creation of the UN* (New Haven, CT, 1997), ix and 11.

27. Roosevelt, "Appendix I," 283, 278, 280, 282, and 286.

28. Freidel, *Ordeal*, 128–129.

29. See note in *PWW* 67, 272–273.

30. See note in *PWW* 67, 272–273; and FDR to Wilson March 23, 1921, in *PWW* 67, 239–240. The animosity continued during the 1920s, see Gene Smith, *When the Cheering Stopped* (New York, 1964), 145 and 275.

31. FDR to Wilson June 29, 1921, in *PWW* 67, 333.

32. FDR to Wilson 29 June 1921 in *PWW* 67, 333.

33. Wilson to FDR July 4, 1921, in *PWW* 67, 341–342; FDR to Wilson July 7, 1921, in *PWW* 67, 346.

34. *PWW* 67, 392 and 448–449; and Wilson to FDR January 30, 1923, in *PWW* 68, 280. See FDR to Wilson April 4, 1923, and J. R. Bolling to FDR April 6, 1923, in *PWW* 68, 319.

35. R. C. Stuart to Wilson April 28, 1921, in *PWW* 67, 273–274. See also Kuehl and Dunn, *Keeping the Covenant*, 35.

36. Kuehl and Dunn, *Keeping the Covenant*, 35. The annoyance of Stuart with FDR and the demise of the Wilson clubs can be traced through his letters exchange with John Randolph Bolling *PWW* 67.

37. Wilson to FDR April 30, 1922, in *PWW* 68, 39; See also Wilson to N. S. Toy February 13, 1922, in *PWW* 67, 543–544.

38. Wilson to N. S. Toy February 13, 1922, in *PWW* 67, 543–544.

39. FDR to Byron R. Newton December 20, 1922, in Freidel, *Ordeal*, 125.

40. See note in *PWW* 68, 365.

41. "News Report" in *PWW* 68, 509. For the Foundation prize history, see Kuehl and Dunn *Keeping the Covenant*, 34–35; Freidel, *Ordeal*, 122–125.

42. Kuehl and Dunn, *Keeping the Covenant*, 35. In 1963, the Foundation placed its activities indefinitely on hold to provide financial backing for the completion of the Papers of Woodrow Wilson. This greatly strained the Foundation and the organization was liquidated. See http://diglib.princeton.edu/ead/getEad?id=ark:/88435/br86b3595, accessed on July 2, 2010.

43. Melvyn Leffler, *The Elusive Quest: America's Pursuit of European Stability and French Security, 1919–1933* (Chapel Hill, NC, 1979), 24 and 32.

44. Frank Costigliola, *Awkward Dominion: American Political, Economic, and Cultural Relations with Europe, 1919–1933* (Ithaca, NY, 1984), 59.

45. Leffler, *Elusive Quest*, 79. FDR continued to blame German aggression for the war—see his column for the *Macon Telegraph* May 2, 1925, in Donald Scott Carmichael (ed.), *F.D.R. Columnist—The Uncollected Columns of Franklin D. Roosevelt* (Chicago, 1947), 64.

46. FDR to James M. Cox December 8, 1922, quoted in Freidel, *Ordeal*, 122.

47. George Marvin to FDR September 3 and 21, 1922, and FDR to George Marvin September 12, and October 10, 1922, quoted in Freidel, *Ordeal*, 131.

48. FDR to George Auld October 13, 1923, quoted Freidel, *Ordeal*, 130–131.

49. The Republicans, preferring order, had no such qualms. See Costigliola, *Awkward Dominion*, 54.

50. Freidel, *Ordeal*, 224.

51. See FDR to Walsh February 22, 1926, quoted in Freidel, *Ordeal*, 224. Louis Howe's report was sent to Senators Walsh, Pat Harrison, and Representative Cordell Hull in March 1926.

52. FDR to George Auld October 13, 1923, quoted in Freidel, *Ordeal*, 130–131; FDR to Frank Kent October 1925 in Fusfeld, *Economic Thought*, 90; FDR "Keynote speech to Democratic State Convention," Syracuse, New York, September 27, 1926, in Fusfeld, *Economic Thought*, 90.

53. FDR "Speech at Hyde Park," July 14, 1920, PVPC Box 20 Scrapbook, FDRL; FDR "We Lack a Sense of Humor If We Forget That Not So Very Long Ago We were Immigrants Ourselves," April 21, 1925, *Macon Daily Telegraph* in Carmichael, *F.D.R. Columnist*, 36–40.

54. FDR, "Shall We Trust Japan?" 478.

55. FDR, "Shall We Trust Japan?" 478 and 526; FDR *The Macon Daily Telegraph*, April 30, 1925, in Carmichael, *F.D.R. Columnist*, 56–60.

56. "F.D. Roosevelt Asks For Naval Holiday," *New York Times* May 5, 1921, 3.

57. Freidel, *Ordeal*, 131–132.

58. FDR, "Shall We Trust Japan?" 477 and 475.

59. FDR, "Shall We Trust Japan?" 475 and 477; See FDR "Letter to the Editor," *Baltimore Sun* August 13, 1923, PF Box 39, FDRL.

60. FDR, "Shall We Trust Japan?" 528 and 478.

61. FDR, "Shall We Trust Japan?" 476 and 478; See also FDR to George Foster Peabody September 26, 1923, PF Box 39, FDRL.

62. FDR to Glenn Frank August 12, 1924, in Freidel, *Ordeal*, 182.

63. Emily Rosenberg, *Financial Missionaries to the World: The Politics and Culture of Dollar Diplomacy, 1900–1930* (Durham, NC, 2003), 123 and 150; See also Johnson, *Peace Progressives*, 5.

64. FDR Speech at Portland, Maine, September 2, 1920, MSF Box 3, Fl 155, FDRL; See also FDR Speech at Cumberland, West Virginia, October 27, 1920, MSF Box 4, Fl 229, FDRL.

65. J. E. Murphy to FDR August 5, 1921. Family Papers 1920–1928 (hereafter FP), Box 35, FDRL; FDR to J. E. Murphy September 27, 1921, FP Box 35, FDRL; Also R Cunningham to FDR March 24, 1922, FP Box 35; and FDR to Ruth Cunningham March 29, 1922, FP Box 35, FDRL.

66. "Democracy's Candidate," *New York Times* July 11, 1920, xx2.

67. FDR was listed as a member the Jefferson Centennial Committee of the Thomas Jefferson Memorial Foundation Executive Committee from at least June 1925. See Elmore Leffingwell to FDR June 17, 1925, FP Box 35, FDRL.

68. FDR to Charles Murphy December 5, 1924, 1924 Election Papers (hereafter 1924 EP) Box 5, FDRL.

69. M. W. Underwood to FDR December 16, 1924, in General Political Correspondence 1921–1928 (hereafter GPC), Michigan File, FDRL; See also Graham J. White, *FDR and the Press* (Chicago, 1979), 146.

70. Freidel, *Ordeal*, 210; White, *FDR and the Press*, 145.

71. FDR to Thomas J. Walsh February 28, 1925, GPC 1921–1928, Box 7 Walsh Folder, FDRL.

72. White, *FDR and the Press*, 145; and Fusfeld, *Economic Thought*, 87–88. For the full *New York Times* exchange, see "Democrats Move to Hold Conference," March 9, 1925, 1; "A Democratic Conference," March 10, 1925, 20; "Democrats

Oppose Early Meeting," April 5, 1925, 5; and "Democrats Escape Clash of Leaders," April 9, 1925, 1.

73. Quoted in Merrill D. Peterson, *The Jefferson Image in the American Mind*, (Charlottesville, VA, 1998), 353.

74. FDR "Jefferson and Hamilton," November 19, 1925, PF Box 41, Fl 64, FDRL; See Hollins N. Randolph to FDR May 4, 1925, GPC 1921–1928, Box 6, FDRL; See also White, *FDR and the Press*, 147.

75. See Claude G. Bowers *Jefferson and Hamilton: The Struggle for Democracy in America* (London, 1925), vii.

76. FDR "Jefferson and Hamilton," November 19, 1925, PF Box 41, Fl 64, FDRL; See also White, *FDR and the Press*, 147.

77. FDR "Jefferson and Hamilton," November 19, 1925, PF Box 41, Fl 64 FDRL. The review was published in the New York *World* December 3, 1925.

78. Ritchie, *Electing FDR*, 86–87; On Lindley's input, see Ritchie, *Electing FDR*, 87.

79. Ronald Steel, *Walter Lippmann and the American Century* (London, 1980), 180–181 and 212–214.

80. FDR, "Reign of Law Sustained By Public Opinion," 1925, PF Box 41, Fl 61, FDRL. This appears never to have been published.

81. FDR, Editorial in *Macon Telegraph* May 2, 1925, in Carmichael, *FDR Columnist*, 64; and FDR, "Our Foreign Policy," 580.

82. FDR Editorial in Beacon *Standard* September 20, 1928, in Carmichael, *F.D.R. Columnist*, 134.

83. H. F. Armstrong to FDR April 25, 1924, PF Box 39, FDRL. Armstrong advised FDR to give more attention to the important maritime law section. FDR, "Our Foreign Policy," 581–582.

84. FDR, *Whither Bound?*, 27; N. H. Davis to FDR April 24, 1928, PF Box 39. FDRL.

85. FDR to Thaddeus A. Adams November 4, 1925, quoted in Freidel, *Ordeal*, 204.

86. FDR to Claude Bowers December 17, 1925, quoted in Freidel, *Ordeal*, 208; FDR to Dr. D. C. Martin December 9, 1925, quoted in Fusfeld, *Economic Thought*, 86.

87. FDR to Norman H. Davis March 30, 1928, PF Box 39. FDRL.

88. FDR to H. F. Armstrong March 22, 1928, PF Box 39, FDRL.

89. FDR, "Our Foreign Policy," 573. The first two paragraphs were almost entirely Armstrong's words, see H. F. Armstrong to FDR April 25, 1928, PF Box 39, FDRL.

90. FDR, "Our Foreign Policy," 573.

91. FDR, "Our Foreign Policy," 582–583.

92. FDR, "Our Foreign Policy," 585.

93. Freidel, *Ordeal*, 234 and 237.

94. Harper emphasizes FDR's Jeffersonianism during the 1920s. See John Lamberton Harper, *American Visions of Europe: Franklin D. Roosevelt, George F. Kennan, and Dean G Acheson* (Cambridge, 1994), 42–131.

95. FDR "Alexander Hamilton," circa 1925, PF Box 41, Fl 58, FDRL.

96. FDR, Speech at Syracuse, New York September 27, 1926, quoted in Fusfeld, *Economic Thought*, 99.

97. This is perhaps the difference with Secretary to the Treasury Mellon who dedicated a statue to Hamilton outside the treasury in 1923. See Peterson, *Jeffersonian Image*, 345. Mellon later became something of a hate figure for FDR who supported tax evasion charges against him when president. See Ritchie, *Electing FDR*, 50; and David Cannadine, *Mellon: An American Life* (London, 2006), 505 and 513–516.

98. Patrick O. Cohrs, *The Unfinished Peace After World War I: America, Britain and the Stabilisation of Europe, 1919–1932* (Cambridge, 2006), 6–11.

99. FDR, "Our Foreign Policy," 585.

100. FDR, "Our Foreign Policy," 573. This was possibly H. F. Armstrong's suggestion, see H. F. Armstrong to FDR April 25, 1928, PF Box 39, FDRL.

101. FDR, "Our Foreign Policy," 585. See also FDR's column in the Beacon *Standard* September 20, 1928, which says much the same thing in Carmichael, *F.D.R Columnist*, 132–136.

102. FDR, "Our Foreign Policy," 577 and 581.

103. FDR, "Our Foreign Policy," 581–582; and FDR, *Whither Bound?*, 30.

104. Michael A. Butler, *Cautious Visionary—Cordell Hull and Trade Reform, 1933–1937*, (London, 1998), 5.

6 INTERNATIONALISM, 1928–1933

1. FDR "Schedule of Speeches for Gubernatorial Campaign," MSF Box 5 Fl 259, FDRL.

2. Daniel R. Fusfeld, *The Economic Thought of Franklin D. Roosevelt and the Origins of the New Deal* (New York, 1956), 118–122. On religion, see Samuel I. Rosenman, *Working with Roosevelt* (London, 1952), 33.

3. James MacGregor Burns, *Roosevelt: The Lion and the Fox* (New York, 1956), 125.

4. FDR to Mrs. H. Lehman February 17, 1930, in *PL III*, 52.

5. FDR "Editorial 20 September 1928," *The Standard*, Beacon, New York in Carmichael Donald S. ed., *F.D.R. Columnist: The Uncollected Columns of Franklin D. Roosevelt* (Chicago, 1947), 134.

6. FDR to Viscount Cecil August 19, 1930, in *PL III*, 57.

7. Frank Freidel, *Franklin D. Roosevelt—The Triumph*, (Boston, MA, 1956), 253.

8. Robert H. Ferrell, *American Diplomacy in the Great Depression—Hoover-Stimson Foreign Policy, 1929–1933* (New York, 1957), 32.

9. FDR "Editorial 20 September 1928," *The Standard*, Beacon, New York in Carmichael, *F.D.R. Columnist*, 135–136.

10. Ferrell, *American Diplomacy*, 107–115.

11. FDR to Sen. Joe Robinson June 25, 1931, in *PL III*, 70.

12. FDR to Josephus Daniels August 1, 1931, in Carroll Kilpatrick (ed.), *Roosevelt and Daniels—A Friendship in Politics* (Chapel Hill, NC, 1952), 108–109.

13. FDR to Cordell Hull May 14, 1929, in *PL III*, 39.

14. Ferrell, *American Diplomacy*, 206.

15. FDR to Arthur Krock July 3, 1931, quoted in Freidel, *Triumph*, 247 and 248 for Lippmann.

16. Freidel, *Triumph*, 245.

17. Freidel, *Triumph*, 250. See also FDR to Josephus Daniels May 14, 1932, in Kilpatrick, *Roosevelt and Daniels,* 116.

18. FDR Address to member of the New York State Grange February 2, 1932, MSF Box 9, Fl 460. FDRL.

19. Donald A. Ritchie, *Electing FDR: The New Deal Campaign of 1932* (Lawrence, KS, 2007), 84.

20. Freidel, *Triumph*, 253. See also Robert Dallek, *Franklin D. Roosevelt and American Foreign Policy, 1933–1945* (Oxford, 1995), 19–20.

21. FDR Address to member of the New York State Grange February 2, 1932, MSF Box 9, Fl 460, FDRL.

22. Gary B. Ostrower, *Collective Insecurity—The United States and the League of Nations during the Early Thirties,* (London, 1979), 199; FDR Speech at Woodrow Wilson Foundation Dinner December 28, 1932, in Edgar B. Nixon (ed.), *Franklin D. Roosevelt and Foreign Affairs I* (Cambridge, MA, 1969), 558–563.

23. FDR to Robert Wolley February 25, 1932, quoted in Freidel, *Triumph*, 257.

24. Frank Freidel, *Franklin D. Roosevelt—Launching the New Deal* (Boston, 1973), 103.

25. FDR Acceptance Speech Chicago, Illinois, July 2, 1932, in Franklin D. Roosevelt, *The Public Papers and Addresses of Franklin D. Roosevelt—Volume One The Genesis of the New Deal 1928–1932* (New York, 1938), 647–659 (hereafter *PPA*).

26. FDR Campaign Address Baltimore October 25, 1932, *PPA I*, 831.

27. Frank Freidel "Election of 1932" in Arthur M. Schlesinger and Fred L Israel (eds.) *History of American Presidential Elections 1789–1968 Volume III* (New York, 1971); and Ritchie, *Electing FDR*, 157.

28. FDR, "Our Foreign Policy: A Democratic View," *Foreign Affairs* 6, No. 4 (1928), 584.

29. FDR to Sumner Welles February 23, 1931, in *PL III*, 66. For the inaugural, see Nixon, *Foreign Affairs,* 20. FDR also applied the "Good Neighbor" specifically to Latin America in a Pan American Day speech on April 12 Address before Governing Board of the Pan American Union, April 12, 1933, *PPA I*, 130.

30. For the argument that FDR accepted Hoover's foreign policies, see Donald A. Ritchie, *Electing FDR*, 133; and Dallek, *Foreign Policy*, 27.

31. Ferrell, *American Diplomacy*, 240; Freidel, *Launching*, 119; See also Bernard Sternsher, "The Stimson Doctrine: F.D.R. Versus Moley and Tugwell," *The Pacific Historical Review* 31, No. 3 (1962), 281–289.

32. Charles Tansill, *Back Door to War: The Roosevelt Foreign Policy, 1933–1941* (Chicago, 1952), 80–119.

33. Ferrell, *American Diplomacy*, 247.

34. Freidel, *Launching*, 23.

35. FDR to Hoover December 20, 1933, *PPA I,* 879–880. On the offer to choose delegates, see also Dallek, *Foreign Policy*, 24–25.

36. Hoover to FDR December 20, 1933, and FDR to Hoover December 21, 1933, *PPA I*, 881–884.
37. Freidel, *Launching*, 42 and 131–132.
38. Ritchie, *Electing FDR*, 37.
39. Freidel, *Launching*, 109; and Henry L. Stimson "Diaries," January 15, 1933 Microfilm (New Haven, CT, 1973).
40. Freidel, *Launching*, 372; Dallek, *Foreign Policy*, 42.
41. FDR to the Heads of Nations at Geneva May 16, 1933; Nixon, *Foreign Affairs I*, 126–128; Dallek, *Foreign Policy*, 48.
42. Ferrell, *American Diplomacy*, 259; Jeannette P. Nichols, "Roosevelt's Monetary Diplomacy in 1933," *The American Historical Review* 56, No. 2 (1951), 301.
43. FDR "Second Fireside Chat," May 7, 1933, in Russell D. Buhite and David W. Levy., eds. *FDR's Fireside Chats* (Norman, OK, 1992), 26.
44. Nixon, *Foreign Affairs I*, 126; Nichols, "Monetary Diplomacy," 306; Dallek, *Foreign Policy*, 37.
45. FDR Inaugural Address March 4, 1933, *PPA I*, 14; FDR "Second Fireside Chat," May 7, 1933, in Buhite and Levy, *FDR'S Fireside Chats*, 25; Dallek, *Foreign Policy*, 49.
46. Dallek, *Foreign Policy*, 47; The delegates were Cordell Hull, James M. Cox, Senator Key Pittman, Senator James Couzens, Congressman Samuel McReynolds, and Ralph Morrison a financial backer of the Democrats. See Nichols, "Monetary Diplomacy," 308.
47. William J. Barber, *Designs Within Disorder: Franklin D. Roosevelt, the Economists, and the Shaping of American Economic Policy, 1933–1945* (Cambridge, 1996), 14–15.
48. FDR to William Phillips July 2, 1933, in Nixon, *Foreign Affairs I*, 269.
49. Dallek, *Foreign Policy*, 55 speculates that FDR had hope for the domestic economy to be on a better footing by the time the London Conference met to discuss international stabilization options.

CONCLUSION

1. Alan K. Henrikson, "FDR and the World-Wide Arena," in David B. Woolner, Warren F. Kimball, and David Reynolds (eds.), *FDR's World: War, Peace, and Legacies* (New York, 2008), 35–36 and 43–46
2. John A. Thompson "Conceptions of National Security and American Entry into World War II," *Diplomacy and Statecraft* 16, No. 4 (2005), 671–697.
3. Alan Brinkley, *The End of Reform: New Deal Liberalism in Recession and War* (New York, 1995), 9–10.
4. Elizabeth Borgwardt, A *New Deal for the World: America's Vision for Human Rights* (Cambridge, MA, 2005), 3 and 6. Cass R. Sunstein, *The Second Bill of Rights: FDR's Unfinished Revolution and Why We Need It More Than Ever* (New York, 2004), 1.
5. Borgwardt, *New Deal*, 6 and 8.
6. Kathleen G Donahue, Freedom *From Want: American Liberalism and the Idea of the Consumer* (Baltimore, MD, 2003), 6–7.

7. Borgwardt, *New Deal*, 6 and 8.
8. Warren F. Kimball, "The Sheriffs: FDR's Postwar World," in David B. Woolner, Warren F. Kimball and David Reynolds (eds.), *FDR's World: War, Peace, and Legacies* (New York, 2008), 93. Reynolds notes FDR's speeches were full of Wilsonian ideology. See David Reynolds, *From Munich to Pearl Harbor: Roosevelt's America and the Origins of the Second World War* (Chicago, 2001), 180.
9. TR "Fourth Annual Message," December 6, 1904, available on http://www.presidency.ucsb.edu, accessed on February 25, 2012.
10. FDR "Speech at Sioux Falls," August 14, 1920, MSF Box 2 Fl 138, FDRL.
11. J. Simon Rofe, *Franklin Roosevelt's Foreign Policy and the Welles Mission* (New York, 2007), 186.
12. William J. Barber, *Designs Within Disorder: Franklin D. Roosevelt, the Economists, and the Shaping of American Economic Policy, 1933–1945* (Cambridge, 1996), 110.

BIBLIOGRAPHY

PRIMARY MANUSCRIPT SOURCES

Franklin D. Roosevelt Library, Hyde Park, New York.
Roosevelt, Franklin D.: Papers Pertaining to Family, Business, and Personal Affairs
Roosevelt, Franklin D.: Papers as New York State Senator, 1910–1913
Roosevelt, Franklin D.: Papers as Assistant Secretary of the Navy, 1913–1920
Roosevelt, Franklin D.: Papers as Vice-Presidential Candidate, 1920
Roosevelt, Franklin D.: Papers, 1920–1928
Roosevelt, Franklin D.: Publications File
Roosevelt, Franklin D.: Master Speech File
Roosevelt, Franklin D.: General Political Correspondence File, 1921–1928
Roosevelt, Franklin D.: 1924 Election Papers

PRIMARY PRINTED SOURCES

NEWSPAPERS AND PERIODICALS

Asia
Association Men
Economic World
Foreign Affairs
Ladies Home Journal
Nation's Business
National Monthly
New York Times
North American Review
Outlook
Scientific American
Scribner's Magazine

BOOKS

Bowers, Claude, *Jefferson and Hamilton: The Struggle for Democracy in America* (Boston, 1925)

Croly, Herbert, *The Promise of American Life* (New York, 1909)

Lea, Homer, *The Day of the Saxon* (London, 1912)

———, *The Valor of Ignorance* (London, 1909)

Mahan, Alfred Thayer, *The Influence of Sea Power Upon History 1660–1783* (London, 1898)

———, *The Interests of America in Sea Power, Present and Future* (London, 1898)

Roosevelt, Franklin D., *Whither Bound?* (New York, 1926)

Roosevelt, Theodore, *America and the World War* (London, 1915)

———, *Fear God and Take Your Own Part* (New York, 1916)

PUBLISHED SOURCES

Carmichael, Donald S., ed., *F.D.R. Columnist: The Uncollected Columns of Franklin D. Roosevelt* (Chicago, 1947)

Cronin, E. David, ed., *The Cabinet Diaries of Josephus Daniels, 1913–1921* (Lincoln, NE, 1963)

Kilpatrick, Carroll, ed., *Roosevelt and Daniels—A Friendship in Politics* (Chapel Hill, NC, 1952)

Link, Arthur S., ed., *The Papers of Woodrow Wilson* (69 vols. Princeton, NJ, 1966–1994)

Morrison, Elting E., John M. Blum, and John J. Buckley, ed. *Letters of Theodore Roosevelt* (8 vols. Cambridge, MA, 1954)

Nixon, Edgar B., ed., *Franklin D. Roosevelt and Foreign Affairs, 1933–1937* (3 vols. Cambridge, MA, 1969)

Roosevelt, Elliott, ed., *The Roosevelt Letters: Being the Personal Correspondence of Franklin Delano Roosevelt* (3 vols. London, 1949–1952)

Rosenman, Samuel I., ed., *The Public Papers and the Addresses of Franklin D. Roosevelt* (13 vols. New York, 1938–1950)

Schewe, Donald B., ed., *Franklin D. Roosevelt and Foreign Affairs, 1937–1939* (14 vols. New York, 1979–1983)

Stimson, Henry L., *Diaries* (9 microfilm reels. New Haven, CT, 1973)

ELECTRONIC RESOURCES

American Presidency Project http://www.presidency.ucsb.edu/, accessed on February 25, 2012.

Avalon Project, Yale Law School http://avalon.law.yale.edu/20th_century/leagcov.asp, accessed on February 25, 2012.

English Speaking Union of the United States http://www.esuus.org last, accessed on February 25, 2012.

New York Times Historical Database, 1851–2006 http://www.proquest.umi.com, accessed on February 25, 2012.

Woodrow Wilson Foundation Records, 1906–1993 http://diglib.princeton.edu/ead/getEad?id=ark:/88435/br86b3595, accessed on February 25, 2012.

SECONDARY SOURCES

BOOKS

Adams, Michael, *The Great Adventure: Male Desire and the Coming of World War I* (Bloomington, IN, 1990)

Ambrosius, Lloyd E., *Woodrow Wilson and the American Diplomatic Tradition—The Treaty Fight in Perspective* (Cambridge, 1987)

Barber, William J., *From New Era to New Deal: Herbert Hoover, the Economists, and American Economic Policy, 1921–1933* (Cambridge, 1985)

———, *Designs within Disorder: Franklin D. Roosevelt, the Economists, and the Shaping of American Economic Policy, 1933–1945* (Cambridge, 1996)

Bartlett, Ruhl J., *The League to Enforce Peace*, (Chapel Hill, NC, 1944)

Beale, Howard K., *Theodore Roosevelt and the Rise of America to World Power* (Baltimore, MD, 1953)

Bederman, Gail, *Manliness and Civilization: A Cultural History of Gender and Race in the United States 1880–1917* (Chicago, 1995)

Bellush, Bernard, *Franklin D. Roosevelt as Governor of New York* (New York, 1955)

Bestor, Arthur E., David C. Mearns and Jonathan Daniels, *Three Presidents and Their Books—Jefferson, Lincoln and F.D. Roosevelt* (Urbana, IL, 1955)

Black, Conrad, *Franklin Delano Roosevelt: Champion of Freedom* (London, 2003)

Blum, John M., *The Republican Roosevelt* (Cambridge, MA, 1954)

Borgwardt, Elizabeth, *A New Deal for the World—America's Vision for Human Rights* (Cambridge, MA, 2005)

Boyle, Francis A., *Foundations of World Order: The Legalist Approach to International Relations, 1898–1922* (Durham, NC, 1999)

Brinkley, Alan, *The End of Reform—New Deal Liberalism in Recession and War* (New York, 1995)

Bundgaard, Axel, *Muscle and Manliness: The Rise of Sport in American Boarding Schools* (Syracuse, NY, 2005)

Burner, David, *The Politics of Provincialism—The Democratic Party in Transition 1918–1932* (Cambridge, MA, 1986)

Burns, James MacGregor, *Roosevelt: The Lion and the Fox* (New York, 1956)

———, *Roosevelt: The Soldier of Freedom* (London, 1971)

Butler, Michael A., *Cautious Visionary—Cordell Hull and Trade Reform, 1933–1927* (London, 1998)

Calhoun, Frederick S., *Power and Principle: Armed Intervention in Wilsonian Foreign Policy* (Kent, OH, 1986)

Cannadine, David, *Mellon: An American Life* (London, 2006)

Casey, Steven, *Cautious Crusade—Franklin D. Roosevelt, American Public Opinion, and the War Against Nazi Germany* (Oxford, 2001)

Casey, Steven and Jonathan Wright eds. *Mental Maps in the Era of the Two World Wars* (Basingstoke, 2008)

Clifford, John Garry, *The Citizen Soldiers—The Plattsburg Training Camp Movement, 1913–1920* (Lexington, KY, 1972)

Cohen, Warren, I., *The American Revisionists—The Lessons of Intervention in World War I* (Chicago, 1967)

Cohrs, Patrick O., *The Unfinished Peace after World War I: America, Britain and the Stabilisation of Europe 1919–1932* (Cambridge, 2006)

Collin, Richard H., *Theodore Roosevelt, Culture, Diplomacy, and Expansion—A New View of American Imperialism* (Baton Rouge, LA, 1985)

Cooper, John Milton Jr., *The Vanity of Power: American Isolationism and the First World War, 1914–1917* (Westport, CT, 1969)

———, *The Warrior and the Priest: Woodrow Wilson and Theodore Roosevelt* (Cambridge, MA, 1983)

———, *Breaking the Heart of the World—Woodrow Wilson and the Fight for the League of Nations* (Cambridge, 2001)

Costigliola, Frank, *Awkward Dominion: American Political, Economic, and Cultural Relations with Europe, 1919–1933* (Ithaca, NY, 1984)

Cox, James M., *Journey Through My Years* (Macon, GA, 2004)

Craig, Douglas B., *After Wilson: The Struggle for the Democratic Party, 1920–1934* (Chapel Hill, NC, 1992)

Dallek, Robert, *Franklin D. Roosevelt and American Foreign Policy, 1933–1945* (Oxford, 1995)

Daniels, Josephus, *The Wilson Era Years of Peace, 1910–1917* (Chapel Hill, NC, 1944)

———, *The Wilson Era: Years of War and After, 1917–1923* (Chapel Hill, NC, 1946)

Davis, Kenneth S., *FDR: The Beckoning of Destiny 1882–1928* (New York, 1971)

———, *FDR: The New York Years 1928–1933* (New York, 1985)

Dickinson, Matthew J., *Bitter Harvest: FDR, Presidential Power and the Growth of the Presidential Branch* (Cambridge, 1999)

Divine, Robert A., *The Illusion of Neutrality: Franklin D. Roosevelt and the Struggle Over the Arms Embargo* (Chicago, 1962)

———, *Second Chance: The Triumph of Internationalism in America during World War II* (New York, 1967)

———, *Roosevelt and World War II* (Baltimore, MD, 1969)

Donohue, Kathleen G., *Freedom from Want: American Liberalism and the Idea of the Consumer* (Baltimore, MD, 2003)

Dunne, Michael, *The United States and the World Court, 1920–1933* (London, 1988)

Dyer, Thomas G., *Theodore Roosevelt and the Idea of Race* (Baton Rouge, LA, 1980)

Eichengreen, Barry, *Golden Fetters—The Gold Standard and the Great Depression 1919–1939* (Oxford, 1992)

Fearon, Peter, *War, Prosperity and Depression: The U.S. Economy 1917–1945* (Oxford, 1987)

Fenster, Julie M., *FDR's Shadow—Louis Howe, The Force That Shaped Franklin and Eleanor Roosevelt* (New York, 2009)

Ferrell, Robert H., *American Diplomacy in the Great Depression: Hoover-Stimson Foreign Policy, 1929–1933* (New Haven, CT, 1957)

————, *Woodrow Wilson and World War I 1917–1921* (New York, 1985)

Finnegan, John Patrick, *Against the Specter of a Dragon: The Campaign for American Preparedness, 1914–1917* (Westport, CT, 1974)

Forcey, Charles, *The Crossroads of Liberalism—Croly, Weyle, Lippman, and the Progressive Era 1900–1925* (New York, 1961)

Freidel, Frank, *Franklin D. Roosevelt—The Apprenticeship* (Boston, MA, 1952)

————, *Franklin D. Roosevelt—The Ordeal* (Boston, MA, 1954)

————, *Franklin D. Roosevelt—The Triumph* (Boston, MA, 1956)

————, *Franklin D. Roosevelt: Launching the New Deal* (Boston, MA, 1973)

Fusfeld, Daniel R., *The Economic Thought of Fraklin D. Roosevelt and the Origins of the New Deal* (New York, 1956)

Gardner, Lloyd C., *Economic Aspects of New Deal Diplomacy* (Boston, MA, 1971)

Goldberg, Richard Thayer, *The Making of Franklin D. Roosevelt—Triumph Over Disability* (Cambridge, MA, 1981)

Greer, Thomas H., *What Roosevelt Thought— The Social and Political Ideas of Franklin D. Roosevelt,* (East Lansing, MI, 2000)

Harbutt, Fraser J., *Yalta 1945: Europe and America at the Crossroads* (Cambridge, 2010)

Harper, John Lamberton, *American Visions of Europe: Franklin D. Roosevelt, George F. Kennan, and Dean G Acheson* (Cambridge, 1994)

Healy, David, *Gunboat Diplomacy in the Wilson Era—The U.S. Navy in Haiti, 1915–1916* (Madison, WI, 1976)

Hildebrand, Robert C., *Power and the People: Executive Management of Public Opinion in Foreign Affairs 1897–1921* (Chapel Hill, NC, 1984)

Hoff-Wilson, Joan, *Herbert Hoover—Forgotten Progressive* (Boston, MA, 1975)

Hogan, Michael J., *Woodrow Wilson's Western Tour—Rhetoric, Public Opinion and the League of Nations* (College Station, TX, 2006)

Hoganson, Kristin L., *Fighting for American Manhood—How Gender Politics Provoked the Spanish-American and Philippine-American Wars* (New Haven, CT, 1998)

Holmes, James R., *Theodore Roosevelt and World Order—Police Power in International Relations* (Washington, DC, 2006)

Hoopes, Townsend, and Douglas Brinkley, *FDR and the Creation of the UN* (New Haven, CT, 1997)

Horsman, Reginald, *Race and Manifest Destiny: The Origins of American Racial Anglo-Saxonism* (Cambridge, MA, 1975)

Houck, Davis W., *FDR and Fear Itself: The First Inaugural Address* (College Station, TX, 2002)

Hull, Cordell, *The Memoirs of Cordell Hull* (2 vols., New York, 1948)

Hunt, Michael H., *Ideology and U.S. Foreign Policy* (New Haven, CT, 1987)

Hurley, Alfred F., *Billy Mitchell: Crusader for Air Power* (Bloomington, IN, 1975)

Isaacson, Walter and Evan Thomas, *The Wise Men—Six Friends and the World they Made* (London, 1986)

Jacobson, Matthew Frye, *Barbarian Virtues-The United States Encounters Foreign Peoples at Home and Abroad 1876–1917* (New York, 2001)

Johnson, Robert David, *The Peace Progressives and American Foreign Relations* (Cambridge, MA, 1995)

Kennedy, David M., *Over Here—The First World War and American Society* (Oxford, 1980)

Kennedy, Ross A., *The Will to Believe: Woodrow Wilson, World War I, and America's Strategy for Peace and Security* (Kent, OH, 2009)

Kiewe, Amos, *FDR's First Fireside Chat: Public Confidence and the Banking Crisis* (College Station, TX, 2007)

Kimball, Warren F., *The Juggler: Franklin Roosevelt as Wartime Statesman* (Princeton, NJ, 1991)

Kleeman, Rita Halle, *Gracious Lady: The Life of Sara Delano Roosevelt* (New York, 1935)

Kloppenberg, James T., *Uncertain Victory—Social Democracy and Progressivism in European and American Thought, 1870–1920* (Oxford, 1986)

Knock, Thomas, J., *To End All Wars: Woodrow Wilson and the Quest for a New World Order* (Princeton, NJ, 1992)

Knott, Stephen F., *Alexander Hamilton and the Persistence of Myth* (Lawrence, KS, 2002)

Kramer, Paul A., *The Blood of Government: Race, Empire, the United States and the Philippines* (Chapel Hill, NC, 2006)

Kuehl, Warren F., *Seeking World Order—The United States and International Organization to 1920* (Nashville, TN, 1969)

Kuehl, Warren F. and Dunn, Lynne K. *Keeping the Covenant—American Internationalists and the League of Nations, 1920–1939* (Kent, OH, 1997)

Langer, William L. and Gleason S. Everett. *The Challenge to Isolation, 1937–1940* (New York, 1964)

———, *The Undeclared War, 1940–1941* (New York, 1964)

Leffler, Melvyn P., *The Elusive Quest: America's Pursuit of European Stability and French Security, 1919–1933* (Chapel Hill, NC, 1979)

Leighton, Isabel and Gabrielle Forbrush, *My Boy Franklin as Told by Mrs James Roosevelt* (New York, 1933)

Leuchentburg, William E., *The FDR Years: On Roosevelt and His Legacy* (New York, 1995)

Levin, Linda Lotridge, *The Making of FDR—The Story of Stephen T. Early, America's First Modern Press Secretary* (New York, 2008)

Lindley, Ernest K., *Franklin D. Roosevelt—A Career in Progressive Democracy* (New York, 1931)

Link, Arthur S., *Woodrow Wilson and the Progressive Era 1910–1917* (New York, 1954)

Livermore, Seward W., *Politics is Adjourned: Woodrow Wilson and the War Congress, 1916–1918* (Middleton, CT, 1966)

Love, Eric T. L., *Race Over Empire: Racism and U.S. Imperialism, 1865–1900* (Chapel Hill, NC, 2004)

Manela, Erez, *The Wilsonian Moment—Self-Determination and the International Origins of Anticolonial Nationalism* (Oxford, 2007)

Margulies, Herbert F., *The Mild Reservationists and the League of Nations Controversy in the Senate* (Columbia, MO, 1989)

Marks, Frederick W. III., *Velvet on Iron—The Diplomacy of Theodore Roosevelt* (Lincoln, NE, 1979)

———, *Wind Over Sand: The Diplomacy of Franklin Roosevelt*, (Athens, 1988).

McCartney, Paul T., *Power and Progress—American National Identity, the War of 1898, and the Rise of American Imperialism* (Baton Rouge, LA, 2006)

McCormick, Richard L., *The Party Period and Public Policy—American Politics from the Age of Jackson to the Progressive Era* (Oxford, 1986)

McGerr, Michael E., *The Decline of Popular Politics—The American North, 1865–1928* (Oxford, 1986)

McLachlan, James, *American Boarding Schools—A Historical Study* (New York, 1970)

Moley, Raymond, *After Seven Years* (New York, 1939)

Morgan, Ted, *FDR: A Biography* (New York, 1985)

Murphey, Lawrence R., *Perverts by Official Order: The Campaign Against Homosexuals by the United States Navy* (New York, 1988)

Neu, Charles E., *An Uncertain Friendship: Theodore Roosevelt and Japan, 1906–1909* (Cambridge, MA, 1967)

Ninkovich, Frank, *The Wilsonian Century: U.S. Foreign Policy since 1900* (Chicago, 1999)

Osgood, Robert Endicott, *Ideals and Self Interest in America's Foreign Policy—The Great Transformation of the Twentieth Century* (Chicago, 1953)

Ostrower, Gary B., *Collective Insecurity—The United States and the League of Nations during the Early Thirties* (London, 1979)

Pearlman, Michael, *To Make Democracy Safe for America—Patricians and Preparedness in the Progressive Era* (Chicago, 1984)

Perkins, Bradford, *The Great Rapprochement: England and the United States, 1895–1914* (New York, 1968)

Perkins, Frances, *The Roosevelt I Knew* (New York, 1946)

Peterson, Merrill D., *The Jefferson Image in the American Mind*, (Charlottesville, VA, 1998)

Range, Willard, *Franklin D. Roosevelt's World Order*, (Athens, GA, 1959)

Renda, Mary A., *Taking Haiti: Military Occupation and the Culture of U.S. Imperialism 1915–1940* (Chapel Hill, NC, 2001)

Renshaw, Patrick, *Franklin D. Roosevelt* (Harlow, 2004)

Reynolds, David, *From Munich to Pearl Harbor: Roosevelt's America and the Origins of the Second World War* (Chicago, 2001)

———, *From World War to Cold War: Churchill, Roosevelt, and the International History of the 1940s* (Oxford, 2006)

Ritchie, Donald A., *Electing FDR: The New Deal Campaign of 1932* (Lawrence, KS, 2007)

Robinson, Greg, *By Order of the President—FDR and the Internment of Japanese Americans* (Cambridge, MA, 2001)

Rochester, Stuart I., *American Liberal Disillusionment in the Wake of World War I* (University Park, PA, 1977)

Rofe, J. Simon., *Franklin Roosevelt's Foreign Policy and the Welles Mission* (New York, 2007)

Rollins, Alfred B., *Roosevelt and Howe* (New York, 1962)

Roosevelt, Eleanor, *This I Remember*, (New York, 1949)

———, *This is My Story* (New York, 1937)

Roosevelt-Longworth, Alice, *Crowded Hours: Reminiscences of Alice Roosevelt Longworth* (New York, 1933)

Rosenberg, Emily S., *Spreading the American Dream: American Economic and Cultural Expansion, 1890–1945* (New York, 1982)

———, *Financial Missionaries to the World: The Politics and Culture of Dollar Diplomacy, 1900–1930* (Durham, NC, 2003)

Rosenman, Samuel I., *Working with Roosevelt* (London, 1952)

Ryan, Halford R., *Franklin D. Roosevelt's Rhetorical Presidency* (Westport, CT 1988)

Sarasohn, David, *The Party of Reform: Democrats in the Progressive Era* (Jackson, MS, 1989)

Savage, Sean J., *Roosevelt—The Party Leader 1932–1945* (Lexington, KY, 1991)

Schwartz, Barry, *Abraham Lincoln and the Forge of National Memory* (Chicago, 2000)

Sherry, Michael S., *The Rise of American Air Power: The Creation of Armageddon* (New Haven, CT, 1987)

Sherwood, Robert, *Roosevelt and Hopkins* (New York, 1950)

Skowronek, Stephen, *Building a New American State: The Expansion of National Administrative Capacities 1877–1920* (Cambridge, 1982)

Smith, Gene, *When the Cheering Stopped: The Last Years of Woodrow Wilson* (New York, 1964)

Smith, Jean Edward, *FDR* (New York, 2007)

Steel, Ronald, *Walter Lippmann and the American Century* (London, 1980)

Stid, Daniel D., *The President as Statesman—Woodrow Wilson and the Constitution* (Lawrence, KS, 1998)

Stiles, Lela, *The Man Behind Roosevelt* (New York, 1954)

Stimson, Henry L. and McGeorge Bundy, *On Active Service in Peace and War* (New York, 1948)

Stone, Ralph A., *The Irreconcilables: The Fight Against the League of Nations* (Lexington, KY, 1970)

Sustein, Cass R., *The Second Bill of Rights: FDR's Unfinished Revolution and Why We Need It More Than Ever* (New York, 2004)

Tansill, Charles C., *Back Door to War: The Roosevelt Foreign Policy, 1933–1941* (Chicago, 1952)

Thompson, John A., *Reformers and War: American Progressive Publicists and the First World War* (Cambridge, 1987)

———, *Woodrow Wilson* (Harlow, 2002)

Trask, David F., *Captains and Cabinets: Anglo-American Naval Relations, 1917–1918* (Columbia, MO, 1972)

Tucker, Robert W., *Woodrow Wilson and the Great War—Reconsidering America's Neutrality 1914–1917* (Charlottesville, VA, 2007)

Turk, Richard W., *The Ambiguous Relationship: Theodore Roosevelt and Alfred Thayer Mahan* (New York, 1987)

Veeser, Cyrus, *A World Safe for Capitalism: Dollar Diplomacy and America's Rise to Global Power* (New York, 2002)

Ward, Geoffrey C., *Before the Trumpet—Young Franklin Roosevelt 1882–1905* (New York, 1985)

——, *A First Class Temperament—The Emergence of Franklin Roosevelt* (New York, 1989)

White, Graham J., *FDR and the Press* (Chicago, 1979)

White, Morton, *Social Thought in America—The Revolt Against Formalism* (7th edn. Boston, MA, 1970)

Widenor, William C., *Henry Cabot Lodge and the Search for an American Foreign Policy* (Berkeley, CA, 1980)

Wiesen Cook, Blanche, *Eleanor Roosevelt Vol I 1884–1933* (London, 1993)

Willis, Resa, *FDR and Lucy* (New York, 2004)

Winfield, Betty Houchin, *FDR and the News Media* (New York, 1994)

CHAPTERS IN EDITED BOOKS

Braisted, William R., "The Evolution of the United States Navy's Strategic Assessment in the Pacific, 1919–1931," in Erik Goldstein and John Maurer (eds.), *The Washington Conference, 1921–22: Naval Rivalry, East Asian Stability and the Road to Pearl Harbor* (Ilford, 1994), 102–123.

Buckley, Thomas H., "The Icarus Factor: The American Pursuit of Myth in Naval Arms Control, 1921–1936," in Erik Goldstein and John Maurer (eds.), *The Washington Conference, 1921–22: Naval Rivalry, East Asian Stability and the Road to Pearl Harbor* (Ilford, 1994), 124–146.

Burner, David, "Election of 1924," in Schlesinger, Arthur M. and Fred L Israel (eds.), *History of American Presidential Elections 1789–1968 Volume III* (New York, 1971), 2459–2581.

Casey, Steven, "Franklin D. Roosevelt," in Steven Casey and Jonathan Wright (eds.), *Mental Maps in the Era of the Two World Wars* (Basingstoke, 2008), 216–239.

Cooper, John Milton Jr., "Fool's Errand of Finest Hour? Woodrow Wilson's Speaking Tour in September 1919," in John Milton Cooper Jr. and Charles E. Neu (eds.), *The Wilson Era: Essays in Honor of Arthur S. Link* (Arlington Heights, IL, 1991), 198–220.

——, "The Not So Vital Center: The League to Enforce Peace and the League of Nations, 1919–1920," in Michael Wala (ed.), *Gesellschaft und Diplomatie im transatlantischen Kontext* (Stuttgart, 1999), 119–132.

Dobson, Alan P., "FDR and the Struggle for a Postwar Civil Aviation Regime: Legacy or Loss?" in David B. Woolner, Warren Kimball, and David Reynolds (eds.), *FDR's World: War, Peace, and Legacies* (New York, 2008), 193–213.

Freidel, Frank, "Election of 1932," in Schlesinger, Arthur M. and Fred L Israel (eds.), *History of American Presidential Elections 1789–1968 Volume III* (New York, 1971), 2707–2806.

Gardner, Lloyd, "FDR and the "Colonial Question"" in David B. Woolner, Warren Kimball, and David Reynolds (eds.) *FDR's World: War, Peace, and Legacies* (New York, 2008), 123–144.

Henrikson, Alan K., "FDR and the World-Wide Arena," in David B. Woolner, Warren F. Kimball, and David Reynolds (eds.), *FDR's World: War, Peace, and Legacies* (New York, 2008), 35–61.

Kimball, Warren F., "This Persistent Evangel of Americanism," in Warren F. Kimball (ed.), *The Juggler—Franklin Roosevelt as Wartime Statesman* (Princeton, NJ, 1991), 185–200.

Kimball, Warren F. and Fred E. Pollock, "'In Search of Monsters to Destroy': Roosevelt and Colonialism," in Warren F. Kimball (ed.), *The Juggler—Franklin Roosevelt as Wartime Statesman* (Princeton, NJ, 1991), 127–157.

Leuchtenburg, William E., "Franklin D. Roosevelt—The First Modern President," in William E. Leuchtenburg (ed.), *The FDR Years—On Roosevelt and His Legacy* (New York, 1995), 1–34.

———, "The New Deal and the Analogue of War," in William E. Leuchtenburg (ed.), *The FDR Years—On Roosevelt and His Legacy* (New York, 1995), 35–75.

Link, Arthur S. and William M. Leary Jr., "Election of 1916," in Schlesinger, Arthur M., and Fred L Israel (eds.), *History of American Presidential Elections 1789–1968 Volume III* (New York, 1971), 2245–2345.

McCoy, Donald, "Election of 1920," in Schlesinger, Arthur M., and Fred L Israel (eds.), *History of American Presidential Elections 1789–1968 Volume III* (New York, 1971), 2349–2456.

Perkins, Dexter, "Woodrow Wilson's Tour," in Daniel Aaron (ed.), *America In Crisis* (New York, 1952), 245–265.

Reynolds, David, "Culture, Discourse, and Policy: Reflections on the New International History," in David Reynolds (ed.), *From World War to Cold War: Churchill, Roosevelt, and the International History of the 1940s* (Oxford, 2006), 331–351.

———, "FDR's Foreign Policy and the Construction of American History, 1945–1955," in David B. Woolner, Warren Kimball, and David Reynolds (eds.), *FDR's World: War, Peace, and Legacies* (New York, 2008), 5–33.

Schlesinger, Jr., Arthur M., "Franklin D. Roosevelt's Internationalism," in Cornelis A. Van Minnen and John F. Sears (eds.), *FDR and His Contemporaries—Foreign Perceptions of an American President* (New York, 1992), 1–16. .

Spector, Ronald H., "Josephus Daniels, Franklin Roosevelt, and the Reinvention of the Naval Enlisted Man," in Edward J. Marolda (ed.), *FDR and the United States Navy* (New York, 1998), 19–33.

Walter, John C., "Franklin D. Roosevelt and Naval Rearmament, 1932–1938," in Herbert D. Rosenbaum and Elizabeth Batelme (eds.), *Franklin D. Roosevelt: The Man, the Myth, the Era, 1882–1945* (New York, 1987), 203–218.

ARTICLES

Ambrosious, Lloyd, "Woodrow Wilson and *the Birth of a Nation*: American Democracy and International Relations," *Diplomacy and Statecraft* 18, No. 4 (2007), 689–718.

Anderson, Stuart, "Racial Anglo-Saxonism and the American Response to the Boer War," *Diplomatic History* 2, No. 3 (1978), 219–236.

Asada, Sadao, "Between the Old Diplomacy and the New, 1918–1922: The Washington System and the Origins of Japanese-American Rapprochement," *Diplomatic History* 30, No. 2 (2006), 211–230.

Bagby, Wesley M. "The Road to Normalcy—The Presidential Campaign and Election of 1920," *The Johns Hopkins University Studies in Historical and Political Science* Series LXXX, No. 1 (1962).

Butow, R. J. C., "A Notable Passage to China: Myth and Memory in FDR's Family History," *Prologue* 31, No. 3 (1999), 159–177.

Clements, Kendrick, "Woodrow Wilson's Mexican Policy 1913–1915," *Diplomatic History* 4, No. 2 (1980), 113–136.

Collin, Richard H., "Symbiosis versus Hegemony: New Directions in the Foreign Relations Historiography of Theodore Roosevelt and William Howard Taft," *Diplomatic History* 19, No. 3. (1995), 473–497.

Cooper, John Milton Jr., "Progressivism and American Foreign Policy: A Reconsideration," *Mid-America* 51 (1969), 260–277.

Costigliola, Frank. "Broken Circle: The Isolation of Franklin D. Roosevelt in World War II," *Diplomatic History* 32, No. 5 (2008), 677–718.

Crapol, Edward, "Coming to Terms with Empire: The Historiography of Late-Nineteenth Century American Foreign Relations," *Diplomatic History* 16, No. 4 (1992), 573–598.

Current, Richard N., "How Stimson Meant to "Maneuver" the Japanese," *Mississippi Valley Historical Review* 40, No.1 (1953), 67–74.

Davis, Kenneth S., "FDR as a Biographers Problem," *American Scholar* 52 (Winter, 1983/84), 100–108.

Divine, Robert A., "Franklin D. Roosevelt and Collective Security, 1933," *Mississippi Valley Historical Review* 48, No. 1 (1961), 42–59.

Eichengreen, Barry, "The Origins and Nature of the Great Slump Revisited," *The Economic History Review*, New Series 45, No. 2 (1992), 213–239.

———, "Understanding the Great Depression," *The Canadian Journal of Economics* 37, No. 1 (2004), 1–27.

Endy, Christopher, "Travel and World Power: Americans in Europe, 1890–1917," *Diplomatic History* 22, No. 4 (1998), 565–594.

Engel, Jeffrey, "The Democratic Language of American Imperialism: Race, Order, and Theodore Roosevelt's Personification of Foreign Policy Evil," *Diplomacy and Statecraft* 19, No. 4 (2008), 671–689.

Gerstle, Gary, "The Protean Character of American Liberalism," *The American Historical Review* 99, No. 4 (1994), 1043–1073.

———, "Theodore Roosevelt and the Divided Character of American Nationalism," *Journal of American History* 86, No. 3 (1999), 1280–1307.

Goldman, Armond S., et al., "What Was the Cause of Franklin Delano Roosevelt's Paralytic Illness?," *Journal of Medical Biography* 11 (2003), 232–240.

Haglund, David, "Roosevelt as "Friend of France"—But Which One?," *Diplomatic History* 31, No. 5 (2007), 883–907.

Hajimu, Masuda, "Rumors of War: Immigration Disputes and the Social Construction of American-Japanese Relations 1905–1913," *Diplomatic History* 33, No. 1 (2009),1–37.

Helbich, Wolfgang J., "American Liberals in the League of Nations Controversy," *The Public Opinion Quarterly* 31, No. 4 (1967–1968), 568–596.

Henderson, Peter V. N., "Woodrow Wilson, Victoriano Huerta, and the Recognition Issue in Mexico," *The Americas* 41, No. 2 (1984), 151–176.

Hodge, Carl Cavanagh, "A Whiff of Cordite: Theodore Roosevelt and the Transoceanic Naval Arms Race, 1897–1909," *Diplomacy and Statecraft* 19, No. 4 (2008), 712–731.

Karsten, Peter, "The Nature of "Influence": Roosevelt, Mahan and the Concept of Sea Power," *American Quarterly* 23 No. 4. (Oct, 1971), 585–600.

Kennedy, Greg, "Depression and Security: Aspects Influencing the United States Navy during the Hoover Administration," *Diplomacy and Statecraft* 6, No. 2 (1995), 342–372.

Kloppenberg, James, "Pragmatism: An Old Name for Some New Ways of Thinking?," *Journal of American History* 83, No. 1 (1996), 100–138.

Kramer, Paul A., "Empires, Exceptions, and Anglo-Saxons: Race and Rule between the British and United States Empires, 1880–1910," *The Journal of American History* 88, No. 4 (2002), 1315–1353.

———, "The Philippine-American War as Race War," *Diplomatic History* 30, No. 2 (2006), 169–210.

Leuchtenburg, William E., "Progressivism and Imperialism: The Progressive Movement and American Foreign Policy, 1898–1916," *The Mississippi Valley Historical Review* 39, No. 3 (1952), 483–504.

Link, Arthur S., "Woodrow Wilson and the Democratic Party," *The Review of Politics* 18, No. 2 (1956), 146–156.

Mallan, John P., "Roosevelt, Brooks Adams, and Lea: The Warrior Critique of the Business Civilization," *American Quarterly* 8, No. 3 (1956), 216–230.

Mckercher, Brian, "Reaching for the Brass Ring: The Recent Historiography of Interwar American Foreign Relations," *Diplomatic History* 15, No. 4 (1991), 565–598.

Merrit, Richard L., "Woodrow Wilson and the "Great and Solemn Referendum,"1920," *The Review of Politics* 27, No.1. (1965), 78–104.

Morgan, William Michael, "The Anti-Japanese Origins of the Hawaiian Annexation Treaty of 1897," *Diplomatic History* 6, No. 1 (1982), 23–44.

Murray, Robert and Tim H. Blessing, "The Presidential Performance Study: A Progress Report," *Journal of American History* 70, No. 3 (1983), 535–555.

Neuman, Walter, "Franklin D. Roosevelt and Japan 1913–33," *Pacific Historical Review* XXII, (1953), 143–53.

Nichols, Jeanette P., "Roosevelt's Monetary Diplomacy in 1933," *The American Historical Review* 56, No. 2 (1951), 295–317.

Ninkovich, Frank, "Theodore Roosevelt: Civilization as Ideology," *Diplomatic History* 10, No. 3 (1986), 221–245.

Pugach, Noel, "Anglo-American Aircraft Competition, 1919–1921," *Diplomatic History* 2, No. 4 (1978), 351–371.

Roberts, Priscilla, "The Anglo-American Theme: American Visions of an Atlantic Alliance, 1914–1933," *Diplomatic History* 21, No. 3 (1997), 333–364.

Rofe, J. Simon, "'Under the Influence of Mahan': Theodore and Franklin Roosevelt and Their Understanding of American National Interest," *Diplomacy and Statecraft*, 19 (2008), 732–745.

Sternsher, Bernard, "The Stimson Doctrine: FDR versus Moley and Tugwell," *Pacific Historical Review* 31, No. 3 (1962), 281–89.

Stromberg, Roland N., "Uncertainties and Obscurities about the League of Nations," *Journal of the History of Ideas* 33, No. 1 (1972), 139–54.

Thompson John A., "Conceptions of National Security and American Entry into World War II," *Diplomacy and Statecraft* 16, No. 4 (2005), 671–697.

Tilchin, William N., "Theodore Roosevelt, Anglo American Relations, and the Jamaica Incident of 1907," *Diplomatic History* 19, No. 3 (1995), 385–406.

Vesser, Cyrus, "Inventing Dollar Diplomacy: The Gilded Age Origins of the Roosevelt Corollary to the Monroe Doctrine," *Diplomatic History* 27, No. 3 (2003), 301–326.

Williams, William J., "Josephus Daniels and the United States Navy's Shipbuilding Program During World War I," *The Journal of Military History* 60, No. 1 (1996), 7–38.

Zasloff, Jonathan, "Law and the Shaping of American Foreign Policy: From the Gilded Age to the New Era," *New York University Law Review* 78 (2002), 239–373.

———, "Law and the Shaping of American Foreign Policy: The Twenty Year Crisis," *Southern California Law Review* 77 (2004), 583–682.

INDEX